Just Wanna Create

Copyright and Fair Use Strategies

Other Titles in the Just Wanna Legal DIY Series

Just Wanna Trademark

A Little Bit of Copyright for Quilters

Just Wanna Quilt Notebook

Just Wanna Patent

Just Wanna Create

Copyright and Fair Use Strategies

By

Elizabeth Townsend Gard

Just Wanna Quilt Publications

An Imprint of Limited Times Publishing House
New Orleans, LA
www.justwannaquilt.com

Editor-in-Chief, Ricardo Gonzalez

Book design/Layout, Eyeridium, LLC.

ISBN: 978-1-7341271-4-0

LCCN: 2020900679

First U.S. Edition, February 2020.

About Just Wanna Quilt

Just Wanna Quilt started as a research project by Dr. Elizabeth Townsend Gard at the Copyright Research Lab at Tulane University Law School. It is now a podcast (available on iTunes and other podcast platforms), a community (on Facebook, www.facebook.com/groups/justwannaquilt), a publishing arm, and so much more. Visit us at www.justwannaquilt.com.

In the end, it all comes down to this: making something again is easy, making something new is brave and making something personal is essential.

-Tula Pink, Tula Pink's City Sampler: 100 Modern Quilt Blocks

Acknowledgments

This project is collaborative, and that means lots and lots of thank-yous. First, to the Quilting Army...you rock! This is a volunteer army that jumped into the immersive research with me -- in every way. We are now over 2800 strong. Oh, so many that have been so influential in this project. We are the Army. To our 300+ guests who have been willing to share through thoughts, experiences, and stories. The project would not be anything without all of you. We talked to inventors, industry leaders, designers, pattern-makers, entrepreneurs, and quilters of all levels of passion and skill. The list of episodes can be found at http://www.justwannaquilt.com.

To *Cheryl Sleboda*, for her expertise and thoughtfulness every step of the way, including taking me in for an impromptu writing retreat that allowed for the first draft of this manuscript. To *Mary Fons*, who featured us early on in Quiltfolk Magazine, and together with Tula Pink had an amazing 2-½ hour Just Wanna Quilt podcast interview at our house that people are still talking about, and then became a good friend to the project and my family. (And to *Tula Pink*, who is just the coolest every in every way.) To *Pam Weeks*, who at the beginning invited Sid and me to a picnic in her kitchen to help me understand the patchwork landscape of the quilting world, and then became my roommate at Quilt Market twice, and became such a trusted friend. To *Scott Fortunoff*, for his conversations and generosity, both in time, expertise and fabric. We went on field trips to both the Jaftex fabric warehouse, and to his offices in New York, which were both amazing. To *Leah Day*, who encouraged us to self-publish, believed in the project and helped us name the book (which changed the direction of the book). To *Paula Nadelstern*, for sharing her copyright story with me, which confirmed the thesis of the book: register your works. To Pam Cobb and Lynn Rinehart, who helped us get ready for both Houston Festival 2018 and then Market 2019, including lending us all of their safety pins; I so adore you both. To *Chawne Kimber*, who puts up with my fangirling juxtaposed with in depth conversations that have so influenced this project. To *Karla Gerome and Nate Erznoznik* at Grace Company, who both are patient, kind and innovative when it comes to dealing with my love of Grace longarms. And to *Bob Ruggiero* at Quilts, Inc. who answered my email, let me come as Press to Quilt Market in 2017, encouraged us to engage with an interactive booth at Quilt Festival in 2018, and was supportive when I asked if we could this time attempt a booth at Quilt Market in 2019. This project would have been so extraordinarily different without your support and kindness.

We always appreciate our famous and industry leaders stopping by to chat on the podcast. To Ebony Love, Marianne Fons, Andi Barney, Alex Anderson, Sara Trail, Sue Bleiweiss, Rob Appell, Barbara Brackman, Ana Maria Horner, Victoria Findlay Wolfe, Sam Hunter, Angie Wilson, Christa Watson, Latifah Saafir, Michael McCormick, Suzy Webster, Joe Cunningham, Janet George, Sandra Scheiber Johnson, Bonnie Browning, Darci Read, Laurie Aaron Hird, Andrea Tsang Jackson, France O'Roark Dowell, Maddie Kertay, Lyric Kinard, Holice Turnbow, Karen Miller, Patrick Lose, Carla Triemer, Tina Hilton, Karla Overland, Kristin Esser, Dora Carry, Jenny Lyon, Jo Westfoot, Deborah Fisher, Stephanie Palmer, Megan Lundgren, Claudia Pfeil, Kim Lepacek, Patty Dudek, Amy Meissner, Susan Goldman Rubin, Amy Newbold, Judel Niemeyer, Thomas Knauer, David Gilleland, Brenda Gael Smith, Jessica Vetor, Karri Vojtechovsky, Nina Paley, Susan Miller Jones, Jeanne Harrison, Eileen Keane, Cely

Pedescleaux, Natalia Bonner, Karen Miller, Laura Flusche, Laura Oswald, Eric Suszynski, Raymond Houston, Mark and Yvonne Darrell, Maria Shell, Leonie and Bill West, Tricia Royal, Janna Thomas, Erica Shockey, Amy Milne, Sherri Lynn Wood, Teresa Duryea Wong, Roderick Kirocofe, Jayna Zweiman, and Karlee Porte who all contributed important information, advice, and support at key moments in this project. We talked to non-quilters too, including lawyers and legal scholars, and I so appreciate their knowledge and time. Thank you to Patricia Aufderheide, Ann Bartow, Sara Benson, Maureen Collins, Dale Nelson, Brandy Karl, Dave Fagundes, Joey Vitale, Brian Frye, David Gantz, Chris Reed, Michael Madison, Chris Sprigman, David Levine, Rebecca Tushnet, Cynthia Burstein Waldmen, John Loken, Kenny Crews, Jessica Silbey, Giancarlo Frosio, Dave Fagundes, Yvette Liebesman, Bobbi Kwall, Lucas Osborn, and Heather Fleniken McFarlane.

To our research sponsors, who sent us samples of things and equipment and everything imaginable so we could experience and immerse ourselves: Jaftex, Michael Miller, the Stencil Company, June Tailor, the Warm Company, Havel's Sewing, Sulky, Honest Fabric, All Brands, AccuQuilt, Superior Threads, Wonderfil, AccuQuilt, The Wool Project, Quilted Twins, Paper Pieces, Quiltsmart, Sulky, Put a Quilt on it, Craftoptics, Martelli, the Grace Company, and the pattern designers, authors, inventors and others who sent us things to review and digest on so many levels.

And especially to the 2 Quilting Army proofing teams that included Scott Murkin, Susan Perkins, Megan Patent-Nygren, Polly Mumma, Randi Hindman, Dominique Newland, Carole Lancon, Misty-Anne Marold, Jo-Anne Vandermey, Christine Weld, Amy Reitzel, Wendy Starn, Jessica Plunkett, Sandra Scheiber Johnson, Brit Staven Eddy, Jeanette Floyd, Laura Houston, Patti Baymiller, Stacy Harding, Suzy Webster, Rachel McAlister Bishop, Melanie McNeil, Anne Vandermey, Ann Wasserman Rose Zapel, Cathy Birkholz, and Carol Stovall McCauley, who all reviewed this crazy, long, detailed book. You kept me going. Really. And to Sandra Hoving Engstrand, Karen Klamczynski, Beth Hennen Strand, Julia Driscoll, Cely Pedescleaux, Lisa Pickering, Hilary Harrison, and Tara Miller who have been especially kind to this ever-growing project.

And to my local QA core team. *Judy Walker*, who started this project with me, took "meeting" walks with me with Rocky and Jazz, taught me how to be a "journalist", let me into her amazing quilting world (and her stash) and became known as "Judy the Neighbor." *Joel Sellers*, who is the most fun to figure out all the longarming with; I love our adventure. *Gigi Baay*, who taught me how to make cosplay jackets, ran our Gypsy Wife sew-along, and became my 'Quilting spouse". *Edith Gross*, whose entrepreneurial spirit, generosity and willingness to have interrupted discussions every afternoon means so much. And *Willow Olson* (not local), who puts up with me and keeps our Inventory Quilt project moving in the right direction. You have lived this project and this manuscript with me every step of the way.

To the law students, especially Corrie Dutton, Ricardo Gonzalez, Madison Manoushagian, Allison Higgins, Rachel Arrison, Katie Dye, and Chris Blexrud. Corrie kept us organized and co-ran the first sew-along with Gigi Baay. Chris was our first podcast producer, and he also helped us to think through the logistics of the sound recordings. And the IP and Entrepreneurship course, the Advanced Copyright Lab, Ron Gard's undergraduate Communications and

Entrepreneurship courses, and the Art Law and Culture class have all jumped in the most amazing ways -- we've had around 125 students work on the project starting in 2018.

To the Dean of the law school, David Meyer, the Provost, Robin Forman, and the Director of the Taylor Center, Kenneth Schwartz, for listening patiently, and providing resources, even when they were not quite sure of the project. To the Newcomb Institute for awarding additional funding through the Greenbaum Fellowship 2019-2020, and to the A.B. Freeman School of Business for the Lepage Faculty Fellowship, 2018- for two years of funding as well. To the Development Office, accounting, and all of the other areas of Tulane that have had to figure out a ton of weird questions. And to Janice Sayas, our Senior Program Manager, who is always my partner in crime, and always positive when the next crazy project needs her help.

Always, to my kid, Sid -- who took a 6-week tour by train, has quilted, worked two booths in Houston, and been willing to be part of this crazy adventure, along with their best friend Sky, whose company, Eyeridium, is responsible for all of our graphics and design. To my partner and husband, Ron, who is surviving (barely) the quilt invasion that has turned our house into something full of fabric, members of the Quilting Army at all hours, and even (now) two big long-arm machines that I keep promising him will find a home at the law school. And of course, to Patrick and Remy, the cats who love to quilt with me, and Rocky and Jazz, who lay by my side as I experiment with English Paper Piecing or put on a binding. I love that they all see a new quilt as the best place to sleep in the house.

And finally, Ricardo Gonzalez, who jumped into the research of this book as a 2L law student, spending multiple days inventorying Judy Walker's stash to crazy quilting adventures from Houston to Nashville and back to Houston to taking on tough research questions as a law student, and now, our Editor-in-Chief in the Just Wanna series. Your patience is remarkable, with all of us in the Quilting Army, and especially me. Your kindness, cleverness, and intellectual rigor make this project just so much better, and I appreciate the babysitting as I sought to finish this ridiculously massive book.

For more about the project, go to http://www.justwannaquilt.com, or visit our Facebook group, Just Wanna Quilt, and our Instagram, JustWannaQuilt. Our shop and podcast can be accessed directly at our website.

Table of Contents

Preface

A Legal Resource for Navigating Copyright and a Little Bit of Trademark

Just Wanna Create: Copyright and Fair Use Strategies attempts to approach the question of copyright as a means of empowerment. Many artists hide from copyright, ignore it, worry about it, or don't know where to get accurate information. We hope this book fills that gap and reorients the relationship of the artist to see copyright as a creative and helpful tool.

First, we look into the process of creation, and the role that copyright does (and does not) play. We also look at the options and realities of what happens once a creation is presented to the public -- for view, for sale, or for commentary. Each chapter explains key concepts to help the artist/author strategize as to how to approach issues that may arise.

You will note that some of the examples are focused on quilting. Quilting is a $5 billion industry, with creators, small businesses, and huge corporations, which we have been studying for the past two years. We have been immersed in understanding other creative industries as well, including video games, art, street art, and tattoos among others. But artists creating are artists creating regardless of the medium. The information presented in this book can be applied in many situations and mediums. Don't be worried that this book is limited to the quilting industry. But if you are interested, you can listen to the podcast, Just Wanna Quilt, on iTunes and other podcast platforms.

Finally, this book concerns U.S. law. Copyright is based on where a potential infringement might occur -- the country of infringement matters. We have included an International copyright chapter, however, as a starting point for those living outside of the U.S.

The following is part of a larger "Just Wanna" Series that assists in understanding various legal aspects of the creative process, including *Just Wanna Patent* and *Just Wanna Trademark*, available at www.justwannaquilt.bigcartel.com.

-Ricardo Gonzalez
Editor-in-Chief

Part 1: Introduction

1: How to Use This Book

Developing Your Copyright Superpowers

This book is an attempt to make copyright more accessible to those who are immersed in it every day: artists, quilters, and other creatives. When we paint a picture, when we send an email, and when we create a quilt, we are engaging in copyright. And yet, most of us are not aware or do not know anything about copyright law. And what we do know is often murky, or sometimes confusing, or conflicting. We believe that having a strong command of copyright increases creativity and confidence and, on the whole, makes for a better community of creativity.

In my office, I have three zebra-print chairs, and not just because I like zebra fabric (although I really do). Copyright is like those three chairs -- it is rarely linear, black-and-white. Rather it jags around, hits unexpected dead ends, and changes with the landscape of how one is using a work. This book is meant to help you understand the physics of copyright, and once you have that, the law and reasoning will make a lot more sense. Embrace its messiness. This is the law supporting creativity, and creativity itself is messy.

This book has been designed as a step-by-step guide. Think of it as a friend helping you along. Copyright has its own physics, its own way of organizing the world. This book in part is helping you understand the physics. Copyright is also a practical regulation system. Register your work. Put proper copyright notice on the work. Do these and other steps. Decide what kind of rights statement you might include on a work. All of these are practical, mechanical issues.

Copyright is also filled with balancing and analyzing, particularly fair use. There are not always answers. But if you understand how copyright works, you will be able to puzzle out solutions. When we are puzzling, we are also thinking, "If this is litigated, how would a court approach the problem?" Of course, there are no guarantees in that answer, but one can do a risk assessment as part of your puzzling. Copyright is also a weird thing. Infringement occurs millions of times a day. Yet, litigation is rare. We have alternative mechanisms, particularly with social media platforms, to regulate behavior. But even then, copyright is difficult to enforce. Social norms and community standards play an important role in this system. We will talk more about this.

Just Wanna Create is part of a larger project, Just Wanna Quilt. Just Wanna Quilt started as a simple project -- learn about quilting and understand the role of copyright within the quilting world. Now over 300 interviews later, the project has grown into a podcast, a sew-along, and so much more. We have a Facebook group of over 2800 active members that we call the Quilting Army. And we are learning about the quilt industry, why we quilt, and who we are. We have also interviewed famous quilters including Tula Pink, Alex Anderson, Mary Fons, Marianne Fons, Ebony Love, Angie Wilson, Rob Appell, Jenny Doan, Chawne Kimber, Christa Watson, Cheryl Sleboda, and Patrick Lose, to name just a few. We've talked to different charities and protest quilters, to historians, and museum curators. We've learned about batting, thread, how fabric is made and learned about lots of tools. I've also asked a lot of questions about copyright and other areas of intellectual property--where it fits within their/our lives in quilting. I also quilted every night -- trying different techniques, experiencing patterns, learning EQ8, marveling at the AccuQuilt system, and thinking, as I worked, about copyright. So, as you read, you will see that a lot of the examples come from quilting.

Do you need to be a quilter to read this book? No. Quilting stands in the place of any creative or scholarly pursuit – something where you have skill, a set of tools, a common language, and with one's own creativity, the production of new creative works. Creative is creative. Quilting stands in that place of creativity.

After all of that work and research, in the end, this book is about copyright. It's about translating what I know about copyright to you -- whether you are an enthusiastic hobbyist, an entrepreneur, an industry leader, a famous quilter, an artist, a scholar or a publisher. This is practical: a book that puts us all on the same page, so to speak. What is copyright? We have to understand creativity to better understand how the law does or does not operate, and in the end, for us to understand the boundaries, tools, and edges of the law.

Our Copyright Approach: New Orleans' Neutral Ground

Copyright is complicated, and it is also political. *Who* is teaching you copyright matters on the approach they take and sometimes colors their expression of copyright. I have spent my career creating tools and work that empower creativity. We all create works. We all base those works and new creations on materials that were already created. Some of those underlying materials will be protected by copyright; others won't. We are trying to understand the system and balance. We are all creators of copyrighted works; we are all users of copyrighted works.

The neutral ground on St. Charles Avenue, New Orleans when there is not a parade. The streetcar runs down the neutral ground. Photo by Sid Gard.

The Neutral Ground: As an author, my philosophy is important. At Tulane Law School, we at the Copyright Research Lab (where this book is originating) have become known over the last decade for being like the city of New Orleans itself. Fun (of course) but more importantly, a neutral ground. In the mid-1800s, New Orleans divided itself into two camps, the French Creoles on one side, and the English-speaking Anglo-Americans on the other.

These groups were divided by Canal Boulevard, which quickly became known as the "neutral ground." We still refer to many green areas on our streets around town as the "neutral ground," and it is where we stand for parades and special times throughout the year, and where we park our cars when the waters get a little bit too high. Copyright, in many ways, is like the divisions of long-ago New Orleans, with different camps about how protectionist and how free to be with cultural works on each side. We remain on the Neutral Ground. This book is about understanding the physics of copyright, and how it applies in various situations. We try to give you a real-world view of the realities of copyright in general, and of the specific field, in this case, quilting. But we are not here to take sides or to espouse opinions. We are here to educate and inform, and provide a context for the decisions you ultimately make. The Copyright Neutral Zone.

About Me

I am a copyright and intellectual property law professor at Tulane University, and I Just Wanna Quilt. For the last two years, I've been immersed in this amazing, crazy, fun project that has taken over my life, my family, my office, the house, and every waking moment. I wouldn't change any of it. All of the activities, the quilts started and some finished, and insanely great new friends made this book.

My first quilt, circa 1980, "A Pink Trip Around the World," constructed with my mom, Sarita (Steinberg) Townsend

I made my first quilt with my mom at age 13 in 1980, at the height of the new quilting renaissance. I remember going to quilting shop filled with fabric, my mom thinking it was a bit expensive, and picking out materials for that quilt--a pink quilt to match my room. I remember hating one of the fabrics (even to this day) and not speaking up. And I remember my mom and me binge-quilting and finishing the quilt within the weekend. We tied it. It remained on my bed until I went to college five years later, traveled to college with me, and now had pen stains from when I fell asleep studying. I still have that quilt today.

Somehow, with all the moves and life events, the quilt has stayed with me. And I can still remember loving each and every step, including the joy of making it with my mom. I've been quilting on and off ever since that pink quilt, with two major intense quilting periods, first in the early 2000s, and now since 2016. (We'll come back to this part of the story shortly). The current project, called Just Wanna Quilt, began two years ago.

I quilt way too late at night, am often impatient, am frustrated by some of the creative mechanics -- I still sometimes hate to iron or rip out stitching, just the way I did with my mom (but as I mature in my 50s, I am trying to learn to love ironing and ripping out), and I love, love, love the sound of the sewing machine. Sometimes I just sew strips to hear the hum. I've made about 40 quilts over the last two years, and have about 20 additional unfinished projects, where I dabbled to understand a particular podcast guest's pattern, technique or invention -- but realized I had to move on to something else. As I quilt, I think about intellectual property, and usually copyright.

In an interview by Abby Glassenberg, I was asked early on what qualified me to undertake the study I was embarked upon. I think my answer was something like "Everything I've done professionally was leading to this moment."[1] Let's take a look.

[1] Abby Glassenberg, "Just Wanna Quilt Podcast Aims to Shed Light on Quilting and Intellectual Property Law", While She Naps, March 20, 2018, https://whileshenaps.com/2018/03/just-wanna-quilt-podcast-aims-to-shed-light-on-quilting-and-intellectual-property-law.html (last visited January 17, 2020).

Cultural Historian by Training: I earned my Ph.D. in Cultural History from UCLA, with a focus on how people express, and sometimes heal, through art and writing from war, and in particular the Great War (World War I). I also studied biography, and worked at the Oral History department at UCLA, where transcribing interviews was one of my jobs in grad school. In 2019-2020, I was awarded the Greenbaum Fellowship at the Newcomb Institute at Tulane University to go back to this work – looking at narrative in fiber arts: how do we write our lives in our crafts?

Law Training: I went to law school after my Ph.D. work because I had a lot of copyright struggles in writing my dissertation, which was a generational biography on the First World War generation. I stayed an extra year to earn an LL.M. in International Trade, along with my J.D. After law school, I had a one-year post-doctoral fellowship at the London School of Economics, where I taught (British) copyright and International Copyright. I also began as a non-resident fellow (since 2004) with the Stanford Center for Internet and Society. Then, we moved from London to Seattle in the U.S., where again I was teaching intellectual property. After teaching a year at Seattle University School of Law, I was offered a tenure-track position at Tulane Law School in New Orleans. I have been teaching intellectual property, art law, entrepreneurship, and social media/advertising law at Tulane University since 2007. I've been cited by the U.S. Supreme Court in *Golan v. Holder* (2012) for my work on the Durationator, a research system I invented that determines the copyright status of any work, anywhere in the world. But I never forgot my roots: creatives and scholars working in a copyrighted world. I took on projects focused on art law, video games, and music. I kept asking the same question: what is the role of law in creativity? I was, and still am, on the hunt for the answer.

Entrepreneurship Training: I also learned a lot about entrepreneurship and became the Jill H. and Avram A. Glazer Professor of Social Entrepreneurship, which funded both the Durationator and the Just Wanna Quilt project for five years. I am now a Lepage Faculty Fellow at the A.B. Freeman School of Business at Tulane University for the last two years. Ron Gard, my husband, and I, started a company for one of my projects, and it was hard. We struggled. That was 2008. Since then, we have both taught entrepreneurship in many forms, and we recognize the needs of entrepreneurs to have understandable guidance and knowledge to move forward. Now I've formed the Quilting Army Krewe, LLC, to study the entrepreneurial arm of the Just Wanna Quilt project, and unlike our first company, I'm all in and will leave no question unanswered. There is no longer hesitation about thinking and understanding what it means to be an entrepreneur. So, I began this project as a cultural historian, an intellectual property law professor focused on copyright for creatives, and an entrepreneur. I was not prepared for what I would learn from the quilting industry and the quilters I would meet. I am transformed.

Just Wanna Quilt Training: For the last two and a half years, I've been immersed--in quilting, in the quilt industry, and in making a Quilting Army. I've gained tremendously from this project. I've learned by doing, listening, and chatting. The friends are real. The quilts are flawed but still amazing. I have dedicated thousands of hours to learn the process, industry and art of quilting to better understand the intersection of law. I feel like this is just the beginning and we're 300+ interviews in, with over 3000 posts, over 24,000 comments, 67,000 reactions, 2,500 active members out of a total of 2,800 members. Every day, I learn a little bit more about the interaction of art, community and the law.

The Story of Two Hats

When I was interviewing for my present job at Tulane Law School, I had to give a presentation to the faculty, after which faculty traditionally ask questions. One of the more intimidating older professors barked at me from the back of the room, "It seems like you want copyright both ways: you aren't taking the side of the creator or the user of culture. Don't you need to pick a team?" My answer to him was: "no." We are always both creators and users of culture.

Creator Hat: We are all creators of culture. Every one of us takes photos, writes email, etc. For many reading this book, we also create all kinds of physical things: art quilts, traditional quilts, baby quilts, protest quilts. Others may create photographs, paintings, drawings, graphic-novels, rugs, woven art, pottery, and many other objects. Each of those is potentially protected by copyright.

User Hat: We are also all users, borrowers of culture. No one creates in a vacuum. We use building blocks, quilters use those found in Barbara Brackman's encyclopedia of quilt blocks. Others may use design motifs on ancient wall art or pottery. We are inspired by art, nature, and our fellow quilters and crafters.

So, when you think about copyright, you think with both hats – you are a creator, who is potentially protective of your works. To create that work, you are a user, relying on others' works, techniques, things in the public domain, and ideas. We are going to work through each of these concepts and more in order to better understand how copyright works. And of course, the hats matter more if you are using the works in a commercial setting. Everything gets more intense. We'll leave that for the rest of the book.

Jeanette Floyd's "Man with Locs" (Handsome). "I purchased a clip art piece and sized it to my choosing. It is an applique felt. Then, I used a walking foot to create a halo effect around him. I faced it instead of using binding because I didn't want to distract from the fact." Jeanette has been quilting for 3 years. This piece as accepted for Road to California Quilt Show. Photo provided by Jeanette Floyd.

Structure of the Book

Part 1 looks at the basics: why we quilt, and the basics of intellectual property.

Part 2 then turns to a deep dive into copyright to provide a basis for further discussions, including copyrightable subject matter, idea/expression, first sale, aesthetic non-discrimination, and useful arts doctrine, copyright terms, the concept of the public domain, and authorship, among other key terms. Part 2 is important and may seem hard to get through. Push through. This is your education into the law that protects your creative work.

Part 3 focuses on the practical: registering your work with the U.S. copyright office, creating notice and rights statements, and strategies when things go wrong.

Part 4 looks more carefully at a working definition and strategy with fair use, both in terms of copyright as well as trademark. This is an important element of any creator's work. It's worth the time to think about carefully.

Part 5 addresses specific scenarios.

Part 6 brings everything together into a Copyright Quilt.

Take it slowly. Read and absorb. You are establishing a way of thinking, working, and interacting with the world. And if you have questions, feel free to email me - townsend@tulane.edu, or join our Facebook Group, Just Wanna Quilt.

2: Why We Create

Why We Create Reflects on Our Relationship with Law

Understanding copyright law means understanding the context of where that law is being applied. The basic questions: who, what, where, and why matter in how and what part of the copyright law applies. This is true for any art. For this book, we are looking at quilting to understand the legal issues, but many of the questions apply to any art medium.

Copyright law governs the creative works of our world – the paintings, literature, films, quilts, street graffiti, woodworking, software, and music, to name just a few. Copyright also governs our everyday activities – posting photos on Instagram, Pinterest, and Facebook, for example. Copyright governs fan works, piracy, and appropriation art. Copyright also allows for Google searches, recording TV shows to watch later, and making copies of software onto your computer. Copyright does a lot of heavy lifting. And yet, in our world, because of the structure of the system, copyright law is not as straightforward or obvious as studying for a driving test. It is more nuanced, complicated, and often includes a risk assessment of how likely someone is to sue or react badly to an unauthorized user. Copyright, in short, is weird. We all interact with copyright every day, and yet, most of us will not be involved in any copyright scuffle, even if we technically commit copyright infringement.

Copyright involves many questions, not only about the object but how you are using an object. Let's look at the quilting world as an example. Are you trying to mass-produce quilts outside the United States? Are you making charity quilts? Are you a hobbyist that enters quilt shows? Are you reproducing a quilt from the 1800s? Are you a fabric designer with a particular "look" to your designs? Quilting can mean many things, and depending on the circumstances, the relationship of the law to the endeavor may alter.

Copyright is about relationships with creative works. We start with the act of creating, and more specifically (for our example) creating quilts. So, I asked the Quilting Army -- what is quilting and why do we quilt?

What is Quilting?

Quilting can be described by its utility: a blanket for keeping one warm. In this way, quilting can be described by its outcome. Quilting can also be described as a series of three layers of fabric.

> *The top:* made in a variety of ways, including bits of fabric sewn together, one whole piece of cloth, sometimes with pieces of fabric sewn on top (applique), and so much more. It is a piece of art.
>
> *The middle:* usually batting (soft, various thicknesses)
>
> *The Bottom:* the back. This again has a wide variety... But it is larger than the first two layers, until it is finished, and can be pieced from a variety of fabrics or be one big piece of fabric.
>
> *Holding it together:* This can be quilted (yes, that is what it is called) where the three layers, either by machine, by hand, or tied with pieces of thread, are connected together. The stitching can be simple or very complicated.

Layers of creativity create warmth, art, and beauty. Quilting can also be described as a means of creating art -- "that was quilted." But quilting is much more than the outcome. It's a way of life, a passion, and an obsession for many. That is true of many art forms.

When we asked the Quilting Army "what is quilting", they said not only these practical things but also: "justification for being a fabric hoarder." (Monica Daigle Pharo); "My life" (Ilse de Koker); "A form of sewing, an art, relaxation therapy (usually after being finished with something that was stressing me out by not going right!) (Julia Driscoll); "Medication for the soul" (Tracy Phillips); "A socially acceptable obsessive-compulsive disorder" (Beth Hennen Strand); and my own, "Materializing Love." So, quilting, from the beginning, is much more than putting three layers of fabric together and stitching them together. This complex of art, purpose, and beauty is found in many art forms. We have to understand this to understand how copyright intersects with what we do.

> Quilting is
>
> an art form
> building someone else's puzzle
> therapy
> community
> shopping
> sharing, love, and giving
> a skill and a talent and a frustration and a joy
> a $5 billion industry
> our history
> our obsession
> our identity
> political, apolitical, religious, agnostic

our family business, our livelihood
our hope that someday we will retire and do nothing else
our escape from the pressures of our everyday life
all of these things and more

Quilting is full of processes, steps, habits, traditions, field trips (to quilt stores, shows, retreats, friends' houses, classes, guild meetings), and learning. It is also filled **with creative choices** (fabric, designing, quilting), learning new techniques, and the sheer will to complete a project (or not). Creative choices are where copyright comes in.

Applique Quilt by Sandy Fitzpatrick

Sewing Solo within a Larger Community

I make quilts for family and friends. While I do enjoy my solitude while working in my studio, I also love working with my quilting friends. We always have so much fun catching up, sharing what we're working on, sharing tips, laughing, eating, and laughing some more. We may not be productive on the project we brought to work on, but we always feel so good when we leave to go home. - Dena Martin, JWQ, August 9, 2019

> I quilt primarily by myself and I enjoy that. However, I also occasionally quilt with guildmates and quilty friends and it's some of my most favorite times :) I'm way less productive in terms of quilting but more productive in terms of filling my need for community. - Jessica Plunkett, JWQ August 9, 2019

For many creatives, we create on our own-- working solo. Quilters are the same. We are often lone quilters, working at all hours of the day and night. I am one of those. I love quilting on my own, with Patrick and Remy, the cats. But even lone quilters sometimes venture out -- to quilt shows, guilds, classes, shops, and retreats, to name a few spaces. Quilters are also part of a community of creatives that guide and influence their work. My friend and neighbor, Judy Walker, who surrounds herself with and creates community wherever she goes (and often drops into my lone space), not only works at a quilt shop, is part of at least two local guilds, but also has two family guilds (yes!) that have annual retreats.

Quilt Guilds: Many join local and national quilt guilds. These can range from a few people to 1000s. The Modern Quilt Guild has branches and national conference, QuiltCon, each year. Locally in New Orleans, we have many guilds and groups. Mostly women gather once a month, on a Saturday or on an evening. They talk about quilting, organize charity events, plan retreats, and often have quilt projects as part of the meeting. And of course, there is show and tell.

Judy's world is filled with a whole quilting world -- family guilds, local guilds, and she organizes the vendors for our regional quilt show, which is an organization of over 40 guilds in four states. I feel lucky to be in that world in a small way. In many ways, Judy is our guide to the community aspect of JWQ. We have done much of our community-building because of ideas from Judy, and we are all richer for that.

Judy Walker's Sampler from her family quilt guild, the Claxton Family Guild

Some find community, like Judy did, in their families. "Quilting is a family tradition as my mother, grandmother, and great grandmother all quilted. My sister and I both do. I've tried a lot of crafts and now just quilt. It's just very satisfying." (Mary Pitchard Furber). And Ann Collins writes, "all of the above: I started very young with my grandmother with a needle and thread, watching her cut her pieces using sandpaper or cardboard. In the final years of her life, her sight was failing her but she never stopped. I remember her taking a piece of fabric and fold it to create perfect squares. So, for me, it is a passion and a privilege to continue for her."

My Christmas Quilt circa 1999, my first attempt at quilt blocks, designed with new husband Ron Gard. We purchased the fabric at Walmart, the blocks came from the Internet, and the cross-stich from patterns my mother mailed me from her collection

For me, quilting has also been connected to family, too. My mom, to begin, but then when I started quilting again in the 2000s, my new (now seasoned) husband would help me design quilts, including this Christmas quilt. And then, once the kid was 5, Sid became my quilting partner, joining in on shopping, sewing, and designing.

Others find community in their friends, in their guilds, in their co-workers. We see retreats year after year of groups of friends and guilds. Some, like Liz Lesher, meet with a friend every Friday to spend time, in her case quilting, while her friend does another craft. For most of us, there is a balance: Linda Newman explains, "I'm kind of an introvert so really enjoy quilting on my own with an audiobook or music playing. But I do participate in a small friendship group and we do handwork (bindings, embroidery), and a couple of retreats a year. I love the feedback and collaboration of a retreat."

Our images of "olden times" (a technical term, of course) are of women sitting around sewing together in quilting bees has some founding in experience. Some of our Quilting Army have stories and memories from their childhood. Anne Vandermey recalled, "My first quilting experience was at the Vermont Quilt Festival in 2003. I sat with a group of women and participated in hand quilting a quilt on a frame. They loved it. I was 12 turning 13 at the time." Megan Patent-Nygren remembered, "My grandma led a community of quilters in the church I grew up in. They met (actually still do) regularly to make quilts for Lutheran World Relief and local charities. Five to six people would be sewing, a few cutting squares, someone pressing and some tying quilts. In the summer, I would help." And Camille Ainsworth tells a story that reminds us that "olden times" is not that long ago: "It wasn't until we moved to Oregon in 1996 that I was able to see a group quilting on quilts using a frame. My mom joined a local church group, while she was working part-time, at their quilting bee. Every Friday the ladies would set up the two frames in the community room of the church and stitch for 2-3 hours on the quilts. They had a list of everyone in the group and they'd rotate quilts on the frame once the current quilt was finished. Part of their service was to make a quilt for the church to raffle off each year. I had the opportunity to go a couple of times and try my hand at hand quilting. Being only 14, I didn't appreciate the experience and what I was doing was a tradition that went back hundreds of years."

After the 2013 Boston Marathon bombing (April 15, 2013,) I took Sid, my kid, to the New England Quilt Museum (Lowell, MA), because there was a community-sewing day to contribute to a memorial quilt of the event. The artist, Clara Wainwright was creating a quilt entitled "Mending Boston." We lived in New Orleans; the sewing day was some 1500 miles north in Massachusetts. So, we planned our trip to visit the family to coincide with this event. I wanted Sid to have the experience of quilting with others for a reason and purpose. (Sid was about 10 at the time; she's the one standing).

An afternoon of community sewing, New England Quilt Museum, sewing "Mending Boston" with Clara Wainwright. Sid Gard (age 10) stands sewing.

We stayed for hours. We had an amazing afternoon. That was long before I met Pam Weeks, now Curator for the New England Quilt Museum. We had an amazing afternoon. I often wonder if we saw Pam that day; she has now become a dear friend.

There is also a middle space of community in quilting held together by meetings and by technology. We share our ideas, plans and aspirations over email and through social media. We get advice, critiques and technique input from people we've never met in person, but are part of our community. We may go to a sewing day with others and their voices and creativity influences ours. We can look at an infinite number of images to get inspiration. Like no other time in history, we can see and find community in both digital and physical space. This may resonate with some other creative works, but feel foreign to others. But, this is part of that messy part of quilting I mentioned above and why copyright is invariably complex in the creative world.

Quilting Online Communities

Community continues to be a huge part of quilting, whether that is neighbors getting together, guilds, churches, quilt retreats, even quilt cruises; social media and even old-fashioned snail mail, where all kinds of blocks and challenges are exchanged. And these communities are often making charity quilts, or collaborative quilts in one way or another. They are teaching, learning and sharing. That is part of who we are, and a big part of the quilting story and ecosystem. But we also see entrepreneurial communities. And of course, the growth of online communities.

When I started this project, I also joined quilting groups on Facebook (FB), and of course, we started the *Just Wanna Quilt* Facebook group. Here are a few examples of the groups I joined and the number of members at the time of publishing (Jan 2020):

- Quilting on a Budget (34,943 members)
- Quilt Pattern Designers (715 members)
- Quilting with David Gilleland (1,387 members)
- Quilters Creative Touch (1,564 members)
- Q'nique 14+/15R (the longarm we have) (1,992 members)
- Threads of Success (entrepreneurial) (98 members)
- Simple Handmade Everyday (671 members)
- Quilted Twins (10,679 members)
- QuiltHistorySouth (777 members)
- Beecher Memorial UCC Quilt group (120 members)
- Christa Quilts (5,059 members)
- Free-Motion Challenge Quilting Along (31,961 members)
- Gypsy Wife Quilt Group (3,482 members)
- Quilting Tula Pink Lovers (4,575 members)
- Machine Applique Adventures (1.103 members)
- Stitch TV (1,539 members)
- Westalee by Me (quilting rulers) (9464 members)
- Hand Pieced Quilt along (1,678 members)
- Muppin (4,069 members)
- Bernina Lovers (18,880 members) and
- Quilt Alliance (7,278 following)

Seth Hackler runs Quilting on a Budget, a Facebook phenomenon of over 30,000 members. We've gotten to know him over the last two years. He has a way of drawing people in and making them feel comfortable. He is starting to branch out and think about next steps with his group. The Stitch TV is a weekly show, with an accompanying FB group, run by Pam Cobb and Lynn Rinehart, where they talk about quilting things; they also have a pattern line. Quilters Creative Touch is a group devoted to discussing the automation software put out by Grace Company, a place where members help each other with various questions and share successes. Quilted Twins is the combination of Becky in Poland, who makes charity quilts and patterns that are spectacular, and her sister Rachel, who has a discount fabric shop in Florida. Each group has its own quirkiness and focus.

The big ones?

- Missouri Star Quilt Company with 110,050 followers
- Quiltville by Bonnie K. Hunter, with 122,289 followers
- Quilt as You Go with 99,677 members
- Scrap Quilt Enthusiasts 67,700 members
- Quilting Space with 77,206 members
- Quilt Along with Pat Sloan with 58,429 members.

Just Wanna Quilt's FB group has been an enormous part of the project. At the time of writing, we are 2800 strong. We also have three subgroups, JWQ-Gypsy Wife Sew Along, JWQ-Inventory Quilt and my personal favorite, the JWQ-Stealth Sewing Squad, where we work on sewing projects needed for the Just Wanna Quilt project. These groups are bringing people together in interesting ways working on projects that help us explore copyright.

Platforms like Facebook and Instagram provide connectivity and spaces to find support, kindness, learning, and problem solving. Many of us are lone quilters but not alone. This project is dramatically richer because of these connections. Quilters go to these groups for friends. We share what we're working on. We learn to fix problems. We find groups specific to a sewing machine brand that we might be thinking of purchasing. We troubleshoot problems with software in the group. The Facebook group is a central component of the quilting world, at least in 2020. This is true for so many creatives -- there exist a myriad of general and narrow "cyber" groups in our space that we can join for support and inspiration.

The thing about the online groups, from my experience, is that they turn into real friendships, where you chat on the phone, meet in person at various events, and share, both quilty things but also the joys of new babies and the sadness of life. These relationships and groups are powerful and important, and so far, underestimated by the quilting industry.

Types of Quilters

You are creating a quilt—from inspiration, from a variety of sources. It's yours. You might be making it for a wedding or birth, or selling the pattern professionally. The context of the resources you use and what you plan to do with it matters. That's what this book is all about! And in many ways, we are rarely in just one of these categories, but they help us start to understand the relationship between the creative process and copyright.

The Quilter

The techniques vary - piecing, foundation piecing, English paper piecing, applique, improv, to name a few. But the focus is on creating works from fabric that are generally meant to be used, not just admired. We experiment. We try new styles. We have favorite color palettes. We try to master the ¼" seam. Some of us care if our points match. We, the Quilting Army, quilt. Over the last two years, I've tried as many techniques as possible, meaning I have about 35 finished quilts and uncountable started/abandoned projects. But I think that there are so many possibilities is part of what makes quilting so alluring, addictive, and awesome. My favorite? Surprisingly machine applique!

The Artist

Quilters are artists, and we have some spectacular, famous ones. Chawne Kimber, Jacquie Gering, Amy Messinger, Claudia Pfeil, and Sue Bleiweiss come to mind. Tula Pink. Wendy Starn, part of our Quilting Army, is making 3 pieces at the time of writing for a show on poverty and homelessness, and she previously finished a piece called "Too Raw" about gun violence. She explains: "I HAVE to make these. My art is my voice." Multi-award-winning quilter Claudia Pfeil describes having to get a quilt out of her creative mind and make it. For some, quilting is just one of many media, as we learned from Victoria Findlay Wolfe, a trained artist who came to quilting after being a sculptor and a painter. You do not have to be famous or a trained artist to create art quilts. Art quilting is a huge part of the quilt landscape. I have had the pleasure of talking to so many art quilters over the last two years.

The Puzzler

We find a pattern, or a kit (a pattern and instructions; often has fabric), and we make it just the way the quilt designer suggested. Or, not. We might alter the colors dramatically. Maybe we substitute a bear for a duck. But when we are finished, it looks like the original. The pattern maker has given the quilter a non-exclusive right to *make that quilt*. No new copyright has been created. Yours is yours. **But you don't have legal rights to do anything but make it.** You can, of course, with your sewing talent, give it away, donate it to an auction, or keep it. Some pattern makers are ok with you selling it, but best practices tell us to ask the pattern maker if the pattern does not explicitly say that you can sell items from the pattern.

The Professional

We had a lot of discussions within our community of what makes someone a professional. Usually it was the focus on earning a living from quilting, rather than strictly a level of skill or dedication to the craft of quilting itself. We see professionals in the quilting industry come from every background. Christa Watson explains: "I fell in love with quilting when I was studying business in college and knew right away that I wanted it to be my business someday as well as my hobby:-) That way I'd have an excuse to quilt whenever I wanted, LOL!!" Some people make their living from quilting, like Cheryl Sleboda. Others are trying to transition from the day job to full-time quilting. Some are retired, but now focused on their entrepreneurial careers. Some maintain a day job and quilt professionally nights and weekends for the income (and the creative release). There are many ways to be professional and to be part of the quilting industry. In many ways, this book is for the professional—someone seeking to commercialize whatever they do within the quilting or craft world. It's when things start to become professional that copyright sits up and takes notice.

But we also see that the industry depends on part-time creatives, submitting their patterns to magazines, designing their fabric lines, teaching a class here and there, and writing a book. The industry is filled with mostly women all over the country doing their part, earning a small bit of money, but being part of a larger world. In many ways, quilting is a cottage industry. And it is not just the companies farming out various tasks to quilters. Think of the longarmers (a longarm is a quilting machine that glides on a carriage that can quilt much faster than with a home machine; some are freehand, some are computerized, some are both) who buy their expensive machines, and take in quilts starting at $.015 per square inch.

The Activist

This is a subset of the art quilters. We talked to Sue Bleiweiss about the political outpouring during the Trump presidency in the U.S. (2017-), and the exhibit, *Threads of Resistance*. We discussed community projects on immigration with Jayna Zweiman and Andrea Tsang Jackson. The quilt as an art form is powerful, dramatic, and beautiful. We talked also to Daric Reed about her powerful piece made for the Women's March 2017.

Daric Reed's "Women Rights Human Rights." Listen to her interview at www.justwannaquilt.com.

We quilt to get our message out, to be heard. And it doesn't have to be big and you don't have to be famous. Sidne Gard made the following quilt in elementary school. We were asked by Coach Dee and art teacher, Susan Holman, to make a quilt for the New Orleans's Anti-Bullying Quilt Initiative. The quilt hung first at New Orleans' City Hall and then at New Orleans Contemporary Arts Center. We'd dealt with bullying issues in 3rd and 4th grade, and Sid really took Coach Dee's lessons about bullying to heart. It was nice to translate that into creation of a message and art. Together, as a family, Sid, Ron and I designed and quilted the 24" x 24" entry. (Sid is great at paper piecing, which is how we created the letters, and is really remarkable at accuracy.) We created this the same year as our Boston trip for "Mending Boston", when Sid was 10 years old.

"Stand Up," by Sid Gard (age 10).

Melanie McNeill's "Resist"

Wendy Starn's "Thoughts and Prayers"

The Solo and Family Business

Quilting is filled with family businesses -- Jaftex, the Stencil Company, Superior Thread, Martelli, Missouri Star Quilt Company, and Christa Quilts, to name just a few. Leah Day's family, along with Tula Pink's, Jenny Doan's, and so many more, all work to support the family business. We saw it with inventors too -- the Bloc Loc, a ruler company focused on the construction stage of a quilt, was created by a husband and wife, as was Westalee quilting rulers, designed by another husband and wife team from Australia. All Brands, that has both five brick-and-mortar shops in Louisiana, along with a strong online presence is also a family affair. For all of these families, quilting is their livelihood either in whole or in part. Quilting is also filled with those doing it all -- they started because of their love for quilting, and now they are running successful businesses that often include teaching, products, and publishing.

Four Generations. I had the pleasure of visiting Scott Fortunoff, both at the fabric warehouse and New York offices of Jaftex, a family-run fabric company that has been in business for 90 years with four generations as part of the business. In their conference room hangs this 85th anniversary quilt, with photographs from the family in each square, and specially made fabric for the occasion. Jaftex includes the fabric companies Blank Quilting Corporation, Studio E Fabrics, Henry Glass & Co, AE Nathan, Fabric Editions, and FreeSpirit Fabrics.

"Happy 85th" provided by Scott Fortunoff, President of Jaftex

The Historian

Quilting is filled with history, and there are many within the quilting world obsessed with understanding and cataloging that history, reproducing quilts from various time periods and so much more. Tara Miller, Barbara Brackman, and Pam Weeks serve as examples of those who focused on the history of quilting. Quilt history, whether it is through study groups, reading and writing books, appraisals, and the art of repairing, is a huge component of the quilt world. This could not be more evident with the advent of major museums dedicated to quilting including the New England Quilt Museum, the National Quilt Museum in Paducah, the International Quilt Museum in Nebraska, the San Jose Museum of Quilts & Textiles, Wisconsin Museum of Quilts & Fiber Arts, and the Iowa Quilt Museum, to name a few.

The Comforter

Many use their quilting skills to comfort others. Comfort comes in a number of forms. The baby quilt or wedding quilt for a family member, friend or colleague. Charity quilting for a cause. Memorializing someone through signature quilts or quilts made out of their clothing. Seth Hackler made a quilt out of his mother's nurses' uniforms and continues to quilt in her memory. Beth Hennen Strand made a signature quilt with a Sawtooth Star pattern when her husband unexpectedly passed away. Quilters spend enormous amounts of time thinking about others and creating and making comforting things to make their lives a little better.

Beth Strand's memorial quilt with signatures and art added to the quilt.

Seth Hackler, "A Son's Loving Tribute," in honor of his mother Angela Mobley-Johnson, made from her nursing scrubs. She spent 21 years as a nurse caring for the elderly. Now, Seth has created the ever popular "Quilting on a Budget" Facebook group.

Camille Ainsworth, and her mother Susan Ainsworth Smith make passage quilts. Ainsworth explains, "Passage or bereavement quilts are donated to local hospitals to be given to family members of dying patients to help give comfort and in remembrance of their loved ones."

Three Passage Quilts created by Camille Ainsworth and Susan Ainsworth Smith.

We talked to so many quilters who quilt for charity -- some at ferocious paces like Amy Reitzel and Becky Tillman Petersen. We talked people who quilted for Project Linus, Quilts of Valor, local charities, foster kids, dog shelters, quilts for firefighters to carry and wrap around a child in need, and so much more. Charity quilting is an enormous part of the quilting world. One of my favorite interviews was with Janice Peachy, who foster cares the most ill of the preemie babies, and when they leave her care, she sends them on with a quilt. We also not only make 10s of 1000s of quilts each year throughout the country. We also make quilts for raffles and auctions for charities.

Carla Triemer of Quilt Beyond Borders and her team of volunteers makes quilts for underserved kids around the world. Carla writes, "This is one of my favorites, taken at a community school for needy children in Ethiopia. It was an amazing experience going there. This picture was taken on a day we went to the Kichene Study Center I'm the blond in the blue raincoat hugging a little boy."

Quilt Beyond Borders provides quilts to kids in underserved areas of the world.

The charity quilting cannot be understated. When I asked for 1-2 images of charity quilting in our Just Wanna Quilt Facebook group, I had 70 comments and images within a few hours. Charity quilting, raffle quilts, and quilts put up for auction are an enormous part of quilting.

We Do Not Need to Choose

We are all of the things described and more. We can do art quilts and charity quilts. We can puzzle one night, and create our own masterpieces. We can sew for our families, and create a business too. We do not need to choose. And we don't....

Holly Hicks fell in love with quilts when she was getting treatments for cancer. Beautiful quilts hung on the wall, and she was given her own charity quilt to keep her warm and raise her spirits. She loved it. Later, while she was recovering, she learned to quilt, which led to the purchase of a longarm, which led to a new business with her two sisters, called Quilting Pantographs, which opened with digital files in October 2019. Holly: recipient of a charity quilt to learning to quilt, to a family business for quilting.

Edith Gross, one of our Core Quilting Army members quilts in many forms. She is an art quilter, with pieces hanging in Houston International Quilt Show, Sacred Threads, Gulf States Quilt Association Quilt Show, North Charleston Cultural Arts Festival, Old Man River Quiltfest, and The Advocacy Project among others. She regularly makes quilts for foster kids in New Orleans, through the Beecher Memorial Quilt Group in the 7th Ward. She has a longarm quilting business. She helped to start a camp to help kids learn to sew. She is all in, and she's only been quilting for five years. Charity quilting, art quilting, a long arm business, and teaching.

This book is for Edith and for Holly, as they each make their way in this quilting world, building their businesses, and expressing themselves in creative work.

Edith Gross' "Sunray's Beauties" created for "Flowers at the Cabin Door" themed show. Based on an idea she had; no photo used.

The Work of Chawne Kimber

Chawne Kimber's work. You know it from across the room. She fills her work with detailed intricate piecing, powerful messages, and color. She uses quotes from life and from books. Sometimes it's just one word, and sometimes that word is naughty or controversial. She is brave in her choices and her politics. Chawne's work is known worldwide. Her famous work, "The One for Eric G" (2015) was acquired by Michigan State University in 2016. She has been featured in the Wall Street Journal, the LA Times, Chicago Tribune, among other publications.

She teaches us patience and slow quilting. She quilts in airports, in silence at home, in the spaces between family and work as a Professor and Department Head of Math at Lafayette College. She embodies so much of what is our world of quilting. Her work is profound and beautiful. But for us, her work is more than that. Here she uses a quote from Eartha Kit's autobiography, *Alone with Me*: "In essence, I am a sophisticated cotton picker." She explained to *The Quilt Show* that the piece is "a direct callback to the make-do utility quilts made by her great-grandmother on a former cotton plantation in Alabama."[2]

Chawne Kimber, "In Essence, I am a sophisticated cotton picker."

The technique of hand-piecing, her particular style, the use of quotes, the quilt itself, the idea of history, the history of our past, her control over where it is hung and if (and when) it is sold, and so much more is what this book is about. My hope is that by providing concrete copyright information you, dear quilter and artist, will be brave and confident in your own choice as you create your own work.

[2] "Cotton Sophisticate," by Chawne Kimber, The Quilt Show Daily Blog, April 13, 2018.

Quilters and Copyright Law

To understand the role of law within the creative process of quilting and other arts, we have to identify what we do. Only then we can begin to ask the legal questions and understand our creative activities in relationship to copyright and other laws.

When We Are Sewists

We buy patterns and kits. We make them. We might give them away. We might keep the final product. We are following the patterns. If we sell the final products, it's our sewing efforts -- the actual physical act of sewing the fabric together -- that people are paying for, not our design. Why? Because we don't own the design when we buy the pattern. **When we buy patterns and kits, are there legal restrictions on what we can do?** Yes! **Can we sell our end-product versions?** There are competing thoughts on that. **What happens if we change the pattern, or choose different colors?** Depends on how much, but merely changing the color, no. **Does this create a new copyright on the quilts?** Depends on a lot of elements. **What is our relationship to the original copyright?**

When We Are Artists

We create patterns. We create quilts. They are masterpieces. They are mundane. We use traditional blocks. We experiment. We improvise. We use different techniques. **What resources can we legally use to create?** That's what the book is about! **What can we be inspired by?** All sorts of things. The question is how close is the inspiration to your new work. **What are the building blocks of our culture?** We'll be exploring that in detail. **What happens when others are inspired by our works?** Depends on how inspired. **How can we protect or works?** Many ways; we'll explore that in this book. **What happens if someone copies our work or if we are accused of copying others' works?** We'll get into that in this book, too.

When We are Inventors

We invent and make tools that help with our quilting endeavors. Sometimes, we patent these. Sometimes, we make businesses based on the inventions. **How do we protect our inventions?** Usually through patents and/or trade secrets. See *Just Wanna Patent*: *The First Steps* by Ricardo Gonzalez. **How do we get our inventions out into the market?** That's the entrepreneurial step. **What inventions are not protectable, and what do you do if your invention falls into that category?** Branding comes into play. See *Just Wanna Trademark* by Elizabeth Townsend Gard.

When We create Businesses

We are pattern makers. We are longarmers. We make memory quilts. We finish bindings. We design fabrics. Our businesses are sometimes part-time, sometimes full-time. Our businesses are sometimes run by one person, multi-generational family endeavors; or sometimes a huge corporation. **What happens to the importance of copyright when something is being done as a business?** We will look at commercial versus non-commercial uses in this book. **Does it change the stakes?** Big time.

When We Quilt for Charity

For strangers. We put our time into quilting for strangers -- for causes, for the sick, for the homeless, for the lost, and the hurt, for joyful occasions, and in memorial. **Can we use any patterns for this activity?** Yes. You can personally use the same pattern as many times as you like, but copyright enters if you are making copies of a pattern you did not create for others to use. **Does charity give more freedom within the copyright system?** No, not necessarily.

When We Quilt for our Families

At key moments in our families' lives, we quilt -- births, birthdays, weddings, anniversaries, sickness, deaths, memorials. **How does copyright impact what we can make and give away to our friends and families?** Non-commercial uses have more freedom under copyright. We'll learn why shortly. **Does this change if our family hires us to make quilts?** As sewists, no. **What if our quilt is so popular with our friends and family that we decide to start an online shop?** Yep, a bit different. Commercial use. **How does that change our relationship with copyright?** Big time.

When We quilt for Ourselves

We quilt because we want to -- as a creative outlet, as relaxation, as therapy. It's our room of our own. It's our time. **Should we care about copyright as we create works in the middle of the night, on weekends, as our kids nap, in the RV as we explore in our retirement the US, or all day long if we have turned our hobbies into our profession?** That will depend on what the ultimate use or outcome of the object you are making is... that's what the book is all about.

When We quilt for Community with Other Quilters

We share our quilting experiences with our friends in quilt guilds, retreats, on social media, and in classes. We quilt with our families. We quilt with our children and grandchildren. **How much can we share our patterns, our fabric, and our ideas?** Ideas are shareable, as is fabric. Patterns are also shareable, but not making copies. **What are the customs of our quilting world, and how does that interact with copyright law?** We will be exploring this more, and the relationship of creativity and community with law.

The answer to these questions helps us to understand your subject position -- your worries, your concerns, when it comes to copyright and other laws surrounding quilting. We'll be exploring that more throughout the book. The answer to these questions always depend on a number of factors. But make no mistake, the variation in the answers does not mean that the answer is not knowable. Copyright is a system. We're going to learn that system, and understand it. In the end, you should be able to answer the questions for yourself.

A Note about Communities and Best Practices

Beginning in 2005, the Center for Social Media and Social Impact at American University (Washington, DC, USA) embarked on a Best Practices project. Patricia Aufderheide and Peter Jaszi embarked on a project. At the time, documentary filmmakers were having a problem. They couldn't clear their films when a baseball game was playing in the background of an interview or a photograph caught a painting. The Best Practices in Fair Use for Documentary Film Makers would start a revolution—how fair use is used by specific communities.

Since the first experience with documentary filmmakers, the Center for Social Media and Social Impact has engaged with many communities to understand the best practices for each community – poets, visual arts, software preservation, journalism, online video, teaching, research and study -- and develop. what makes sense for each community, (I was on the legal review team for the poets' Best Practice.) We haven't had a crafts, and more particularly, a quilting Best Practices. But we can glean the key ingredients.

Communities make their own standards within the context of legal principle, which in turn influence how copyright is interpreted. We'll see that along the way as well. Quilting has a rich public domain, history of sharing, vast and complex culture, and insatiable consumer appetite, even from its modern beginnings in the 19th century. We'll be looking at this aspect of the relationship of quilting, community and copyright throughout this text. Communities also then have the obligation of understanding the law to create and police their own community standards. One of the things that I have seen throughout the project is that there is sometimes a disconnect, a fear, and/or confusion about copyright law -- and with it can come community strife and divisions. But I also am seeing continuity and a common language developing. This is what the project was about in part -- helping artists, quilters and others find their way through copyright within their own artistic experiences.

What You Will Learn from This Book

This book is a long slog (or perhaps an amazing journey) through copyright, I know. But I hope you will come out with the following:

- You will have a strong understanding of copyright, when it matters and how to tackle various issues and scenarios that arise.
- You will know the basics of how copyright interacts with your own creative process.
- You will learn how to protect your copyrighted works, and alternatively how to make them more accessible for others to build and use your works.
- You will have a toolbox for addressing copyright infringement, both if you find yourself being accused, or if someone else infringes on your work.
- You will be able to address various uses, including non-commercial and commercial uses.
- You will be able to help educate others in understanding the relationship of the law to the creative process, and selling creative works in the marketplace

Learn from the book. Share the book (yes!)—lend it to a friend, teach your guild, and post in Facebook groups about what you learn. Knowledge is power. And try to be a good citizen – understand that your actions matter, that you are part of a creative community that is historical, personal and commercial. Understand that copyright can be complicated, but leads to amazing results. We make beautiful work that people appreciate, cuddle with, and love.

The Intersection of Copyright and Quilting: When It Matters

Can't wait till the end of the book? Impatient? Reading this in a quilt shop, and not ready to purchase it? This is the page to "steal." (And for this page only, it's totally ok. Take a photo. Post it online. Do what you want. I give you permission.)

□ **Right of Attribution.** Most people want credit for their work. Don't be a jerk.

□ **Commercial Use**. Many people do not like it when others take their work and make money from it without their permission. Any time you are selling your work, all kinds of considerations come into play. Copyright suddenly cares greatly.

□ **Many Things are Not Protectable**. Techniques, methods, basic shapes, most fonts, and many more things are free for anyone to use.

□ **Idea/Expression**. Ideas are not protectable. The expression of the idea is.

□ **Selection, Arrangement, and Coordination.** How you put together non-protectable things gives you copyright.

□ **First Sale Doctrine.** When you purchase something, you get certain rights to do things...but copying is not one of them.

□ **Copyright Notice and Rights Statements.** Let the world know what matters to you, but learn what is legally supported from this book.

□ **Register Your Work.** If you really care about your work, register it with the U.S. Copyright Office.

□ **Fair Use.** So very, very important to any artist. As one of our Quilting Army members said, "Learn it, live it."

□ **Enforcement.** There are degrees of enforcement: through social media platforms, social pressure, attorney's letters, and of course, a lawsuit. We may also have a new mechanism for enforcement, a small claims court, but it has not yet passed through Congress. But enforcement is also impossible in many situations. It's part of the world we live in.

□ **Derivative Works.** Harder to create than you think. You may have made a mere copy.

□ **Public Domain.** So very, very important to an artist. Learn more about it in this book.

□ **Piracy.** People don't like it when someone steals their patterns by making copies.

□ **Creativity.** Copyright helps to create new works! That's the best part. We'll learn about the public domain, first sale, and fair use, just to name a few copyright tools.

This book helps navigate many situations that arise, both when you are creating works, using other works, and when someone else uses your work.

3: Basics of Intellectual Property

Identifying the Differences Between Patent, Trademark, Trade Secret, Right of Publicity and Copyright

For artists, musicians, filmmakers, quilters, and other creators, copyright law is important, and often ignored until it becomes a problem. The core of what we do as creators is regulated by copyright. Copyright law fits into a larger group of laws called intellectual property. Intellectual property is the legal system that protects our inventions, creative works, our business secrets, and even the economic rights of famous people. Intellectual property includes five topics: copyright, patent, trademarks, trade secrets, and right of publicity. Intellectual property rewards creativity and invention. Each area has different requirements, rules, and exceptions.

Intellectual property is like any other property – land, a table, your dog. It can be purchased and sold; a painting, a quilt, a book of music are all physical, tangible property. But what makes intellectual property *intellectual* is a second set of rights – for the intangible elements. Your house is tangible. An apple is tangible. A song – the song itself – is not. We call it a "public goods problem." There is no natural way to keep you from singing my song, telling your own version of a story or copying that really cool art quilt you saw at a museum. And so, copyright law comes into play. The government gives to the author a limited monopoly to exclude others from singing the song for a certain period of time. The same is true for inventions and other intellectual property topics, the creator or controller of the intellectual property is granted a limited monopoly.

Laws help exclude others from using your invention, creation, or logo. But right behind those exclusive rights there also exist exceptions that allow others to use your work without permission. **This is the bargain of copyright law: you get a bunch of rights to the work you created but so do others.** Another distinction is that song is coming from you – and so many see the right connected to that song as personal, special, and deserving of attribution that is different from the company that built your house or assembled your toaster.

Types of Intellectual Property

There are five basic types of intellectual property, and a thing can fall under more than one type.

Patents: Patents protect inventions, like elements in a sewing machine, medical devices, and some interesting Chemical X. Officially, it is a grant by the federal government that gives the inventor the exclusive right to exclude others from making the patented object for a specific period of time. Then it comes into the public domain, and we all can make our own. The trade-off is that you have to disclose the invention at the time of filing so that when it comes into the public domain, everyone can use the invention. There are a number of different types of patents - design, utility, and process, and patents generally last for about 20 years. You must apply for a patent with the United States Patent and Trademark Office. They are not easy to obtain and can be expensive. Examples of patents in the quilting world include Bloc-Loc rulers (https://www.shop.blocloc.com/), the thread cutter Cutterz (which has both utility and design patents, https://www.threadcutterz.com) and a whole host of June Tailor products (https://www.junetailor.com/). Jill Repp of June Tailor, Inc. has been on the Just Wanna Quilt podcast a number of times. She talked about the importance of patents, and how some inventions are big hits, while others, no matter how inventive, never quite work. Her thoughts on the inventive entrepreneur are refreshing, honest, and fun and offer a relevant perspective to inventors outside the quilting world. Why do people spend time and money on patents? It gives them the right to exclude others from manufacturing the patented work and also gives them advantages in the business world. If you have a process, invention, or something that is functional, you can investigate whether the work might qualify for patents. For more, see *Just Wanna Patent: The First Steps* by Ricardo Gonzalez.

Trade Secrets: Anything that is economically valuable to a business that is kept secret, and not disclosed to the public or others, is a trade secret. Customer lists, business strategies, and recipes are examples. These are protected by both federal and state law, as long as the secret remains secret. You have to take reasonable measures to keep it secret. I was recently at Wizard World Comic Con in New Orleans, and I saw a booth where an artist had created old-time-y sheet music and then overlaid them with images -- the musical composition was his interpretation of the theme song from the show/character depicted in the image. When I asked him how he made them, he responded "trade secret." "Really?" I followed up. "Yes. Really. No one can know how I make it. It's my competitive advantage."

Trademarks: Trademark law is for the purpose of protecting your brand, and to help identify your company and products. Logos, business names, and product names and packaging all fall under trademark. Bloc Loc may have a patent on the little groove that keeps a quarter inch seam from moving when cutting but it's the trademarked name "Bloc Loc" that lets us know what it is. The idea is to inform and keep you, the consumer, from being confused as to the source of the product, and to cut down on your time in looking for a particular product. If you can quickly identify "Bloc Loc" that cuts down the "search cost" in your purchase. The same is true in fabric lines. You can tell the shop that you are looking for Island Turtle Hand Batik, Kaffe Fassett Collective, or Michael Miller – that's trademark in action. Trademark can be a powerful tool. Quilt companies use trademark in many ways. You buy particular tools because you trust

Havel's, Olfa, or Quilter's Select. You like a particular sewing machine company and buy a Juki, Brother, or Janome again. You only buy Tula Pink fabric. Your long-arm is made by Grace Quilting Company. These are all trademarks that help you and others identify a product or service. The trademark stands at their goodwill, what you think of when you see the mark. You buy more products from companies with a trademark you know and trust. Artists in other fields may only use paints, paper, pens, brushes, or software from specific companies as they have loyalty to that trademark

We found, however, that many companies, especially new companies, are <u>not</u> filing for federal trademark. This leaves them vulnerable in myriad ways. We wrote *Just Wanna Trademark* to help with this problem. Through the last two years, we have been encouraging and teaching people how to register their trademarks, either on their own or with an attorney. We've seen *the Quilt District, Quilted Twins, What's Your Stitch,* and many more register their works. If you use your trademark as a hashtag, you are vulnerable that someone else might start using it if you have not registered your trademark with the USPTO. That's what *Just Wanna Trademark is all about.*

Right of Publicity: It's the law that protects the economic value of one's name and likenesses from being used without our permission. If you are famous, there is an economic right in your likeness, image, voice, name, etc. And if you are a regular person, you are asked to sign waivers to have schools post pictures of your kids on the school's website. In this instance, you are waiving the child's right of publicity and/or privacy. We've talked to a number of celebrities in the quilting world, including Alex Anderson, Mary Fons, and Marianne Fons, all who discussed in interviews the value and issues that arose around their right of publicity in legal contracts.

So, when Mary Fons brought Tula Pink to the house to be interviewed on *Just Wanna Quilt*, the power of their right of publicity was palpable. The house has never been cooler. Not in its 100+ year history. And it's still the interview that is most listened and most commented upon when people talk about the show. For both, wherever they go in the quilting world, people line up see them, get their autograph, and take selfies with them. There is value in just being around them. That's part of their economic power, and that is protected by right of publicity. (Listen to the interviews with Marianne, Alex, Tula and Mary for more discussion of right of publicity.)

Copyright: Copyright protects creative works. We'll learn a lot more soon.

Other Big Concepts

Object versus Intellectual Property: You buy a new sewing machine from Bernina, a very exciting day. You own the sewing machine. You can give it away, resell it, break it, or love it forever. But by buying it, you do not *own* the intellectual property embedded in the sewing machine – you don't own the patents, the copyright in the software, the trade secrets of the company, or the logo of the company.

Economics: When people earn their living from copyrighted works, they often care a great deal when someone uses the work without permission. A copyright attorney from MGM studios once said to me that every time someone pirates a copy of one of their films, they are hurting the families of those who depend on the income from that pirated work – from people working as janitors, scriptwriters, prop masters, and drivers.

Attribution: The other situation is when someone is not given credit that the work is theirs. The right to be named, along with a host of other moral rights, is important. Copyright in the United States has not been as interested in moral rights, and only gives them grudgingly to certain visual artworks, and only for a certain period of time. But we, as a community and as a society care a great deal about moral rights, even if the copyright law does not. The other instance where moral rights come into play is disparagement. Your quilt on a religious theme is hung next to a quilt using animal poop as a component of the design. (These cases often include poop and religious elements). You feel like your quilt is disparaged because it changes the message, now it has some relationship to the poop quilt.

> **What if I post my work online?** Attribute the pattern maker (so others can find them), which currently is the hashtag associated with the company or artist (take a minute to find the correct spelling and hashtag). Don't take credit for work that is not your own. Attribution matters.
>
> **What about if I show my work publicly, like at a quilt show or gallery?** If you are using someone's pattern, they would like credit so that if a quilter comes by and likes the pattern, they can seek it out.

Commercial versus Non-Commercial Uses: Copyright is an economic system. It was designed from the beginning to set rules and boundaries between competing publishers in the 1790s. So, not all copyrights are the same, and that's important. We have a system that rewards and punishments. *Copyright matters in a number of scenarios*: when you are selling more than one copy commercially. Then, all of the elements that will be discussed in this book matter a great deal. These are generally considered commercial uses. *Copyright matters much less in these scenarios:* when you are selling a unique work, and when you are making/gifting a work to someone. These are usually considered non-commercial uses.

A Little Bit of Copyright History

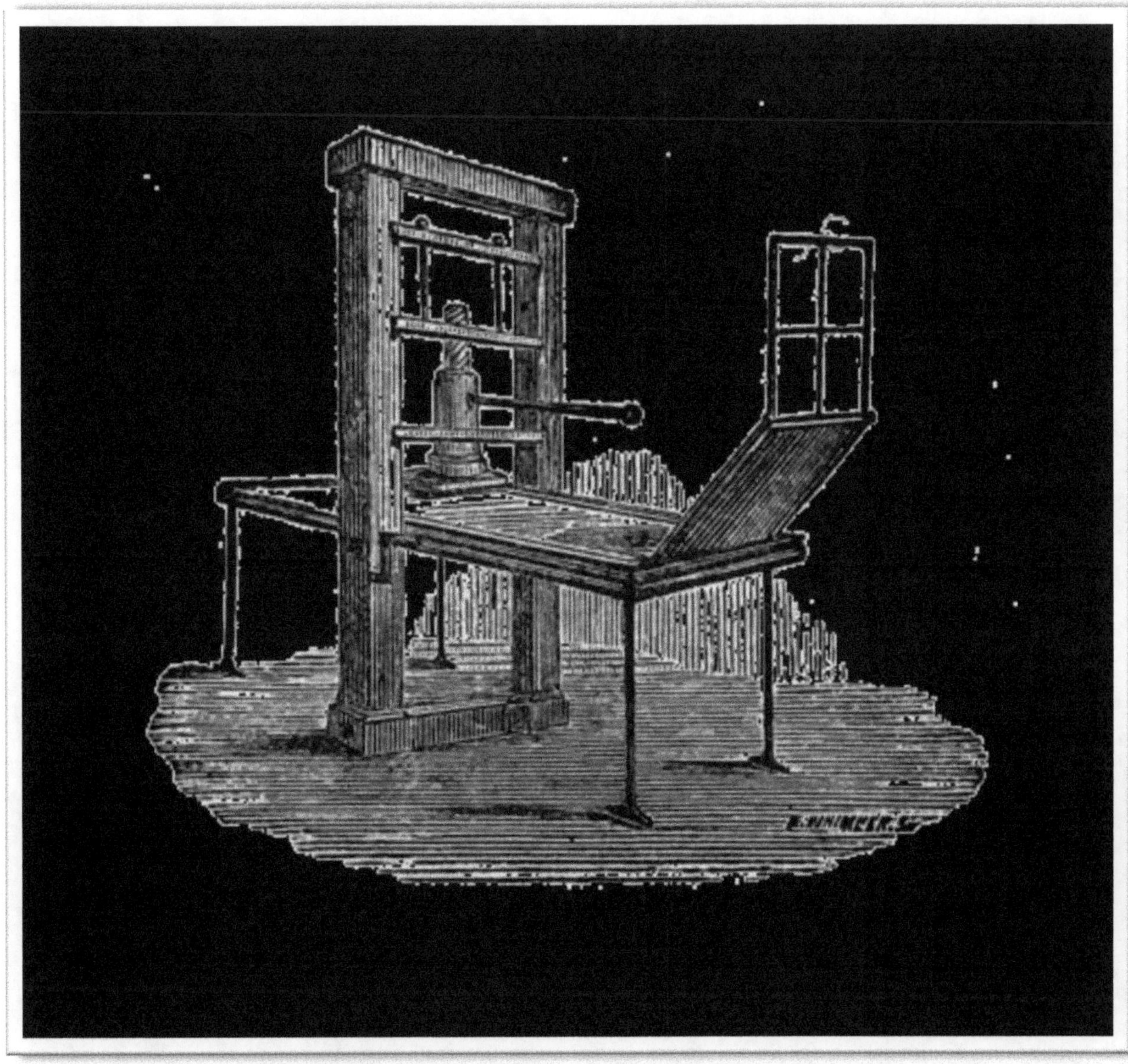

Early Press, etching from Early Typography by William Skeen, available at https://en.wikipedia.org/wiki/Printing_press

Technology and copyright have always gone together from the beginning. Copyright only became a legal concept after the invention of the printing press, because it was only then that copies could be easily and economically made. So, there became a need to develop laws to decide who could print a book and when that right expired. So, copyright is about copying. Get it? It's in the name. Copy right. It's also about limiting who can make copies. And then, after a while, allowing everyone to make copies. The first copyright act was the British: The Statute of Anne (1710), and is what the first U.S. Copyright Act was based upon in 1790.

Technology played another role in copyright, particularly beginning in the 19th century. New things could be created *by* technology. Photographs, films, sound recordings, digital art, and 3-

D printing are examples of technology that created new forms of art. Copyright had to adjust and protect them. It did. And then, at the end of the 20th century, technology began to create new mechanisms of transmission of creative works. From the photocopier to CD burner to the Internet, reproductive technology moved quickly. And then the user-generated content hit.

Before the age of the Internet, copyright really only mattered to the big players – the publishers, the movie industry, and the recording industry. We consumed products. Now, we make products. We make patterns; we don't just buy them. We post pictures of our versions of quilts. The dividing line has become much murkier, and as discussed in the previous chapter, it took content owners time to adjust.

Theories of Copyright

Before we dive into the specifics, we have one more topic to discuss: theories underlying the incentive to create, and in turn the rationale for copyright.

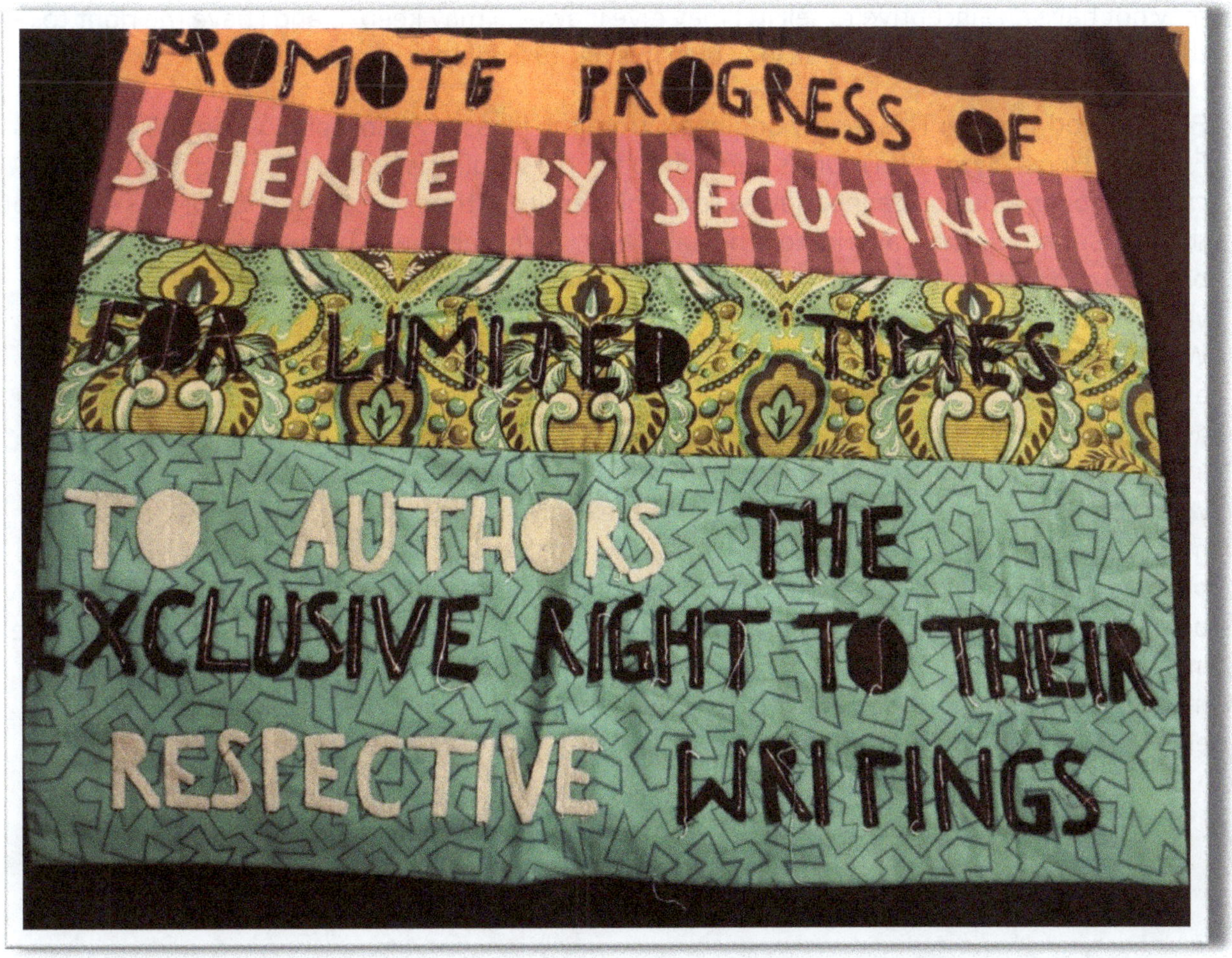

"I Believe in 1.8.8" by Ricardo Gonzalez and Elizabeth Townsend Gard

An Economic System (again): Our copyright laws are enacted by Congress to fulfill one of the requirements in the U.S. Constitution. The Copyright and Patent clause (sometimes called the IP clause) creates a *bargain* between the United States and the author: when someone creates something, they get to control its use for a set amount of time, and then the work comes into the public domain. The Constitutional Clause (I.8.8) reads: "to promote the progress of science [copyright] and useful arts [patent] by securing for limited times to authors and inventors the exclusive rights to their respective writings and discoveries." What we want to understand right now is the bargain. It benefits society to give you control of your creation. Then, you work hard to market it and make it available to us. Or you work hard to get the creations into museums so we can view them. Or you publish a book with your new techniques or creations. This is called utilitarianism. This idea of a **utilitarian economic system** is important.

Lockean Labor Theory: John Locke (1632–1704), a political philosopher, was looking to explain how property is created. We start with a world where no personal property exists. Then, someone comes along and picks an apple off a tree. Locke asserts that by mixing one's labor in picking the apple with the object itself, you create ownership. Most artists and quilters fall into the Lockean Labor Theory. I mix my creativity with resources and create a work. It is mine and I may not have any incentive to sell it; I may give it away, I may keep it, and I have the right to let the world know it's mine. The reason I own it is because it is my creative labor.

Personhood Theory: This theory originates from the ideas of philosopher Georg Wilhelm Friedrich Hegel (1770–1831). One's personhood or personality is tied to the things that they create or own; a person cannot have a sense of identity without the protection of these parts of their personhood. That favorite toy the baby won't sleep without, your wedding ring, that baseball cap from 'a thousand' years ago – they are imbued with more than just economic value. They have greater meaning and worth. Think of the quilt you spend 100 hours making. We see discussions about the economic worth of the quilt, that quilters should be respected and paid for the worth of their work. But not all quilters are quilting in a capitalist, get-it-done-as-fast-as-possible way. Instead, we see that we are taking the time to create something imbued with our own personhood, our labor, our creativity. The work has more value than what someone would pay for it. Let's look at the example of charity quilting, where quilters make quilts that they give away as a charitable act. If one wanted to be most efficient with providing blankets to those in need, having a guild spend a year creating 100 quilts would not be the best idea. But those quilts are again imbued with something more, a message to people in need or in hard times that they matter. That someone they didn't know took the time to make something unique and beautiful that signals that they are worth the time. Quilters are engaged in these activities all of the time.

One Person's Hobby is Another Person's Business

One thing we have seen in copyright in the last decade is conflicts between those creating on a utilitarian model (think record companies, publishers, movie studios) and the fans/consumers that create out of love of the thing. Both feel a Lockean labor sense of property. It took a while for content owners to understand that in the Internet age, their fans were going to create, post and sell things. Now a decade in, they seem to have created a balance in protecting their copyright and understanding spaces for creativity for fans. And so, we will see there are interesting boundaries.

Tula Pink is one of the most famous fabric designers, and her works are insanely popular. She is like the Elvis of the quilting world. When Tula Pink creates her new line of fabric, she plans to exploit her works within a utilitarian economic system: her creations are protected by law, and the law is there to incentivize her to keep creating *and selling*. She gets a set of rights for a period of time to exploit her economic opportunities. She uses her celebrity and brilliance to market, license and promote her work. But Tula might also feel that she mixed her labor, in this case her hand-created drawings, and that means those drawings become her property. Lockean Labor Theory. She also might care deeply about the creations, regardless of whether they make money or not. In fact, she feels so connected to the sample quilts she makes, she keeps them and never gives them away, even though they would be worth a lot of money. In an interview, she talked about how she never gives away her quilts, that they are not for sale, and when she has given one away on a rare occasion, she finds herself making it again to replace it. That feels not only like Lockean labor theory, but personhood. They mean something to her, and she doesn't want to part with them. Copyright law protects that empire so that she can license her creations. In 2019, she announced that Bernina Sewing company was putting out an exclusive line of limited-edition sewing machines that start at $4300. She was lending her name and trademark, and her distinctive style also influenced the aesthetic design and features. Her trademark, her look would sell these systems.

An example of Tula Pink Fabric, "All Star" line, piecing by Elizabeth Townsend Gard, and quilting by Edith Gross

Tula creates a work. She holds the copyright in that work. She is then able to license the art to FreeSpirit, and to others to use the work for a set amount of time and under certain circumstances. She gives them to the right to produce fabric. She still holds the right to create other items from the same designs. (Copyright allows this). This includes English paper piecing kits at Paper Pieces, embroidery designs, long-arm patterns, and so much more. She licenses to each of the manufacturers the right to use her art.

Fans buy her fabric in quilt shops. They are free to make quilts, clothing, bags -- anything they want. They may resell fabric, when it becomes rare (fabric lines are often only available for a few months each). How far can fans go? That's what this book is all about: to understand the relationship we have with designers like Tula, and to understand the boundaries of copyright law in our creation using others' fabric and patterns. And finally, to understand how copyright law protects our own creativity.

The Power of Expression

Not all quilting is motivated by economics. We've discussed charity quilting as an example, along with protest and activist quilting. I asked Sara Trail to write about why she started Social Justice Sewing Academy, which is a non-profit organization that has taken the world by storm: youth voices on fiber hanging in museums, expressing their stories. The motivation is not economic; the expression itself, and having a platform for that expression is the focus. I think her work is the essence of personhood theory. Here are Sara's words:

> Young people are presented in the popular media to be apolitical, deviant, and in need of intervention. Some have even relegated youth, particularly youth of color, to be a problem population that needs to be controlled. In spite of popular discourse that suggests young people are problems, young people have always been the vanguard of social change. From the Civil Rights Movement to the current Black Lives Matter movement, youth have been the ones to lead progressive social movements that have fundamentally transformed the daily lives of so many marginalized populations. After attending UC Berkeley and learning the impact of social inequality on communities of color, particularly youth; my educational experiences inspired me to develop the Social Justice Sewing Academy (SJSA). This program facilitates free programming that teaches youth methods for engaging in social change in community context while creating participatory art as a vehicle for personal transformation and social change.

Sara Trail, "Rest in Power, Trayvon,"

> When I was 16-years-old, I was saddened to learn Trayvon Martin was murdered. Trayvon and I were born only days apart and our lives, both valuable and precious to our families, had very different outcomes. My first portrait art quilt, "Rest in Power: Trayvon Martin," was designed as a memorial for the young Black teen who was murdered due to fear of the unknown, felt by another man, which was largely due to Trayvon's race. These events inspired me to create the Social Justice Sewing Academy (SJSA). SJSA is a critical education program that fosters participatory art as a vehicle for personal transformation, community cohesion, and social

change. It is a place where people come together to create art that provides healing, self-expression and a call to action.

SJSA has workshops to create quilt blocks that are designed by young people who may have never worked with fabric before. These quilt blocks are constructed with colorful fabric by a new fabric artist who speaks his or her heart through the message and meaning placed on the block. The blocks are designed by young folks who may not have had the opportunity to take expensive sewing or art classes, and may have never had their voices heard. After the workshop is completed, the blocks are distributed across the nation to experienced volunteers who embroider and embellish the blocks with their own special touch!

The final product is a quilt block, perhaps designed by a 13-year-old girl, about her desire to motivate her community to combat gang violence. That same block might be embroidered by a 70-year-old woman who lives in Vermont and has never felt the pain of losing a family member or friend due to gang violence, but wants to help start a movement.

By bridging the two fabric artists together through sewing, a common ground of understanding and empathy is found; and the collaboration creates one piece of an amazing art quilt! The art quilts that I sew together bind Americans from all walks of life, age, gender, sexuality and socioeconomic backgrounds together to create an art quilt that will speak to joy and pain felt individually and as a whole in a collective, non-threatening and non-judgmental dialogue. I believe that by having productive dialogue, people can drive out hate and replace it with love.

Personhood theory and empowerment together.

The Clash: Pattern Designers Unite

Pattern designers feel that when they mix their creative labor with elements in the world and make a pattern that they hold a property right, a copyright in the pattern. They have fixed their creative labor into a concrete form. This is Lockean labor theory at work.

Then, we see all kinds of people -- other pattern makers, shop owners, guilds, and groups. They come upon the pattern. And they do upsetting things, in the pattern maker's mind, to the pattern:

- They take a picture, and reverse engineer it
- They think because it is free it is fair game to distribute widely and even rewrite the pattern
- They think that they can make copies
- They think they can teach the pattern to a class without the class purchasing the pattern.
- They make their own, changing things only slightly, like "10%".
- They post it on the Internet for all to see, as a form of "sharing"
- They make a copy of their friend's pattern to save money.

Why? They are not seeing the economic value of the pattern. They are not doing the same thing with fabric. They can't. But they can in our current world with patterns.

Free patterns seem to confuse them the most. If it is free, there is no utilitarian value placed on it, and therefore they interpret free as "free for all" or "without copyright." Free does not put something into the public domain. But they see it as less valuable.

Fabric companies put out free patterns to sell the fabric line. They are using the pattern as a tool, and it is not the focus of their business model. But they have paid for the pattern behind the scenes--it is not actually free; there is a cost.

So, why do people steal patterns? I used to believe it was because they had a dark heart, or that they were stupid. I couldn't understand the disconnect. But now I think it *is just that*: a theoretical disconnect. They do not see the pattern as Lockean. They think the pattern is put out for their benefit. But the benefit is utilitarian. The copyright holder is incentivized to make us beautiful patterns in exchange for an exclusive economic right to exploit and control that work. Somehow the message was lost.

We will also see that just because someone feels that it is theirs --that Lockean labor feeling -- doesn't always mean it is protectable by copyright. That's a discussion for Section 2, Creating Works, and Section 3, Protecting works.

A Summary Before We Dive In

So here is a way to think about copyright.

1. There is a **system of copyright.** It's how we understand the world. You will understand it shortly. The next chapters guide you through all the basic elements of the copyright system.

2. There is **enforcement of copyright.** There are varying degrees of enforcement. There are lawyers involved. Scary words like "cease and desist" get thrown around. We'll talk about that. You won't get sued for $1 million every time you violate copyright, which you do on a daily basis, whether you know it or not. But you might if you violate it with Dr. Seuss! Just kidding. There are ways to understand when it matters, and again, levels of enforcement. And the flip side: what do you do if someone violates your copyright? We'll discuss that, too.

3. **Non-commercial, fair and personal uses.** We have a huge space for non-commercial uses, fair use, nominative use, and personal uses of copyrighted works. So, not every violation of a copyright is actionable. And that's really important. And not everything is covered by copyright. We'll learn about that, too. There is a common pool of resources that we all can use.

4. **Copyright law is a lot like speed limits.** In our world, there's the speed limit. But unless there are automatic cameras, most of the time, there's leeway. Copyright law, at the moment, has some cameras (especially on platforms like YouTube), and we may shortly be getting more mechanism. (At the time of the writing of this, the CASE Act had passed the House, but not the Senate.) If you know the rules of the road, you should be able to better understand when it matters to follow the speed limit, when no one really cares, and most importantly, what the speed limit is (and how it varies). There is also the custom and community standards part, and the reality of enforcement of copyright. But, you also shouldn't litter, even if the police aren't going to arrest you.

Let's get you comfortable with copyright – its rules of the road, its physics, its way of working. And then you can make your own decisions – on when to follow the rules and when to break them. You'll understand the potential consequences. You'll stand up for your rights – as users, as the copyright holders, as teachers, and as quilters. And you can make informed decisions on your own creative process in relation to the law.

Intro Quiz

1. I have a great idea for a new kind of thimble! It's different than anything I have ever seen. What law potentially protects the invention?

a. Trademark
b. Patent
c. Copyright
d. Right of publicity

2. I want to call my company "ThimbleLand". What protects the name of my company?

a. Trademark
b. Patent
c. Copyright
d. Right of publicity

3. My grandmother's quilt has been passed down to me. It's in tatters, but I love it. The theory that best describes my relationship to the quilt is

a. Lockean labor theory
b. Personhood
c. Utilitarianism
d. String Theory

4. I take a picture with Tula Pink at a quilt show, and she is wearing my thimble! I want to use it on the packaging. Can I, without getting her permission?

a. Yes! It's my photograph. Copyright rules.
b. No. She's famous. She controls her right of publicity
c. Yes! But keep it a secret.
d. No. I'm not sure why.

5. I buy a copy of the book *A Little Bit of Copyright*. I want to teach my guild all of the things that I learned from it. I photocopy the whole book and give it to 100,000,000 people. Is that ok?

a. Yes! You own the intellectual property rights in the book because you bought a copy of the book at the local bookshop.
b. No!!! That violates the authors' copyright right. You are taking money out of their pockets and they won't be able to repay their student loans!
c. Yes! Because it's just for my 100,000,000 favorite friends. (An argument actually made in Professor Townsend Gard's law class once)
d. I'm not sure. I'm going to keep reading the book.

Answers: 1.b, 2.a, 3.b, 4.b, 5.b or d

Part 2:
Create Your Work

4: Seven Key Concepts

Basic Terms that Every Creative Should Know

Copyright can be complicated. Let's learn a few key concepts that every quilter should know. In this chapter, we're going to walk through seven of these concepts before diving into how copyright is created, what gets protected, and what to do when you believe someone has infringed your work.

In many ways, copyright is a system that provides boundaries of use: who gets to do what and when with a creative work. We're going to start thinking about each work—every work—having these boundaries and we need to be able to identify what boundaries apply.

We have big concepts that help us understand the boundaries of what we can do with creative works: **first sale doctrine**, **doctrine of functionality,** and **aesthetic non-discrimination.** There are pairs of boundaries that are particularly important: **copyright/public domain, infringement/permissible uses, and idea/expression** being the key three.

1. First Sale Doctrine

You purchase fabric, a book, or a pattern. You own the physical copy. You can do many things: write in it, resell it, lend it to a friend, make a quilt, and even throw it away. The copyright holder does not control the physical copy after the first sale.

> ***But***
>
> First sale also does not allow you to make copies of the book or pattern. You can't copy your purchase and give that copy to a friend. That violates the exclusive right to copy and distribute under the U.S. Copyright Act. Again, first sale allows you to do what you want with that physical object you bought--that version--but not make copies.

Example: As part of our project, we ripped up a Pat Sloan and Jane Davidson's Splendid Sampler book and sent different pages with patterns to people to make the 6 ½ inch squares. That was the first sale doctrine in use.

First Sale Does Not Apply to Digital Copies. First sale does not include digital copies. First Sale doesn't apply to any digital copy. You can't email or make a copy of a PDF for a friend. There's no First Sale, rather it is seen as a license (like software). And first sale does not include making a copy, which is what would have to happen if you gave someone a digital copy, whether in an email or printing it out. No sharing of digital copies.

Sixteen embroidery blocks from "Splendid Sampler" by Pat Sloan and Jane Davidson, created by the Stealth Sewing Squad, Quilting Army, and donated to the Just Wanna Quilt project at Tulane Law School, 2018-2019.

Quick Quiz: Do you think we purchased the paper or the Kindle copy for this exercise?

If you guessed paper copy, you are correct! First sale allows us to do many physical things with the book, including sending different pages to people throughout the country. We did not make any copies at all. We would send 2-3 patterns to an individual to avoid such a copyright infringement.

First sale is a super important concept for copyright. You couldn't have used book stores or resell your car (which includes copyrightable software) without it. You couldn't bring magazines to a quilt guild meeting for recycling. And, you couldn't rip up a book and send pieces of it to different people to make a quilt.

2. Doctrine of Functionality

Copyright does not protect functional things. Patents do that. That includes techniques, methods, math, and steps. You learn to do something in class. You can teach others. You can use it yourself. Techniques and methods are not protectable.

But

The expression of the technique is protectable. The handout or book describing the technique is likely under copyright. This includes a recorded class (e.g. YouTube video). This is protectable under copyright.

You can't take notes of a lecture and then publish or post them without permission, or worse, secretly record a session and post it on the Internet. That's covered by the anti-bootlegging laws and the "teacher exception." That's someone else's intellectual property. Again, the expression is protected, but not the technique or method itself.

3. Aesthetic Non-Discrimination

Copyright does not judge. Really. Whether it is a two-year old's drawing or a great work of art. Copyright does not judge. I was giving a lecture at QuiltCon, and I asked which of my quilts would qualify for copyright, and a snippy woman in the audience said, "None." Clearly, she didn't like my quilts. But she was wrong. They may not be protected for other reasons, but aesthetics is not one of them.

4. Limited Times

Copyright lasts for "limited times." That's the exact phrase from the U.S. Constitution. The exact amount of time has varied over the last 230 years of copyright law in the United States. At first the term was 14 years, and if the author was still alive, another 14 years. The term increased over time. The 20th century is a particularly messy period. (We'll talk more about that later). Now, the term is life of the author plus seventy years, or if it is anonymous or a work for hire, 120 years from creation/95 years from publication, whichever is shorter. (Again, more later). This is a long, long time. But once the term is over (and this varies again through history, and even with work we might want to use today), the work is in the public domain. Today, this term arises automatically in everything we make. But to get that term, the work has to qualify for protection. We'll discuss that more shortly.

5. Copyright/Public Domain

A work must qualify for copyright, and if it does, copyright protection arises automatically. But not everything is protectable. Many things are not. We'll talk about that soon. Some are out of copyright. Some things never could meet the requirements. So, we have to know what qualifies when we are using works. It gives us more freedom and confidence as creators.

6. Infringement/Permissible Uses

You create something. You post it. Then, you find someone else has swiped your pattern and is claiming it as their own. We have mechanisms to deal with that. But there are also permissible uses – fair use, library uses, and others. The rights in copyright are not absolute. We'll learn about those rights and the limitations to them.

7. Idea/Expression

Copyright does not protect ideas. I have an idea for a fabric line with fruit. That is not protectable. Kaffe Fassett creates fabric with oranges. That is protectable. But it doesn't keep others from making their own fabric with fruit, or even oranges. The idea is not protectable. The question is one of degree; when does someone else's expression of an idea start to infringe on your version? We look to the levels of abstraction test to figure it out, but it's not easy, and courts struggle with this, too. The next chapter will take a deeper dive.

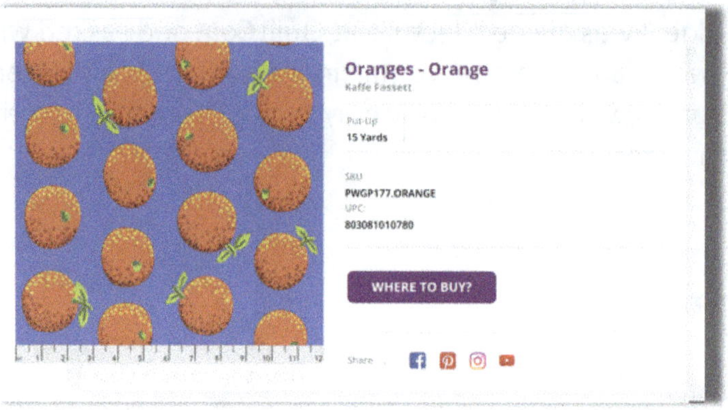

From FreesSprirt Fabrics, an image of Kaffe's fabric for fabric/quilt shops to review for purchase. https://www.freespiritfabrics.com/oranges-orange/

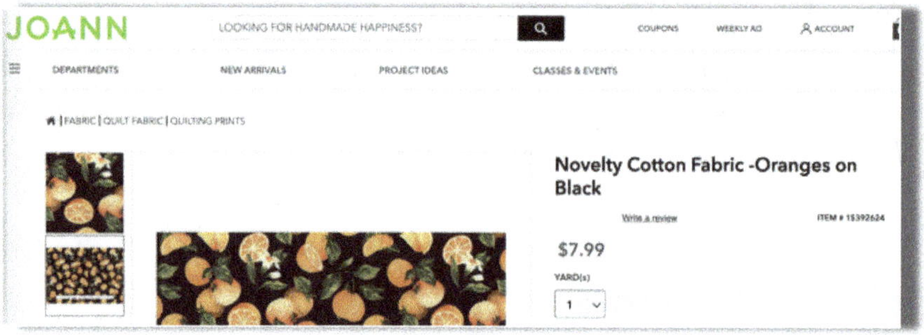

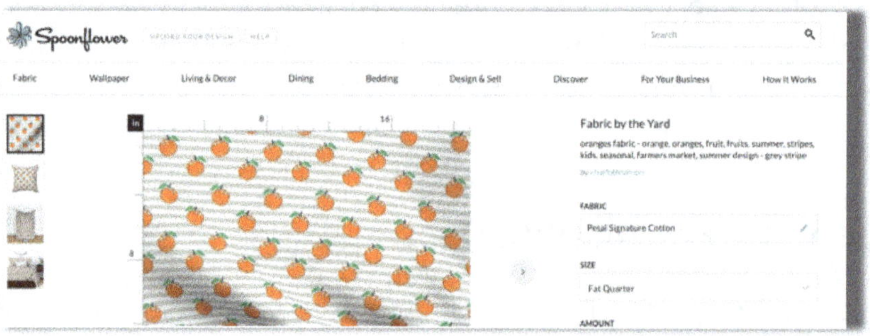

Now you know some basic concepts. You understand theories. You recognize that economics and attribution are important. Now, we're going to start from the beginning again, this time walking step by step through copyright to understand what is not protectable, what is, and then we'll look at the rights and rights statements, copyright notice, infringement, and permissible uses, including fair uses. Finally, we will look at strategies in different creative scenarios.

5: The Idea Before Copyright Begins

When an Idea Turns into Something More

Do you know the moment when you are in the midst of a project -- you've planned it, you've started to sew it together, you're about halfway through...you've been thinking "I'm brilliant? I have the best idea ever." Now you are in far enough that you think -- "Oh, No! This is horrid." That moment, when you are making your quilt, where you have begun putting it together -- that's fixation. And that moment of horridness, the law rewards your pain with copyright. Copyright begins when you fix an idea. When you sew those pieces together and make that quilt top. Now your sketches are protected too. Everything fixed is potentially protected by copyright. But the idea is never protectable.

When we asked the Quilting Army where their ideas came from, here are some of their responses:

> Sometimes I start with fabric. Now, I often start with fabric because I think the colors or patterns go well together and I just want to see what happens. I may see stripes or shapes together and see how it flows. This is why I have so many unfinished projects. - Michelle Curney Willis
>
> A blinding flash of inspiration followed by a period of obsession.... - Beth Hennen Strand
>
> I usually fall in love with fabric first and then look for a pattern that will showcase it best. - Leah Holland
>
> Fabric inspires me - most always fabric reminds me of a person who needs a quilt. - Vickie Menasco
>
> For art quilts, I start with a picture in my mind and put it on paper. - Celeste Poulin
>
> I usually start with color. -AJ Grossman
>
> I love fabric, but I also collect patterns. It may just be a block I want to try. With a modern quilt, I'll start with an idea. - Cosette Ripley Blackmer
>
> It could be anything that gives me an idea even a conversation, seeing something in nature, a color or a texture of something and an art piece, etc. - Jeannette Floyd
>
> Being inspired by a photo that I'd like to incorporate into my life. - Jennifer Davis Digiovanni
>
> Most often, I start with an idea and then figure out what fabrics and techniques will express it the best. - Ann Wasserman
>
> A lot comes from Pinterest and Instagram because it's so readily available. - Camille Ainsworth
>
> I start with the life experiences of the person who will be the quilt recipient. I designed a triathlon quilt for a close friend and a family tree quilt with 250 ancestors for a holocaust survivor. - Eileen Howell Zito

Architecture and nature most of the time. I'm always on the lookout for interesting patterns when I'm out of the house. Occasionally inspiration will come from art, although rarely from other textiles directly. Lately, I have been designing foundation paper pieced animal quilts based on photographs I have taken at the local zoo. - Cassandra Beaver

And how did professional pattern makers answer the same question?

Because I'm both a pattern designer and fabric designer, I create patterns that will support my fabric. So, I start with basic shapes, or an overall idea, then I tweak it so that it will showcase my fabric well. I might change the sizes of the blocks, or add more or fewer blocks to accommodate a specific fabric collection, knowing that if it looks good in my fabrics, it will work with other fabric lines, too. - Christa Watson

For me, it depends on my mood.. sometimes I see a fabric I love and I design something to showcase the fabric.. sometimes I doodle in a sketchbook and they will evolve from a sketch. - Jennifer Scranton McClanahan

I have yet been inspired by a particular fabric, I start by sketching in my graph paper notebooks and it evolves from there. - Jen Gibbons Shaffer

I start with shapes or a block idea that I want to explore. I will usually start with solid colors and then substitute fabric as appropriate. I'm both a fabric and pattern designer. If I'm working with a specific manufacturer to showcase a fabric line, I'll look to the fabric for inspiration but it's usually a shape that sparks the initial idea. - Ebony Love

As I design bag patterns, I'll generally start with a general sketch of an overall design, then add measurements and draft out my pattern pieces based on some math - fabric generally comes in after the fact, since I can re-size for any type of print, or tweak later. - Tara C Sinclair

Not usually inspired by fabric but inspiration comes from everywhere else - tiles on a cathedral floor, Roman mosaics, embroidery books, Celtic/Pictish designs, my daughter's geometry books, attempts to tesselate unusual shapes, etc, etc.... - Diana Eaton

I usually start with an idea and find the fabric later. - Robin Koehler

I start with a technique I've developed. A quilt, then workshop, then quilt pattern may follow. - Anita Grossman Solomon

Play around with Electric Quilt (software program) when I have an idea. Dark/light/ mediums first, then colors/fabrics. - BrendaLou McNally Scott

I'm a total weirdo. I usually have an idea for a specific way to quilt something then work backward to create a pattern that will accommodate my quilting idea. - Vicki Ruebel

I start with an idea or shape. Or a block. And I sketch first. Then choose colors. Then choose fabrics. Then do the math. Illustrator diagrams. Cutting diagrams, expected fabric requirements. Instructions. Then sew it up checking my instructions as I go, making notes. Then I double-check the math, finalize instructions. - Emily Lang

I don't start with fabric normally. Sometimes it's designing to use a certain type of precut, sometimes inspired by a tile pattern, sometimes it's a doodle. Anything that gets the ideas flowing really. - Lori Suss

> Antique quilts. - Virginia Berger
>
> Usually, I start with blocks, and values (rather than specific colors or fabrics), and then add the fabrics later. I like to start with a traditional block and then change it around, and I also like to mix blocks together to get secondary patterns. If I'm working with a specific fabric collection (e.g. for a fabric company that is promoting a new line), I'll start with the fabric - but I usually find that a bit more of a challenge. - Pam Nourse

And finally, Sam Hunter: "Sometimes I have a fully formed idea and need to just make what I see in my head. Sometimes I play until I have a block I like. Sometimes a fabric will prompt an idea. Sometimes I throw fabric at the wall until I like where it lands, sometimes I sketch, sometimes I wrangle 20 versions in Illustrator. I don't think it's possible to say that pattern designers all do it a specific way. Probably the common thread among us is attention to looking for inspiration that can be patterned!"

Ideas are not protectable. The expression of that idea is potentially eligible for copyright protection. Before that fixation, an idea is not itself protectable. So, what happens when you tell someone your idea? Can they use it too? Yep. Unless you have a contract in place – stating that if they use your idea they agree to pay you. Otherwise, you are a victim of the blurting out doctrine. If you blurt out your idea, no one has any responsibility, financial or otherwise, to you. Don't blurt if you want to protect your idea before it is fixed.

How Fixed Does It Have to Be?

A sketch, a recording, a sample all count. Any fixation works. ☺But if you end up in court, what is fixed will be the basis of the infringement claim. Think of the difference between the musical compositions and the performance on a sound recording of the same song

The Idea of Inventory Quilts

Jessica Vetor, otherwise known as @Jessicaquilter created what she called an "Inventory Quilt." She made a small hexagon from each fabric from her stash. And it was stunning.

The idea of an Inventory Quilt, even calling it this, is not protectable. Her specific version is. I interviewed her and told her I made my own, but mine was made of 3-inch squares instead of hexies. Putting the samples into a rainbow configuration also is an idea. But we also, out of courtesy, asked Jessica if she was ok with this, and gave her credit for the idea. This is an important issue in the community. Attribution--giving credit--and asking permission from the inspiration is something many people want. This is a custom. Copyright does not demand it. There are benefits too. If I include Jessica, our ecosystem expands. Not only is it polite, but it builds good feelings and community. Everybody wins.

Now, what if Jessica had said, "No." I'm a bit feisty. So, I think I would have probably turned to copyright to sort out whether I could do what I wanted to do, or alternatively, I would have decided to do something else. It wouldn't be worth the trouble. It would also depend on whether I was making the work for personal, private use, for a teaching purpose, or commercial selling.

My version of an Inventory Quilt, using 3-inch squares.

And then the idea grew. We now have a JWQ-Inventory Quilt Group. Here are some Inventory Quilts from the group. We're just getting started. Here are some of our in-progress Inventory quilts so far. And now, we now have over 35 designers participating with our Quilting Army to make quilts from new patterns and using our inventory. So, the idea is still to reacquaint ourselves with our fabric. We're just branching out.

Rachel Rose

Carol Stovall McCauley

Willow Olson

Michele Forstall Ernst

Have you done your own Inventory Quilt? They can be all of your fabrics, a subset, anything. What would happen if I took a bit from every pink fabric that I have? Or how many ways can I come up with using panels? The idea of Inventory Quilts has morphed into something more than what we started with Jessica.

Levels of Abstraction: Idea to Expression

Ideas are not protected. Only the expression of the idea. Your version. Your selection, arrangement, and coordination of that idea. That's expression. The question is where is that boundary between an idea and expression. "Nobody has ever been able to fix that boundary, and nobody ever can," wrote Judge Learned Hand, a famous judge writing in the early 20th century.

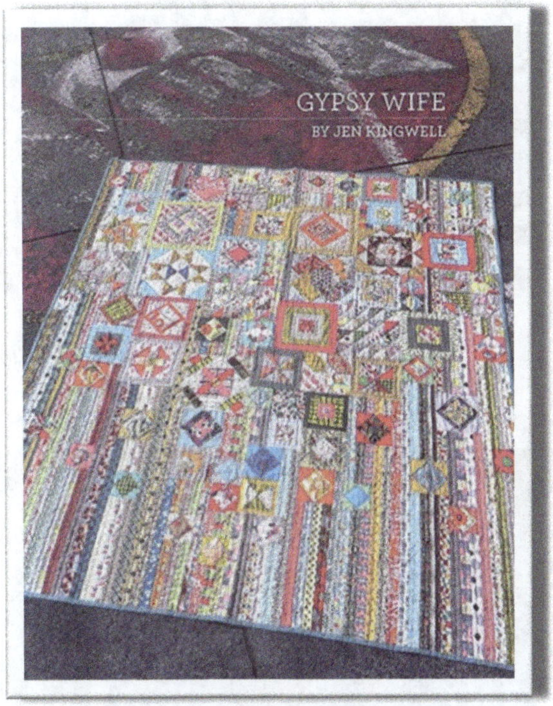

Jen Kingwell's Gypsy Wife quilt is striking because it lays blocks against vertical 1½ inch strips. The idea is brilliant. But that doesn't mean others can't use that idea. The pattern itself -- her selection, arrangement, and coordination of strips and blocks -- is protected, of course, but the idea of vertical strips is not. The question is, where does her expression start as compared with the idea? Can others use vertical strips to set common blocks? What if they were 1-½ inch strips, too?

We had a Gypsy Wife sew-along as part of Just Wanna Quilt. We each bought the pattern and then Gigi Baay took us through strategies in constructing particular blocks.

Here are some of our versions:

Version by Janice Young

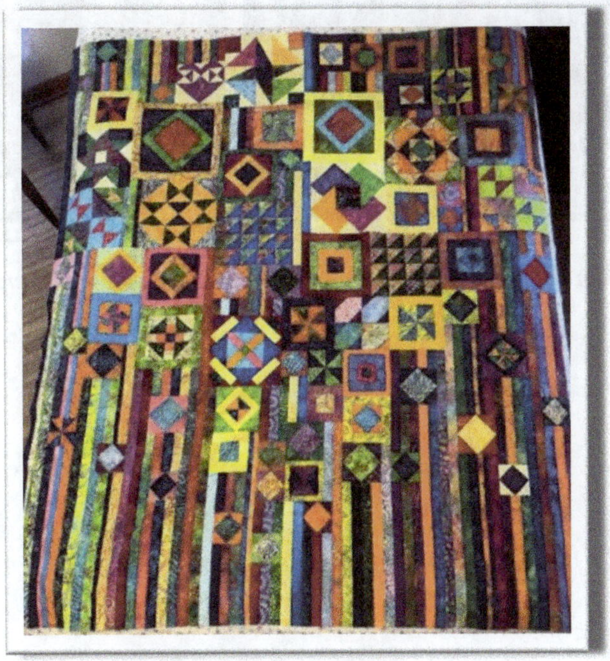

Version by Amy Reitzel

Mine in progress, using Tula Pink and Halloween themed grey, purple and green fabrics.

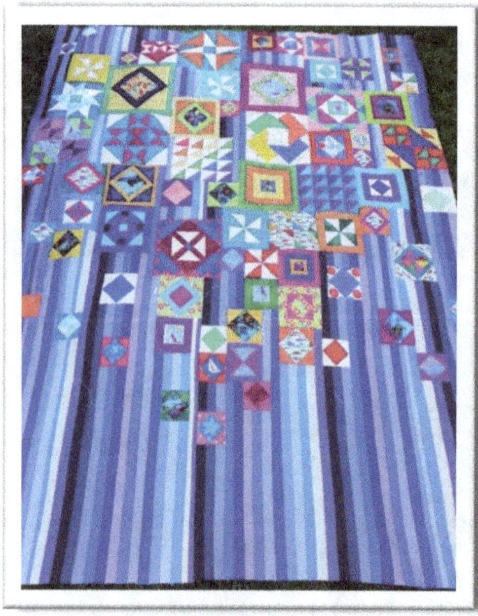

Version by Ilse de Koker

In progress version by Sonia Simone

The Idea of Vertical Strips

Let's look at the idea of vertical strips in a number of contexts.

Here is Melanie McNeill's quilt from 2013, using vertical striping. The idea is not protectable. The quilt is. This looks very different and would not be mistaken for a Jen Kingwell inspired quilt.

But we also turn to common sense, community standards, and history. When the question of strip quilts is posed to the Quilting Army, they respond: Melanie McNeil writes, "Oh goodness, strip quilts are as old as bed quilts. EQ (a software program) has a bunch of designs built-in. Let me find a couple..." Patricia Kelly Spuries finds the "McCord Vine Quilt," ca. 1850 in a Fons and Porter book, *Quilts from the Henry Ford* (p. 40).

Quilting Army member Karen Klamczynski turns to design a few vertical strip quilts for us in a computer program commonly used by quilters called Electric Quilt, or EQ.

The Idea of Strips + Common Blocks

And while they are responding on Facebook, I go upstairs to my Quilt Studio to make my GW inspired by Gypsy Wife sample. I take out some 6- 1/2" squares that the Stealth Sewing Squad of the Quilting Army has made, and I start to think about the idea of Jen Kingwell's Gypsy Wife quilt. Her strips are mostly 1-½", and I realize this makes it easy to add blocks -- they finish at 1" and so there's very little math.

I decide to do that, too, 1-½" strips. I also decide to do it in the JWQ colors: blue, green, pink, orange... I start thinking about how I constructed the Gypsy Wife, what I learned. And I start. At first, I feel like I'm imitating what she did.

I realize I need to move beyond the idea of vertical stripes, and how Jen did it. I need to think about ways to take the *idea* and make it my own. And so, I started to experiment. Now, the idea started with the Gypsy Wife pattern. I learned construction and techniques. I even made (am still making) my own version, even though sometimes I substitute easier blocks or get off a bit. I'm puzzling. But the Common Block/Strip Quilt is really my leaping point from the ideas and techniques I learned from the Gypsy Wife quilt into my own creation. This is the essence of the story of copyright. It all starts with an idea. And so, this is what I create.[3] Again, Amy's GW for a comparison. What do you think?

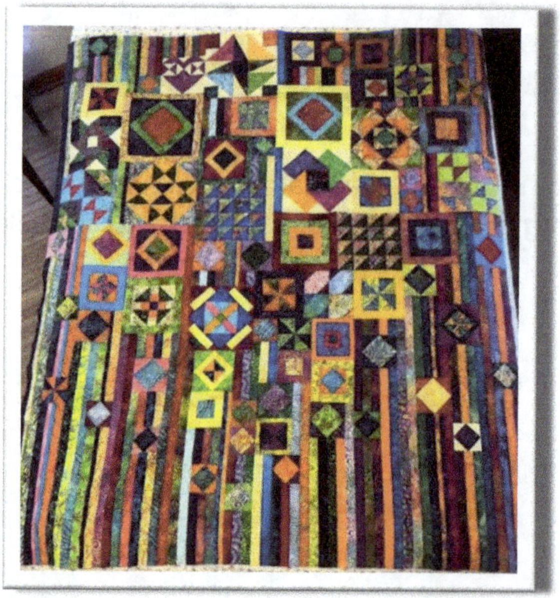

[3] Blocks provided by Vicki Holloway, Shelly Weeks, Misty-Anne Marold, Willow Olson, Carole Lancon, Beth Henna Strand, Brandy Pettit, Barbara Webb Castle, Anne Vandermey, and others. This is part of our Common Pool Block Challenge to create a known, familiar block using JWQ colors. We'll return to the Common Block quilt blocks later in the book

I've used 1-½" strips to put together a series of basic quilt blocks, the same idea as Jen Kingwell. Do you think mine is different enough? Too inspired? That's what the courts are looking for -- the boundary between an idea (not protectable) and expression (protectable). If I turn it so the quilt is horizontal, does it change the idea?

The Test for the Difference between Idea and Expression

We turn to an old test by Judge Learned Hand, a famous judge from the first half of the 20th century. This is a famous quote, in which he is analyzing a play. "Upon any work, and especially upon a play, a great number of patterns of increasing generality will fit equally well, as more and more of the incident is left out. The last may perhaps be no more than the most general statement of what the play is about, and at times might consist only of its title; but there is a point in this series of abstractions where they are no longer protected, since otherwise, the playwright could prevent the use of his "ideas," to which, apart from their expression, his property is never extended." 45 F.2d 119 (2d Cir. 1930) As something goes from **details to abstraction**, we find that what is protectable diminishes.

The case, Nichols v. Universal Pictures Corp, 45 F.2d 119 (2d Cir. 1930) concerned the play "Abie's Irish Rose," by Anne Nichols and the potentially infringing film, "The Cohens and the Kellys." In both, a young Jewish man marries an Irish Catholic woman, and both fathers are against the marriage. Both are comedies. The court looks to the similarities as well as elements that were stock characters and other elements that would be available to everyone. General motifs and characters are not protectable.

We will discuss infringement and other aspects of comparing works later in the book. For now, it is important to understand that there is no fixed formula to tell if someone has taken more than an idea and has nudged into expression. It's a complicated copyright world. We'll also learn how courts do an infringement analysis later in the book and return to this example. For now, what we want to concentrate on is the idea of vertical strips is not a property right of Jen Kingwell's. The question is when are we too close to her expression, and when have we created a new work? Before we get there, we have to learn a little more about copyright.

Take Away

So, what if you want to protect your idea before you have gotten around to expressing it?

- **Don't blurt.** The blurting out doctrine says that if you go about telling people or posting about it online, you can't get too upset when they use it without including or asking you. You gave it away to the world. (QA member Wendy Starn points out, "this includes posting progress photos of your quilt if it will be entered in a competition. Some entry rules specifically prohibit sharing online.)
- **Contract.** In some fields, you sign a contract that if they use your idea, they will pay you.
- **NDA**. Non-disclosure agreements when you are pitching something to a company.
- **Make it.** Make it first. Get it fixed in a tangible medium of expression. Then share it.
- **Levels of Abstraction** (introduced). When you compare one expression to another, you look to both the big ideas (not protected) through to the details (that might be protected).

6: Steps to Copyrightability

Obtaining a Copyright is Easy

As of January 1, 1978, copyright arises automatically. When you create something, you have a copyright. Exciting, yes? The two basic elements to create a copyrightable work are fixation and originality. You also need to be aware of the categories of proper subject matter in copyright. The Copyright Act is our guide in making these determinations. Here is Section 102(a) of the 1976 Copyright Act that governs copyrightable subject matter:

> (a) Copyright protection subsists, in accordance with this title, in original works of authorship fixed in any tangible medium of expression, now known or later developed, from which they can be perceived, reproduced, or otherwise communicated, either directly or with the aid of a machine or device. Works of authorship include the following categories:
>
> (1) literary works;
> (2) musical works, including any accompanying words;
> (3) dramatic works, including any accompanying music;
> (4) pantomimes and choreographic works;
> (5) pictorial, graphic, and sculptural works;
> (6) motion pictures and other audiovisual works;
> (7) sound recordings; and
> (8) architectural works.

We'll look at the following concepts that appear in Section 102(a):

☐ original works of authorship,
☐ fixation in any tangible medium of expression, and the
☐ categories of authorship.

Original Works of Authorship

Copyright protects original works of authorship. The originality requirement has two parts: modicum of creativity and independent creation. Note: you do not have to be the first one to ever have thought of that particular idea of how to paint a flower. Originality is a constitutional requirement. The Intellectual Property clause reads that Congress can secure "for limited Times to Authors...the exclusive Right to their respective Writings." U.S. Constitution, I.8.8. We define "Writings" broadly, but we require original writings based on the creative powers of the mind.

Independent Creation

You must have created the work and you have to be human.

Human: No animals—think painting elephant or selfie-taking monkey. Under the 1976 Copyright law in the U.S., you have to be human. If you are not human and you create a work, you will not be given copyright protection. Works created by artificial intelligence also do not gain protection. One scholar, Yvette Joy Liebesman explained that you can't recover damages against artificial intelligence, and so animals and AI are judgment proof. That's why she explained, they do not receive copyright. See our interview with Yvette Liebesman at http://www.justwannaquilt.com. This also means that if you claim your work is written by God or dictated by a spirit from another planet, you will not gain copyright.

Not copied: An author creates a work independently. Copyright is rewarding you for your creativity and creative work. How much creativity is key.

Modicum of Creativity

How much creativity do you need to have? A little bit, that's all. Traditionally, we believe that if it is more than alphabetizing or basic patterns, you can obtain copyright. We'll see in the next chapter that the bar is a little bit more complicated and harder to get over. But for now, you have to have just a little bit of creativity.

The case that helps us understand how much creativity is *Feist Publications v. Rural Telephone Service*, a U.S. Supreme Court case, written by Justice O'Connor, about competing telephone books. 499 U.S. 340 (1991). There, Justice O'Connor eloquently explained originality:

> The *sine qua non* of copyright is originality. To qualify for copyright protection, a work must be original to the author. Original, as the term is used in copyright, means only that the work was independently created by the author (as opposed to copied from other works) and that it possesses at least some minimal degree of creativity. To be sure, the requisite level of creativity is extremely low; even a slight amount will suffice. The vast majority of works make the grade quite easily, as they possess **some creative spark**, "no matter how crude, humble, or obvious" it might be. Originality does not signify novelty; a work may be original even though it closely resembles other works so long as the similarity is fortuitous, not the result of copying...

We will learn in the next chapter what does not qualify as enough creativity. But for now, assume that as long as it is more than a modicum, you have enough creativity.

Creative Labor

You also have to have creative labor. Just because you worked hard on something or spent a lot of money doesn't mean copyright will reward you. We call that "sweat of the brow" (This is not necessarily true in the United Kingdom, or in other parts of the world.) Copyright is about creativity, and so the labor that is protected is creative.

I often hear pattern makers complaining about people copying their patterns because *they worked hard on creating the pattern.* Now, I completely appreciate this. And we as a community should respect the hard work, and buy the pattern. *But...hard work alone is not enough.* If that hard work is tracking down the supplies, no. If that hard work is figuring out the math, no. If that hard work is recreating a common block in the public domain, no. So, why make a log cabin pattern? Because quilters will buy it for the convenience that you have done the math and made a beautiful version. You may be a beginner quilter who has never been exposed to a particular pattern. You might be very experienced, but just want the math done for you. But the pattern itself is not necessarily protected by copyright.

Fixation

For artists, this is an easy step. Fix the work, and copyright automatically begins. Where it gets complicated is in ephemeral work, like sandcastles and ice sculptures. Ideas are not protected. Sketches of ideas and the work itself are. If you sketch an idea on a napkin, that sketch itself is protected. It could be seen as the underlying copyrighted work for the finished version. That's why keeping notes on your preparation material becomes important if there is a dispute. Not only does it prove that you created the work (if you are being accused of copying from others), but the work itself is protectable, too!

Photographs of sandcastles are protectable. That is fixed. And QA Wendy Starn points out, "This is part of how artists like Andy Goldsworthy (https://www.goldsworthy.cc.gla.ac.uk/) and Christo and Jeanne Claude (https://christojeanneclaude.net/) make a living from creating ephemeral works. They make photographs, and books while the work still exists. They sell preliminary drawings. Christo sold pieces of fabric from some of his completed projects." (Notes from Wendy on reading the manuscript).

Quick Quiz: At what stage of your work does copyright begin?

A. The moment I have an idea
B. The moment I put a sketch of the work onto paper
C. The moment I have completed the work.
D. When I file an application for copyright with the U.S. government.

Answer: B. Fixation creates copyright in that creation. The sketch is protected. Once you fix the work itself -- that too is protected. Unpublished and published, finished and unfinished works are protected.

Who Is the Author?

Copyright law presumes that the creator is the author. Copyright ownership is found in Chapter 2 of the 1976 Copyright Act. Let's take a look:

> *17 U.S.C. Section 201(a) Initial Ownership.—*
> Copyright in a work protected under this title vests initially in the author or authors of the work. The authors of a joint work are co-owners of copyright in the work.

The default is that the author is the owner. The author controls the exclusive rights of copyright, when to give permission, and when to sell and license the work. The copyright term is based on the author's death, or if there are joint authors, the last surviving author's death.

To be a joint author, there are a few requirements. First, here is the definition from the Copyright Office. "A "joint work" is a work prepared by two or more authors with the intention that their contributions be merged into inseparable or interdependent parts of a unitary whole." 17 U.S.C. Section 101. There are a couple of key points.

You must as joint authors believe you are joint authors at the time of creation, and intend to integrate your creative work. You also must contribute creative work, and not merely financial or "sweat of the brow." You don't have to do equal shares, but the contribution must be substantial enough to stand on its own as copyrightable expression. The ownership is considered a "tenants in common," meaning that each joint author can exercise any and all rights without permission of the other authors, but there is a duty to account for the shares of the profits from any use or license. Joint authors must all agree to exclusive licenses or transfers/assignments of rights in writing.

You cannot after the fact decide to be joint authors. If you feel that you contributed a great deal but didn't get credit, that's not the time to claim joint authorship. It is something that is decided *jointly* at the time of creation. Who is named matters. Registering with the U.S. Copyright Office matters, as it provides a record of who is the author.

Work for Hire

Work for hire is a legal term. You may be working for hire, but not count as a "work for hire." There are two ways that your creative work can fall under work for hire: an employee in the course of their employment, or a commissioned work that falls under specific, enumerated categories in the Copyright Act. Let's take each of them for further discussion.

Employee in the course of their employment

A sculptor was hired to create a sculpture for a non-profit. He was given an idea – a statute in the form of homeless man, woman and child that harkened back to Mary, Joseph and baby Jesus. But the parties did not indicate who was the copyright holder, and there was a conflict on who owned the statute. *Community for Creative Non-Violence v. Reid* is the U.S. Supreme Court *case* that helps us determine whether someone is an employee under the meaning of the law, and an independent contract – an art case! 490 U.S. 730 (1989). What we are trying to see if you do regular work, have health insurance, are covered by taxes, etc., or whether you have been hired to do a specific job (think wedding photographer) and control the means by which you do that job.

Why does it matter? Again, whoever is the copyright holder controls the use of that work. You may assign, transfer or license those rights, but if you don't have those rights, you don't have the right to do anything, and may even be stopped from creating further copies or derivative works. Here is the statutory language:

> 17 U.S.C. Section 201(b) - Works Made for Hire.—
> In the case of a work made for hire, the employer or other person for whom the work was prepared is considered the author for purposes of this title, and, unless the parties have expressly agreed otherwise in a written instrument signed by them, owns all of the rights comprised in the copyright.

Let's look at how to determine the hiring party's right to control the manner and means by which the product is accomplished. This would mean that the hiring part was any employee, rather than an independent contract. Here are the factors:

- skills required
- source of the instrumentalities and tools
- location of the work
- duration of the relationship between the parties
- whether the hiring party has the right to assign additional projects to the hired party
- extent of the hired party's discretion over when and how long to work
- method of payment
- hired party's role in hiring and paying assistants
- whether the work is part of the regular business of the hiring party
- whether the hiring party is in business
- provision of employee benefits
- tax treatment of the hired party

The court found that the sculptor was the copyright holder. He had special skills, had his own tools, a studio where the work was done, and the relationship was only lasting as long as it took to create the sculpture. The hiring party could not assign additional tasks. The hiring party was not directing when and how long to work, and it wasn't the business of the non-profit to make sculptures. The sculptor received no employee benefits, and he was taxed as an independent contract. Reid held the copyright; CCN had a non-exclusive license to the sculpture.

Commissioned Works

A proper work for hire situation can also come up with commissioned works. This has to be one of nine categories defined in the Copyright Act:

- a contribution to a collective work,
- as a part of a motion picture or other audiovisual work,

- as a translation,
- as a supplementary work (Supplementary work includes works for publication like introductions, conclusions, illustrations, explanations, revisions, commentary, forwards, afterward, maps, charts, tables, editorial notes, afterward, editorial notes, musical arrangements, answer material for tests, bibliographies, appendices, and indexes.)
- as a compilation, as an instructional text,
- as a test,
- as an answer material for a test, or
- as an atlas.

If your work fits into one of these categories, there has to be an express, signed agreement in place as well. For most of us, our work does not fit into one of these categories.

Independent Contractor

If you are working for someone else, and your work does not fit into employee or commissioned works, then you are an independent contractor. Unless there is an agreement to the contrary, you retain the copyright in the work, even though a third party paid you to make/create the work. They receive a non-exclusive license to use the work. But unless there is a contract in place, no assignment or exclusive license has been created by the act of creating it for someone else or even getting paid.

This is interesting, yes? You quilt someone's quilt. No copyright agreement is in place. You created your own design on their quilt You hold the copyright (and not the object of the quilt itself), not the person who owns the quilt. You see how this could be powerful? You can use that design elsewhere. Now, there is an implied non-exclusive license for them to do all the things people normally do with a quilt. *But there is no implied non-exclusive license* to publish it, make directions on the quilting itself, etc. You retain the copyright on that portion.

Now, let's take the reverse. You create something on Spoonflower, a company that does custom printing of fabric. (See http://www.spoonflower.com). You are the copyright holder. You upload your image to Spoonflower. Are they now able to 1) sell it to the world, and/or 2) has the copyright transferred? Let's look the Community standards section. "**Your control of your own designs.** In order to run Spoonflower, we have to be able to do things like reproduce and distribute the designs you upload, actions outlined below in the section titled Proprietary Rights . But at all times you retain both copyright and control over your designs. We will not sell, share, or reproduce your work except as necessary to run our service and our website. We started Spoonflower to empower creative people, not to take advantage of them." https://www.spoonflower.com/terms. And to the question, "Do I keep the copyright for my designs," Spoonflower responds, "We value the copyright of all images. The designer owns the rights to their artwork. You can find more information about copyright in our terms of service. https://support.spoonflower.com/hc/en-us/articles/204444560-Do-I-keep-the-copyright-for-my-designs- This means you decide when a work is released to the public, and when it is not.

Summary

Kurt Saunders in *Intellectual Property Law: Legal Aspects of Innovation and Competition* (West Academic, 2016) compiled a useful table (which I have modified) to help us sort out when someone is an employee versus an independent contractor, using the *Reid* factors.

Works Made for Hire	
Employees	Independent Contractors
The work was created by an employee within the scope of employment: • during the time of the employee's work, • while doing the type of work the employee was hired to do, • in the employer's work place, and • for the employer's business purpose • [I would add they receive benefits, vacation days, and/or a W-2 for tax purposes]	*Specially Commissioned Work* • The work is one of the following: a contribution to a collective work, part of a motion picture or other audiovisual work, a translation, a supplementary work, a compilation, an instructional text, a test, answer material for a test or an atlas • There is a written agreement signed by both parties. *Copyright Held by Independent Contract* • Supplies own instruments • Cannot be assigned other tasks • Uses own space to create • Business is based on the work being done, and not the specialty of the client. • No benefits or taxes paid • Any assistants chosen by IC, and not client

If you are an independent contractor, you hold the copyright, unless you assign it in writing signed by both parties.

Contributions to Collective Works

Pat Sloan and Jane Davidson's *The Splendid Sampler* contains contributions from a variety of authors. Those are considered a contribution to a collective work. They are each a separate contribution to a collective work, which carry a distinct copyright from the whole. Think anthology. I'm currently writing a piece for law anthology that will be published by Oxford University Press. I retain copyright of that article, unless the Editors require me to assign copyright. So, I could take it and write a longer piece or even an entire book! But I couldn't do that if I did not hold the copyright in that original work without getting permission from the editor(s)/press. Here is the copyright law portion for contributions to collective works:

> *17 U.S.C. Section 201(c) Contributions to Collective Works.* —
> Copyright in each separate contribution to a collective work is distinct from copyright in the collective work as a whole, and vests initially in the author of the contribution. In the absence of an express transfer of the copyright or of any rights under it, the owner of copyright in the collective work is presumed to have acquired only the privilege of reproducing and distributing the contribution as part of that particular collective work, any revision of that collective work, and any later collective work in the same series.

Categories of Works

Copyright protects the following categories of works: literary works; musical works; dramatic works; pantomimes and choreographic works; pictorial, graphic, and sculptural works; motion pictures and other audiovisual works; sound recordings; and architectural works. 17 U.S.C. Section 102(a). It's not a closed list because the word "include" is used. But these are the common categories, and when you register your work at the U.S. Copyright Office, you are asked to choose which category you are registering.

Where do quilts fall?

- The quilt itself: artist work
- Book about quilting: literary work
- Pattern booklet: literary work
- Fabric: artist work
- YouTube videos: audiovisual works
- Podcasts about quilting: sound recordings

If it has words and directions, it is likely a literary work. If it is the quilt or resources for a quilt (e.g. fabric), it is likely an artistic work. Individual images/quilts within a book, of course, are likely artistic works. This will matter later with the right of attribution and moral rights. We'll come back to these categories a number of times in the book, but for now, recognize that quilting and crafting involve a variety of categories. Let's look at how the U.S. Copyright Office defines each category.

Literary Works

The Copyright Act defines "literary works" as "works, other than audiovisual works, expressed in words, numbers, or other verbal or numerical symbols or indicia, regardless of the nature of the material objects, such as books, periodicals, manuscripts, phonorecords, film, tapes, disks, or cards, in which they are embodied." 17 U.S.C. § 101. Here's a list from the Copyright Office:

☐ Abridgements	☐ Anthologies	☐ Blogs	☐ Catalogs (text)
☐ Advertisements (text)	☐ Articles	☐ Autobiographies	☐ Dictionaries
☐ Board games (text)	☐ Books	☐ Cookbooks	☐ Craft books
☐ Dissertations	☐ Directories	☐ Workbooks	☐ Fiction
☐ Genealogies	☐ Historical Works	☐ How-To Books	☐ Instructions
☐ Interviews	☐ Magazines	☐ Manuscripts	☐ Newsletters
☐ Newspapers	☐ Periodicals	☐ Poems	☐ Reference works
☐ Research papers	☐ Serials	☐ Short stories	☐ Tests
☐ Text	☐ Text w/art	☐ Textbooks	☐ Translations
☐ User Manuals.			

In the quilting and craft world, we do a lot of these activities. Can you check which ones might apply? Can you think of others? Can you think of others that might qualify as literary works?

Performing Arts: "Works of the performing arts are works that are intended to be performed for an audience. This category includes a wide variety of creative works, including music, lyrics, sound recordings, scripts, screenplays, choreography, motion pictures, video games, and similar types of works." https://www.copyright.gov/registration/performing-arts/index.html The Copyright Act states that performing a work "means to recite, render, play, dance, or act it, either directly or by means of any device or process or, in the case of a motion picture or other audiovisual work, to show its images in any sequence or to make the sounds accompanying it audible." 17 U.S.C. § 101. Here is a list from the Copyright Office:

- ☐ Albums
- ☐ Comedy Routines/Standup
- ☐ Choreographic Works
- ☐ Instrumentation
- ☐ Interviews (recorded)
- ☐ Musical Instruction Books
- ☐ Live Concerts
- ☐ Mix Tape
- ☐ Music Editing
- ☐ Musicals
- ☐ Musical Arrangement
- ☐ Spoken Word Recordings
- ☐ Audio books
- ☐ Podcasts
- ☐ Musical Theatre
- ☐ Music and Lyrics
- ☐ Stage Plays
- ☐ Jingles
- ☐ Lyrics
- ☐ Sampling
- ☐ Screenplays
- ☐ Pantomime
- ☐ Remix/Mashups
- ☐ TV/Radio Broadcasts
- ☐ Beats
- ☐ Drama
- ☐ Music
- ☐ Songs
- ☐ Scripts
- ☐ Treatments
- ☐ Vocals
- ☐ Soundtracks
- ☐ Synopses
- ☐ Teleplays

Quilt-related products/projects can fall under these categories: think Podcasts, musical theatre, songs, scripts, audio books, and tv/radio broadcasts. The podcast, *Just Wanna Quilt*, fits under performing arts as a category.

Visual Arts

"Works of the visual arts include a wide variety of pictorial, graphic, and sculptural works, as well as architectural works. Examples of visual arts works include paintings, sculptures, photographs, and other types of works. https://www.copyright.gov/registration/visual-arts/index.html. The Copyright Act states that "pictorial, graphic, and sculptural works include two-dimensional and three-dimensional works of fine, graphic, and applied art, photographs, prints and art reproductions, maps, globes, charts, diagrams, models, and technical drawings, including architectural plans." 17 U.S.C. § 101 The Copyright Act defines "Architectural Works" as "the design of a building as embodied in any tangible medium of expression, including a building, architectural plans, or drawings. The work includes the overall form as well as the arrangement and composition of spaces and elements in the design, but does not include individual standard features." 17 U.S.C. § 101. Here is the list from the Copyright Office:

- ☐ Advertisements (visual)
- ☐ Architectural works
- ☐ Artwork (2d/3d)
- ☐ Blueprints
- ☐ Board games (art)
- ☐ Buildings
- ☐ Carpeting
- ☐ Cartography
- ☐ Cartoons, comics
- ☐ Catalogs (visual)
- ☐ Craft Kits
- ☐ Drawings
- ☐ Fabric Designs
- ☐ Flooring Designs
- ☐ Illustrations
- ☐ Jewelry Designs
- ☐ Logos
- ☐ Photographs
- ☐ Geologic Charts
- ☐ Graphic Designs
- ☐ Greeting Cards
- ☐ Label (visuals)
- ☐ Maps
- ☐ Masks
- ☐ Models
- ☐ Paintings
- ☐ Posters
- ☐ Prints/Reproductions
- ☐ Product Packaging
- ☐ Puppets
- ☐ Scientifics Drawings
- ☐ Sculptures
- ☐ Stationary
- ☐ Stencils
- ☐ Technical Drawings
- ☐ Textile Designs
- ☐ Toys
- ☐ Vessel Hulls
- ☐ Wallpapers
- ☐ Website
- ☐ Wrapping Paper

Again, there are number of these that relate to the quilting world. (Vessel hulls, of course). Advertisements, artwork, catalogs, craft kits, graphic design, posters, textile designs, fabric designs, and logos, to name a few.

This is obviously an important category for quilting. But books *about quilting* would be filed under literary works.

Photographs

Photographs have their own special category, where you can register up to 750 photographs in one registration form. Here is the list of categories:

- ☐ Commercial
- ☐ Events
- ☐ Personal
- ☐ Scientific
- ☐ Portrait
- ☐ Documentary Photos
- ☐ Fine Art
- ☐ Photojournalism
- ☐ Sports
- ☐ Editorial
- ☐ Forensic
- ☐ School
- ☐ Wedding

Motion Pictures and Other Audiovisual Works

"Motion Pictures are works that contain a series of related images that are intended to be shown with a projector, digital display, or other device. When the images are shown in successive order, they create an impression of movement that is perceptible to the eye. Examples of motion pictures include movies, television shows, video games, animations, and similar types of works." https://www.copyright.gov/registration/motion-pictures/index.html. Again, here is the list:

- ☐ Animations
- ☐ Commercial (video/audio)
- ☐ Motion Picture
- ☐ Slide Presentations
- ☐ Audiovisual Works
- ☐ Concert Videos
- ☐ Multimedia Works
- ☐ Television Shows
- ☐ Banner Advertisements
- ☐ Documentaries
- ☐ PowerPoints
- ☐ Videos

We will come back to the Copyright Office and how to register your works later in the book. For now, I wanted to give you a better understanding of what is protected by copyright, and in what categories. Bear in mind that there are different forms and requirements, depending on the category. The Copyright Office has one more category

Other Digital Content

It's not actually a category, but a guide to help you figure out which category your work fits into: The Copyright Act protects a wide variety of works that are used with computers, tablets, smartphones, video game platforms, and other electronic devices. It also protects works that are used or distributed on the internet, such as websites, blogs, and other online content. To register these types of digital content, determine the predominant authorship and submit as a literary work, work of the visual arts, or work of the performing arts.

For any work, you have to fit it into the category that makes the most sense. What happens if you get it wrong? That's ok. Under the previous 1909 Act, it made a big difference on what was covered under copyright, but now that is not the case. Do your best. And reach out for help if you are not sure.

The Key to Everything: Compilations and Derivative works

We need to understand two concepts of law: compilations and derivative works. We understand that not everything is protectable. And we know that it takes a certain degree of creativity to achieve a copyrightable work. Compilations and derivative works may help us understand *when* a work is copyrightable.

Compilations

The selection, arrangement, and coordination (SAC) of pre-existing materials is key to understanding how a copyrightable work is created. This can include copyrighted and non-copyrightable elements. As long as the SAC has a modicum of creativity, the work gains protection. When we choose blocks, fabric, and how we will quilt the top, we are creating a compilation. Our compilations are protectable because of our selection, arrangement, and coordination. This is a way to think about the creative process.

Compilations can also be collective works like anthologies or books where different authors contribute independently protectable works, like short stories.

Feist teaches us that individual parts need not be copyrightable, but the whole, with the requisite creativity can be. That the compilation is protectable does not change the status of the underlying, individual parts. 17 U.S.C Section 103.

Now, not everyone believes that we should define everything we make as a compilation. I understand. But, I think it is a useful way, a shorthand, to help us identify the elements of creativity. Patti Baymiller, for example, created this text quilt.

The design was her own, and she hand drew the words, cloud and snow flake. She made decisions. She selected, arranged, and coordinated borders, clouds, fonts and a phrase, and in the process created a copyrighted work.

The individual parts, as we will see, may not be protectable (fonts, the shape of a cloud, a phrase), but put them together, and they are.

We are looking to see if we have created something with a modicum of creativity that achieves copyrightable status. It doesn't take much, but it does take a little. The question is how little. And we will see, just because you have a copyrightable work, doesn't mean someone else couldn't think of the same thing independently themselves, and moreover, without registration, you do not have much hope of protecting your work should it really be infringed. I

Derivative Work

We hear the word "derivative" used quite a bit. Not everything we make becomes a derivative work. First, we will see that the copyright holder has the exclusive right to create derivative works. So, one needs permission (implied or explicit) to create derivative works. Second, merely changing the color of something does not create a derivative work. Third, in creating a derivative work (with permission), you gain certain rights to the new creation, but the underlying work still belongs to the copyright holder.

Here is the definition from the 1976 Copyright Act: "A "derivative work" is a work based upon one or more preexisting works, such as a translation, musical arrangement, dramatization, fictionalization, motion picture version, sound recording, art reproduction, abridgment, condensation, or any other form in which a work may be recast, transformed, or adapted. A work consisting of editorial revisions, annotations, elaborations, or other modifications which, as a whole, represent an original work of authorship, is a "derivative work"." 17 U.S.C. Section 101.

Let's break down the definition of a derivative work into elements:

- A derivative work is "a work based upon one or more preexisting works." You have to have a work that is your base. So, Romeo and Juliet is a play. That's our preexisting work.
- "such as a translation, musical arrangement, dramatization, fictionalization, motion picture version, sound recording, art reproduction, abridgment, condensation, or any other form."
- "in which a work may be recast, transformed, or adapted." This is really important. The derivative work must be "recast, transformed or adapted" in such a way as to be distinct and identifiably different from the original. There are many cases that go in depth into what qualifies as a derivative work, and whether it meets the threshold of originality required for a derivative work.

There's an origin point -- the pattern, a picture, a traditional block. Then, you make something. You choose the colors. Now you have made a derivative work of the original. We will return to derivative works a number of times throughout the book, including when we discuss exclusive rights, infringement, and fair use.

Lyric Kinard, "Still Yearning"

Here is Lyric Kinard's amazing fiber collage work, particularly related to immigration. (https://lyrickinard.com/) How did she make it? She took public domain photographs she finds on the New York Library website, and transformed them into amazing pieces. Her piece, "Still Yearning" combines her own vision of immigration as part of the exhibition, "Threads of Resistance."

Here is one of the original photographs: Ruthenian woman, 1906.[4] See her in the front? Lyric hasn't done much to change her, but she Is part of a bigger context. We'll see artist Jeff Koons learn to do the same thing after three lost court cases. And here, unlike Koons, Kinard is using public domain images. (We'll learn more about that in a later chapter). For more images, go to http:///digitalcollections.nypl.org.

[4] Manuscripts and Archives Division, The New York Public Library. (1906). Ruthenian woman. Retrieved from http://digitalcollections.nypl.org/items/510d47da-dc92-a3d9-e040-e00a18064a99

Fiber Artist Eric James Suszynski-Soifakis created an amazing 40" by 60" piece of work. It is based on the photograph taken by Cayton Cox. Here is the original photograph by Cayton Cox:

Original Photograph by Clayton Cox

Then, Eric did the following: "To make the quilt, the substrate itself was sewn with over 50 different polyester and polyblend fabrics. The original photo was then broken it into smaller rectangles, printed onto transfer paper, and sublimation transferred to the fabric substrate. Once all the pieces were printed, they were then sewn together and quilter.

Authorized Derivative Version by Eric James Suszynski-Soifakis

The Concept of Puzzling

What about a kit? Usually, you are making someone else's selection, arrangement, and coordination. So, you are the sewist. You are using your skill to make someone else's copyrighted work. I make Tula Pink's All-Star kit. I decide to change the background from half black/half white to all black. That small change does not give me a legal derivative work. I've merely altered the color of part of the pattern. We will see shortly that merely changing the color of something is not necessarily enough creativity to gain copyright protection.

What if I add something? I may have created a derivative work, yes. But the copyright notice and rights statement on the pattern I've used as an underlying work may limit what I can do with that derivative work. If I want to commercially exploit my derivative work, I will need to get permission from the underlying copyright holder. Take for example, Cheryl Sleboda's "Pleats to Meet You" pattern. She taught me how to make it! She explicitly knew I was making it. And it is a pattern she teaches all over the US. I added my own touch, including beads and "Just Wanna Quilt Now." Hers is a table runner. Mine is a sign. Now, some could argue my amazing creativity meets the derivative work standard, that I've recast, transformed, and adapted the pattern with enough creativity. Even if this is the case, if I want to use it within a commercial context, I need to ask Cheryl's permission as the underlying copyright holder. Here's Cheryl's pattern, available at http://www.muppin.com/, and here is my version, made under the guidance of Cheryl (at her home). See the differences? Is this puzzling (no new copyright) or a derivative work?

There are many ways we puzzle. Kits. Following a pattern. We will learn later that merely changing the color of something does not create a new copyright.

So, if I take Christa Watson's fabric lines, and make my own version of KimberBell's "Make yourself at home" pattern, is that merely changing the color? Any copyright bestowed?

Not likely. I've merely changed the color. I've followed the pattern. I don't get a "new" copyright.

Puzzling in Action

We do kits and patterns because it brings us joy. We learn new skills. For me, I get to immerse myself in the art itself as I put together each piece. It's not about copyright. It's about the skill and beauty of making someone lovely.

Celeste Poulin explains, "My sister gave me a kit called Compass Roses by Christine Stainbrook. I decided to make a practice center for it since I wasn't sure if I could do it. I liked it so much, I kept going with my own fabrics (all batiks.) This kit was the WHOLE reason that I decided to buy a longarm. I still haven't quilted this. I just need to do it!!"

Celeste Poulin creates the Compass Rose

Summary

So, we are on our way to understanding *what is protected by copyright*: independent, creative work. We are just at the beginning of our journey. Let's look now at what elements within a creative work are not protectable, and how that interacts with obtaining copyright in your own creations.

When you think about copyright, you have to think with both hats. What can I use as a creator – what is not protectable, what I may need to get permission to use, what is covered by other parts of the Copyright Act like the First Sale doctrine, and what permissible uses might not require permission, like fair use. And then, what is protectable once I create a work? How should I think about the work that I created? Do I actually own anything protectable? Is the protection thin or thick? What additional steps must I do to strengthen my copyright, or alternatively share it with the world?

Let's look at the elements that are available to all of us to help with that creative process.

Steps to Copyrightability Quiz

1. **My talented cat, Patrick, intentionally paints a painting. Is it protectable under copyright?**
   a. Yes
   b. No

2. **I work really hard to replicate the Mona Lisa in a quilt. It takes 100s of hours, and I get it just right. Is it protectable as a new work?**
   a. Yes
   b. No

3. **I take a photograph of the Mona Lisa and I draw cat eyes onto it in pace of the human eyes. Is it protectable as derivative work?**
   a. Yes
   b. No

4. **I make a quilt with ten blocks, each with a flower in the center. Later, I found out that someone else had done the same thing 20 years earlier. Can I obtain copyright even if someone else had already thought of the idea?**
   a. Yes
   b. No

Answers:

1. B. Sadly, Patrick cannot obtain copyright because even though he thinks he is, he is not human.
2. B. Nope. Sweat of the brow does not get me protection. One could argue that I've recast it in quilt form, but there would be very little to protect if it is an exact replica.
3. A. Yes! Recast, transform or adapt!
4. A. Yes! Independent creation. Happens all the time. We'll discuss subconscious copying leading to infringement in a later chapter. That's where you saw it but don't remember, and infringe on someone's copyrighted work. Happens a lot in music.

7: Our Common Pool: Non-Protectables

We All Want Things to be Both Protected (our work) and Not Protected (our common pool)

Copyrightable subject matter, as we have learned, is governed by 17 U.S.C. Section 102. Section 102(a) tells us what is protected, including suggested categories of work and the requirements for protection. Section 102(b) helps us understand what is *not* protected. We all draw from a common pool of materials and resources to create works. This chapter looks more carefully at the various aspects of non-protectable elements. Here is Section 102(b) of the 1976 Copyright Act:

> In no case does copyright protection for an original work of authorship extend to any idea, procedure, process, system, method of operation, concept, principle, or discovery, regardless of the form in which it is described, explained, illustrated, or embodied in such work.

You can start to see a pattern. Copyright protects fixed creativity. Ideas are not protectable. We know that. Things that make things go are not protected under copyright either. We know that, too. Those are protected by patents and trade secrets. But Section 102(b) includes a bunch of other elements that are less obvious, and that's what this chapter is about. We will look at many non-protectable elements, but first a story.

Learning to Sew at the Public Library

I sit in a sewing class at Mattison Area Public Library District, in a suburb of Chicago. Five brand new sewing students learn to make PJ pants. (I do, too). The room is strangely quiet. Each kid is absorbed in pinning, cutting, sewing, and reading directions. We hear the hum of the sewing machines. And throughout the two hours, the librarian/sewist, Julia Driscoll works with each child (and me), creating a running commentary on the basics of how to pin, cut, sew, and follow directions. It is strangely soothing. Here we see five kids voluntarily learning to sew during the summer. It's a four-week class to make one pair of pants. This is their third night. Each kid has picked out the fabric. They are all at different stages. They are serious. They want to learn. They are becoming sewists. But what they are doing is not protected by copyright.

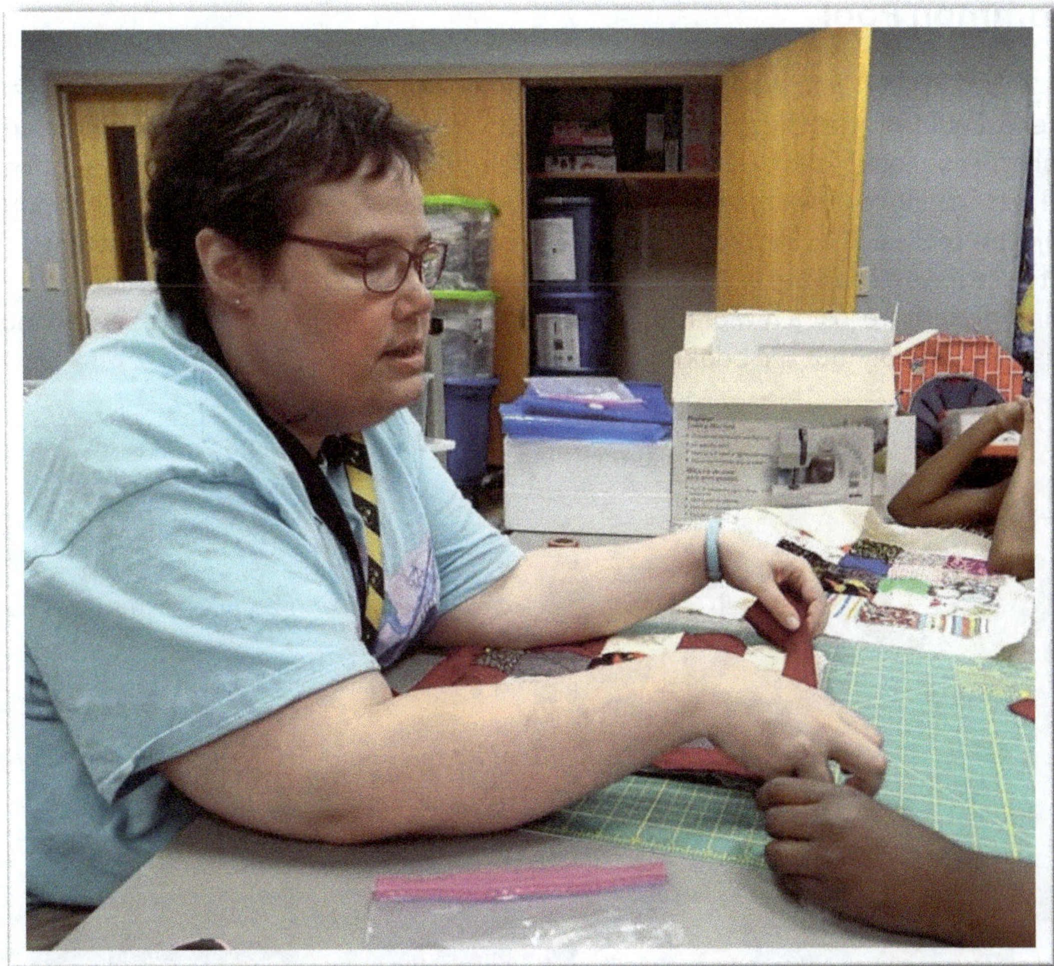

Julia Driscoll teaches kids how to sew at the public library.

Copyright does not protect clothing patterns or useful articles. PJs are useful. We don't protect recipes either. Julia freely teaches techniques to her students. Making pants this way has been handed down and now these Generation Z kids are learning too. Learning how to put in the inseam. How to add an elastic waistband. Quilting is also full of techniques. Some are even named after a particular person. But none—NONE—of those techniques are protectable by copyright. How to make a Flying Geese unit using a particular ruler is not protected by copyright. Now, you can check the ruler to see if it has a patent number on it. If it doesn't, the ruler isn't protected either. What is important at this moment is that rulers, techniques, and methods are *not* protectable by copyright. What is? The expression of those methods may be protected. We'll come back to the example of Flying Geese shortly.

This chapter is the story of why we can learn to make PJs at a local library, why we can create quilts from blocks we all know well, and why when a new way of binding or putting in an inseam is created, we all can partake of that technique.

Our Common Pool

We have a sub-group in Just Wanna Quilt called the Stealth Sewing Squad. It started out as an experiment. Could you get the shy members of Just Wanna Quilt to interact more if the group was smaller? (You totally can). I also really needed samples of things made, and I was falling behind. I was hoping to enlist them in sewing various things. We started with our Common Pool project -- make a 6- ½ inch square with JWQ colors that is of a well-known pattern. I wanted to see if we all had the same idea of what the common pool was. I was not disappointed. Here are just a few of the 100+ blocks that were mailed to Tulane Law School. (We'll see more throughout the book).

Twenty-five of our Common Pool blocks made by the Stealth Sewing Squad of the Quilting Army

Ann Wasserman's "Beggar's Block,"

Here is what Ann Wasserman wrote about her block: "A 6" version of the first block I made in my first quilting class c. 1978. Beggar's Block (Brackman #1758). With vintage prints. Yea! The class block was finished as a pillow, and I symbolically used it as a seat cushion at my sewing machine for many years. When it started to wear, I put it away for safekeeping. Somewhere. I'd love to show it to you all, but can't find it. This has set me off on an overdue sort and purge and organize in my sewing room....." Quilting has a rich tradition of common blocks, techniques, and motifs. We know that as quilters. This chapter explains why that is legally.

For every creative, there are a bunch of things, tools, and objects available for us all to use to create: colors and shapes, for example. Copyright recognizes that there are basic elements that should be common to all. Some of these are also because copyright law does not protect them—they don't fall under copyright's jurisdiction. Others are because they are too old or didn't follow proper formalities, and are now in the public domain. Think Shakespeare. (That's the next chapter) And some come into the common pool because of custom –they are just so common to their particular field of art that no one would think of locking them up. (That's the chapter after next.) In this chapter, we will now look very specifically at elements that are not protected by copyright. Keep your creative hat on. I hope you recognize the gift and the importance of having a strong, healthy common pool of creative resources.

The List of (Mostly) Non-Protectable Elements

None of these are protectable by copyright. We'll go through them one by one.

- Ideas and concepts
- Procedures, methods and techniques
- Useful things: the doctrine of functionality and useful articles doctrine
- Facts
- Shapes
- Mere Change in Color
- Some fabrics
- Mere Copies
- Layout or Format
- Typeface and fonts (with exceptions)
- Letters, words, titles, and slogans
- Ingredients
- Restoration
- Stock characters/Scenes a faire/Common elements
- Expired copyrighted works now in the public domain (the next chapter)
- Works that did not meet the required level of creativity (the previous chapter)

The Copyright Office has created a huge and helpful resource to help us, called the Compendium. It helps us understand the law and its interpretation in case law in a variety of situations. We'll refer to it throughout this section. For more info, see https://www.copyright.gov/comp3/ . Let's look at them one by one.

No Ideas and Concepts

Ideas are not protectable. Expression of the idea is. Your version. Your selection, arrangement, and coordination of that idea is protectable. We've learned that already.

Judy Kump's Ocean Quilt

Can you identify the ideas behind this raw edge applique by Judy Kump? Here's what she wrote about creating this quilt: "My friend's son and his wife were doing an ocean themed bedroom for their baby. I just pulled batiks that reminded me of water, made a bunch of half square triangle blocks. I played with them till I had the right effect. Then I added the Fish and seaweed. I spent a lot of time staring at it from different angles till it made me happy.

Procedures, Methods, and Techniques

Copyright law does not protect procedures, methods, techniques or other ways of doing things. Patents and/or trade secrets protect functional elements, not copyright. So, the techniques you develop or learn from a YouTube video are not protectable by copyright. (The YouTube video itself, of course, is protected, in its expression). You can use the techniques, teach them to others, and profit from them. If, however, they are protected by patents, that is another story. Here are three examples of techniques:

Glue Basting

QA member Edith Gross loves to baste almost everything with glue first. Glue basting is both an idea and a technique. Anyone can do it. And anyone can suggest it in a pattern. You can use products that may or may not be protected by patents. But the technique is free. Edith's work is gorgeous. She swears by the glue. One time Edith glue basted a quilt's binding for me, and I forgot, and washed it. So, maybe not glue basting for me.

Bloc Loc we have discussed previously, Bloc Loc is a patented invention. Bloc Loc is a ruler system that locks the seam so that when cutting a pieced seam doesn't move, whether a half-square triangle or something more complicated. Block Loc has a patent on the technology and a trademark on the name. They created a pattern book. That is protected by copyright. I can use Bloc Loc with any pattern or quilt that I am making. There's no restriction on that. But I can't take their technology and reproduce it on a 3d printer at Tulane. That would-be patent infringement.

Quilt Math

Whether it is how to construct a half-square triangle, the perfect ¼-inch seam, or strategies on the best way to bind a quilt, all of these are not protectable by copyright. But what about rulers, papers, or books produced with that method? The book is protectable as a copyrightable expression. Rulers may or may not be protected by patents. Paper systems may be known by their trademark, but the system itself is not under copyright.

A quilt may be protected by copyright. But the directions – the math is not. Strange, yes? It's one anomaly. The math is seen as functional, even though the math is another version of the quilt. Expression of the directions are protected, of course. Just not the math. Some believe the math should be protected as an expression of the art That makes sense. But you can't lock up component parts, and the directions teach you how to make the parts. The question is *when does* math become something protectable?

The Example of Flying Geese

Jessica Vetor's Flying Geese

Flying Geese are my least favorite thing to make, but they are very pretty. The ones above are made by Karen Grote. Flying Geese are strangely difficult to make, and so everyone has their own technique to make them. Karen Klamczynski describes Flying Geese: "The finished Flying Geese block is half a finished square-on-point in a square (cut along midpoints on sides)." This is a Flying Geese.

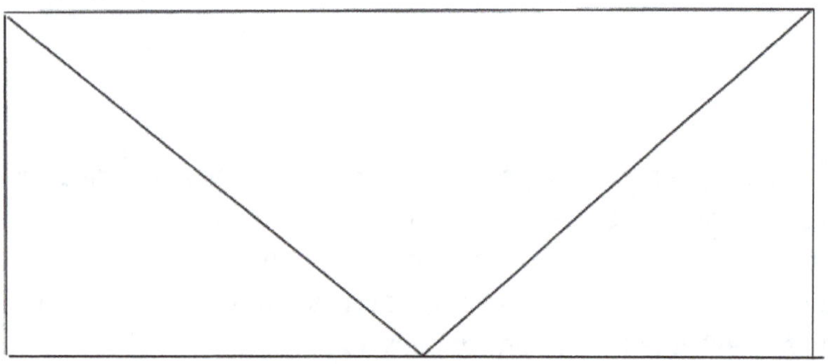

Linda Newman explains the basic concept: "A rectangle where the height is about half the width. Along the bottom of the rectangle is the base of a triangle and the apex of the triangle is the midpoint of the top of the rectangle. Generally, the top angle is an oblique angle and the two side angles are equal acute angles. The rectangle and triangle are contrasting fabrics in color, value or pattern."

So, there are many, many ways to make Flying Geese, and they are a staple within quilt patterns. Here is a list of a few methods:

- AccuQuilt cutting system[5]
- No Waste Flying Geese
- Four at a Time Method

---

[5] For transparency purposes, AccuQuilt sent us two Go system to try, a s part of our research.

- Deb Tucker's Wing Clipper
- Lazy Girl No Math
- Quilt in a Day Flying Geese Rulers
- Stitch & Flip
- Marti Mitchell Flying Geese Ruler
- Caryl Bryer Fallert-Gentry's Version
- Foundation Piecing
- Thangles Flying Geese
- Kimerbell's machine embroidery technique.

We have tried nearly all of these. I'm still not very good at them. I'm not sure why. It's like playing golf, I think. Always working on that swing that put. For me, it is Flying Geese.

Stephanie Kucera Jacobson's Flying Geese

"AccuQuilt has specific Flying Geese dies, but you can use the quarter square triangle (die #4) and half square triangle (die #5) in any Qube set to make Flying Geese. Let me see if I can find a picture.", explained Stephanie Kucera Jacobson

And here is an amazing example by Celeste Poulin of Flying Geese incorporated into an art quilt. As Karen Klamczynski explains, "People do creative things with them, altering the proportions as in Celeste Poulin's example below. So maybe the working definition today is "a triangle of fabric turned into a rectangle with the addition of two matching triangle corners."

Celeste Poulin's Flying Geese

The expression is protected, but the method she used is not. In this case, Celeste also used her AccuQuilt. She explains: "Before I got my GO! Cutter, I tried every method I could find. I called my Flying Geese, broken winged geese because they came out so wonky. The best method I found at time made four at once. You put small squares on a larger square and sew then cut on the diagonal and repeat with the other corners."

Here are Stephanie Kucera Jacobson's improv Flying Geese. Here's how she explained her technique: "It doesn't have a name that I know of. (I'd like to think I invented it, but I'm sure it's been done before!) The colored triangles are the leftover pieces from making binding. For the "wings" I cut squares in half and sewed half on each side of the center triangle." And Carolyn Oppenheim writes, "I think 'Flying Geese' is my favorite! And I love the pattern expanded. I've made two quilts with each triangle from a 16" square."

And Scott Murkin's example of a Flying Geese Quilt.

For each of these, the method of making the Flying Geese is not protected by copyright. The expression—the quilt--is protected.

Christine Van Buskirk created a pattern called ""Crazy for Geese" where she used Eleanor Burn's method of Flying Geese, along with Creative Grids rulers and their ultimate Flying Geese Tool.

Christine Van Buskirk's "Crazy for Geese"

Christa Watson published "Geese I the Garden," with oversize geese. She explained, "Because it's a simple design and one that could be easy to knock off, the math is done a little differently so that someone would need to purchase the pattern in order to make this quilt."

There are many patterns out there using Flying Geese. Nann Blaine Hilyard created "Twenty-Cent Geese" for The Quilter in 2006. Sara Bond created "Release the Geese, a circular pattern. Bonnie Hunter created "Wild and Goosey."

Joanne Kerton writes, "Wandering Geese was the first pattern I wrote to sell. (I design and sell as Canuck Quilter Designs)." She used the four-at-time technique for the Flying Geese. Again, why would you purchase the pattern? For the directions, to support the artist, to make what she made. But copyright did not lock up Flying Geese when Joanne made the pattern.

Joanne Kerton "Wandering Geese"

Joanne Kerton also wrote a booklet, "Flying Geese Skillbuilder," where she went through each of the methods. Again, the methods are not protectable, but her version -- the booklet is.

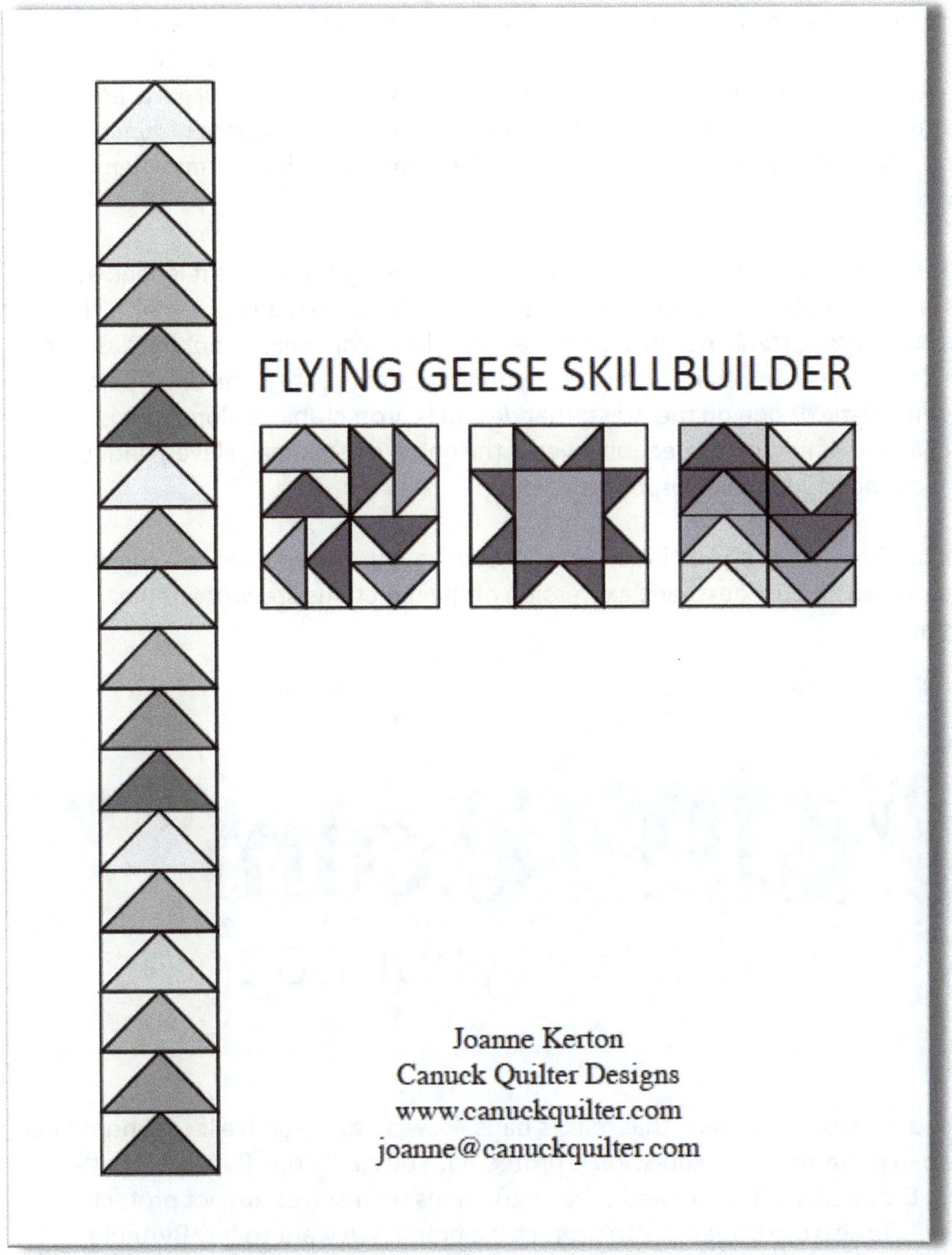

And we have others too – writing blog posts on how to tackle Flying Geese, and describing all kinds of methods and techniques to be successful. A whole industry made upon Flying Geese.

Not Useful: Doctrines of Functionality and Useful Articles

A work cannot get protection for its usefulness. It has to be un-useful. That's the useful articles doctrine. So, a lamp that is also a statue of Uncle Sam can get protection as a statue of Uncle Sam, but it can't get protection for its lamp qualities. So, too, for quilts. This is called aesthetic separability. You take the artistic parts (the top, the quilting designs) and separate it from the functionality (a warm thing to put over a loved one on a cold night). The useful parts are not protected by copyright. That's patent's job. Get it? It is also called the doctrine of functionality. Functional elements are not protectable under copyright. That will be important when we get to patterns and directions.

Also, an important note. Clothing is not protectable under copyright because it is seen as functional. That means that patterns for clothing are not protectable under copyright. No protection. We buy dress patterns because they are helpful and convenient, not because we can't make the dress unless we pay its author. Copyright does not protect the dress pattern. Now, if there is an artistic design on the dress, that design is protectable, as long as it is aesthetically separable. If not, no protection, even if the pattern is original, clever, and full of creativity. The clothing's functional purpose wins out.

What about bags? Those are useful articles. Not protectable. But the expression—the way the directions are arranged and the aesthetic expression of the directions are protectable. Functionality is not.

byannie.com™
...what's in your bag?

ByAnnie is a famous pattern company that makes bags. How do they survive if copyright does not protect the bag patterns? The expression is protected. You can't copy ByAnnie's patterns and put them on the internet. But the math, the instructions themselves are not protected. Can you see why? We also use trademark to protect the brand. We want to buy ByAnnie products because we like the techniques, style and way the bag turns out. Same with clothing. You choose to go to the Gap or the Loft because you like how their clothes feel and look. Trademark does the heavy lifting with useful articles, not copyright. (Trademark doesn't necessarily protect the individual design of the bag or clothing, but creates brand loyalty). For more see, www.byannie.com.

We also see that ByAnnie's business model is not only about patterns, but more importantly, all of the extra notions you need to make the bag: the small zippers, pieces of plastic, mesh, etc. During the Holiday Season 2018, ByAnnie sent out free packets of 25 patterns for cell phone holders that look like badge holders. We received a pack. How generous, you say. Yes. But it also meant that to make them, you now likely would order at least three pieces needed to make the free pattern. Brilliant. Genius. You see why?

No Facts

We learn that facts are not copyrightable in *Feist*, the U.S. Supreme Court case we discussed in the previous chapter. Justice O'Connor writes, "'No one may claim originality as to facts.' This is because facts do not owe their origin to an act of authorship. The distinction is one between creation and discovery: the first person to find and report a particular fact has not created the fact; he or she has merely discovered its existence. Census takers, for example, do not "create" the population figures that emerge from their efforts; in a sense, they copy these figures from the world around them. Census data therefore do not trigger copyright because these data are not "original" in the constitutional sense. The same is true of all facts—scientific, historical, biographical, and news of the day. 'They may not be copyrighted and are part of the public domain available to every person.'" (additional citations omitted)
Facts are not created. So, there is no modicum of creativity. That seems simple enough. Copyright, of course, has to complicate it. What about facts that are actually fiction? If they are presented as facts, then they are treated as facts.

What about fiction, or "created" facts? Those are *not* facts. So, the fact that Harry Potter lives under the stairs while growing up is not considered a fact. Fictional stories are not facts. We have a case where someone wants to create a trivia book based on *Seinfeld*, and the Second Circuit court declares that the "facts" in the episodes are copyrightable, and therefore, to create a trivia book, you have to get a license from the copyright holders of *Seinfeld*.

What if you create "fictional facts"? You make up things that you claim are facts? The courts take them as *facts*. You can't later say, "Oh, I made those up." The courts use copyright estoppel: people relied on those as facts, and so you can't change your mind.

What else are facts? Math. Dates. Historical information. No one owns these elements. And why? Because there is no authorship, says copyright, they just exist in the world—no one created facts. And going back to Section 102(a), you must have authorship to have a copyrightable work.

Turning back to quilting and crafts, can you identify facts that would not be protected? Math is the easiest one. If you have 1-½ inch strips, once they are sewn with a ¼-inch seam, they will be 1 inch wide. That's a fact. Not protectable.

Shapes

According to the U.S. Copyright Office, the Copyright Act does not protect common geometric shapes, either in two-dimensional or three-dimensional form. There are numerous common geometric shapes, including, without limitation:

- straight or curved lines
- circles
- ovals
- spheres
- Triangles
- cones
- squares
- cubes
- rectangles
- diamonds
- trapezoids
- parallelograms
- pentagons
- hexagons
- heptagons
- octagons
- decagons

Compendium III, 906.1

For quilters, this is particularly interesting, and it is why when asking Jake Kleiner of Paper Pieces, he rightly answered that they have no copyright or property right in the shapes that they make for English Paper Piecing. They have a property right in the convenience of hundreds of specifically shaped hexagons or diamonds. And the patterns made by those basic shapes are the selection, arrangement, and coordination of basic shapes, and so are likely under copyright. But when you combine the shapes, you get something that has enough originality to be protectable. Katja Marek created one of the best-selling books, *The New Hexagon*, which combines various shapes into beautiful hexagons.

Here is our in-progress version from the Quilting Army of some of those blocks.

Our in-progress version of the New Hexagon

At what point do individual shapes combine together become copyrightable? The Copyright Office actually provides an example that is very quilt relatable of what is and is not protectable by copyright law. A purple rectangle with eight evenly spaced dots (that looks like a domino) is *not protectable*.

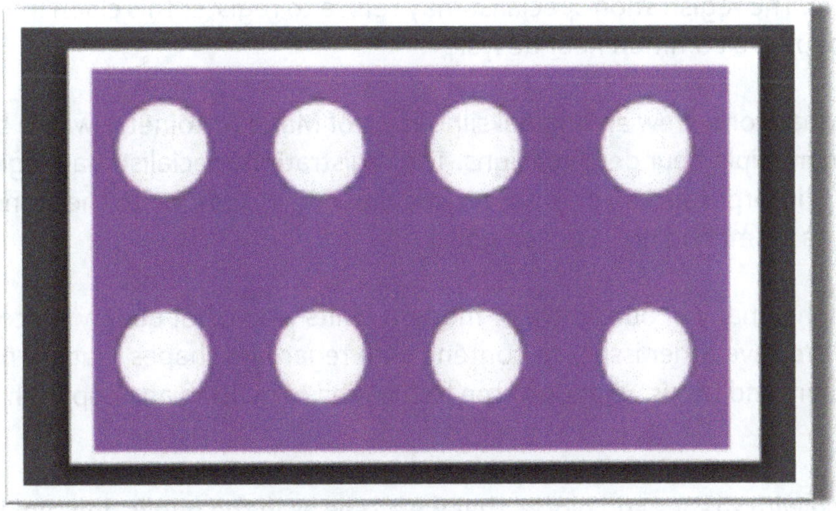

From the Compendium

Circles are not the only shape being denied protection, as the Copyright Office explains: "Geoffrey George creates a drawing depicting a standard pentagon with no additional design elements. The registration specialist will refuse to register the drawing because it consists only of a simple geometric shape." Familiar objects, like a fleur-de-lis, are also not protectable.

But an image with lots of shapes is protectable. The Compendium explains: "The registration specialist will register this claim because it combines multiple types of geometric shapes in a variety of sizes and colors, culminating in a creative design that goes beyond the mere display of a few geometric shapes in a preordained or obvious arrangement." Compendium, Section 906.1. What is considered "preordained or obvious?" No further suggestion is given. That's where copyright gets interesting. The following is the example given for protectable:

From the Compendium

For both shapes and familiar objects, once an author has used a familiar symbol in a "creative manner", it is then protectable. The question is what is a creative manner? Here are examples the Copyright Office provides:

> • Francis Ford created a sketch of the standard fleur de lys design used by the French monarchy. The registration specialist may refuse to register this claim if the work merely depicts a common fleur de lys.
>
> • Samantha Stone drew an original silhouette of Marie Antoinette with a backdrop featuring multiple fleur de lys designs. The registration specialist may register this work because it incorporates an original, artistic drawing in addition to the standard fleur de lys designs. Compendium, Section 906.2.

This also means that many of our simple or modern quilts would not qualify for copyrightable subject matter. We have other issues to contend with regarding shapes that are not mentioned in the Compendium and this is what drew me to the idea of quilting and copyright in the first place.

Our world is filled with shapes and blocks that we all see as in the public domain. How does that occur, and why? We'll discuss it soon. But for now, basic shapes are not protectable, but selection, arrangement, and coordination of a bunch of shapes are.

Quilting is made up of common shapes. The question is when do those shapes become protectable. Here is an example from the Compendium that could easily be a quilt:

> Grover Gold creates a painting of a beach scene that includes circles of varying sizes representing bubbles, striated lines representing ocean currents, as well as triangles and curved lines representing birds and shark fins. The registration specialist will register the claim despite the presence of the common geometric shapes.

When I read this, it made me think of Juli Seydell Johnson's amazing quilt based on a photograph of her family. She used Michael Miller fabrics (because I had received some as a brand ambassador,) and make this amazing work.

Juli Seydell Johnson's use of Michael Miller fabric 2019

So, where is that boundary between non-protectable shapes and protectable selection, arrangement, and coordination? The following four quilts were made by Misty-Anne Marold.

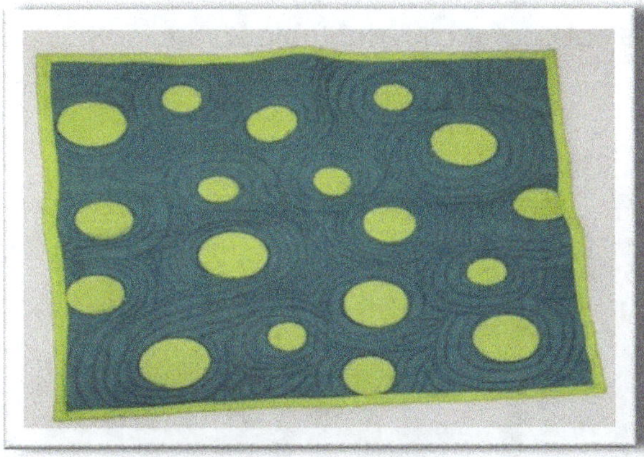

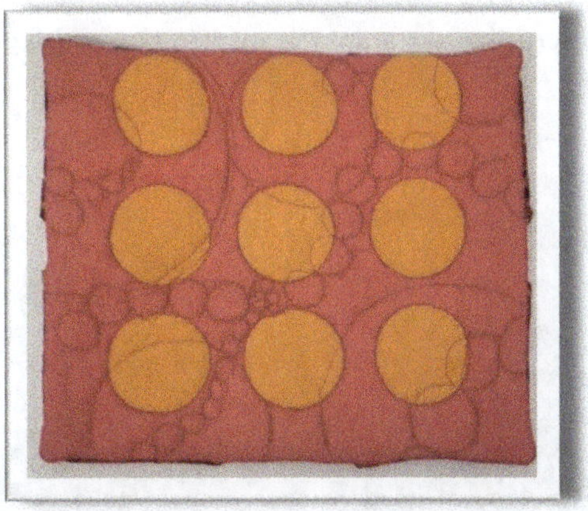

Would they qualify without the quilting? Likely not. But they are minimalist art. Do you think there is enough creativity to qualify for copyright protection? We're going to put in an application for registration with the U.S. Copyright Office and find out.

This last one was created by Ann Wasserman. Again, enough creativity? I think likely, yes. How do you feel about this? Where *should* the line be between protectable and not-protectable.

When is Changing the Color Enough

Mere Change in Color

Quilters don't fare well with this one either: "Merely adding or changing one or relatively few colors in a work, or combining expected or familiar pairs or sets of colors is not copyrightable, regardless of whether the changes are made by hand, computer, or some other process." The Compendium uses a particularly poignant example that makes me think of my alterations of a pattern. "For example, the Office will not register a visual art work if the author merely added relatively few colors to a preexisting design or simply created multiple colorized versions of the same basic design." So, changing the background on a Tula Pink pattern from black and white to just black does not create a new copyright.

It may be safe to say that following the pattern and altering the colors does not create a derivative copyright in the new work. It is more like a coloring book, where mere alterations in color are not sufficient to create a derivative copyright. Can you think of examples where you made the quilt pattern but altered the color, changed the colorization? In many ways, the Gypsy Wife quilts are this. Changing the colors does not confer copyrightable status.

By Judy Krupala Holik

By Karen Jong Brewin

By Susan Vincent Eubanks

Can you see why mere change would not produce a new copyrightable work?

Creative Authorship + Colorization = copyrightable subject matter

If you combine creative authorship with colorization, the Copyright Office recognizes that this is copyrightable. Here are the three examples they give:

> Cleo Camp took a photograph of a tree and digitally edited the image to add new shades of red and blue. Cleo submitted an application to register the altered photograph and described her authorship as "original photograph digitally edited to add new shades of blue and red in certain places." The registration specialist will register the claim because the creativity in the photograph, together with the alteration of the colors, is sufficiently creative.
>
> Charles Carter took a digital image of Leonardo da Vinci's Mona Lisa and added different hair color, colored nail polish, stylized clothing, and darkened skin. Charles submitted an application to register the image, and described his authorship as "changed public domain, Mona Lisa, to green and pink-streaked hair; purple nail polish; prisoner-striped black-white clothing; and darkened rouge on cheeks." The registration specialist will register the work because the changes in color are sufficient to constitute a new work of authorship.
>
> Clara Connor found a black and white photograph that is in the public domain. She altered the image by adding a variety of colors, shades, and tones to make it appear as if the photo was taken in a different season. Clara submitted an application to register the revised photograph and in the Author Created and New Material Included fields she described her authorship as "adapted public domain black-white image by adding different colors, shades, tones, in various places of derivative work." The registration specialist may register the work if Clara made sufficient changes to the preexisting photograph. Compendium, Section 906.3

This makes me think of Lyric's work with New York Public Library's photograph collection. We will return to photographs in fair use, but for now we should recognize that adding things to photographs – aside from whether they are under copyright or in the public domain, creates a copyrightable work, separate from the underlying work. When you take a photograph and then alter it with all kinds of elements, that is likely protectable. The question we will answer later is whether you need permission to do that to the photograph, if the photograph is under copyright, and a second question, how do you tell when a photograph is in the public domain. Obviously, if you take the photograph yourself, you are presumed to be the author, and you can do with it what you want. The only issue would be if you took that while an employee, or if you have a contract (think wedding photographer) that limits what you can do with that photograph.

Here is Carla Triemer's applique work based on a photograph: "This is probably my most famous quilt. This is called "Card Shark." it was made for a guild challenge. It's from a photo of the grandson of one of the Quilts Beyond Borders regional coordinators. He was doing the drawing of the winner of our Fat Quarter Challenge. In the original photo Jonah is holding the name of the winner. But the guild challenge was "Playing with a Full Deck" and I'd drawn the 5 of diamonds, which doesn't lend itself to a lot of inventive imagery, like the King or Queen of Heats would. So, I asked permission of the photographer, Jonah's mom, Karisa Harriman if I could use the photo, and she agreed to let me do it. The quilt has won a few ribbons, and has been Pinterested by a lot of people. He's raw edge applique. The technique is that I build him by starting at the furthest back element (in this case the eyes), and build out from there. All the sewing is done from the back, and excess fabric is cutaway. Not really "reverse applique", more "foundation applique."

Carla Triemer, "Card Shark."

So, altered photographs have sufficient creativity. Modifying an image of the Mona Lisa also has sufficient creativity. But, if someone follows the directions in a coloring book, the Copyright Office might refuse registration "if the changes were dictated by the coloring book and the addition of color was not sufficiently creative." So, if the pattern calls for pink, and you choose green, that might not be sufficiently creative to create a new copyright in your work. That makes sense.

Fabric and Color

The Compendium included an example about fabric!

> Colette Card registered a fabric design called "Baby Girl Fabric," which contains a pink background with stylized images of cribs, rattles, and pacifiers. Colette then created a fabric design called "Baby Boy Fabric" that is identical to the "Baby Girl Fabric" design, except that the background color is blue instead of pink. Colette attempts to register the "Baby Boy Fabric," disclaiming the prior registration for the "Baby Girl Fabric." The registration specialist will refuse to register the blue variation because it is identical to the preexisting "Baby Girl Fabric" design aside from the mere change in background color.

Changing color is not enough creativity -- it just doesn't meet the modicum of creativity standard, according to the Copyright Office.

Some Fabrics: When is Fabric Not Copyrightable

We use a lot of fabrics that are not copyrightable.

- Solids
- Basic polka dots
- Gingham
- Chevrons
- Stripes
- Houndstooth
- Plaids

You can probably think of others. The Copyright Office also will not register textures. Here is a recent refusal for fabric.

The Copyright Office described the work as "a two-dimensional graphic pattern consisting of white, dark blue, medium, blue, and light blue rectangles arranged in a check pattern." The application was filed by Hastens Sanger, and a copyright registration was refused. The company appealed the decision twice. "The Work falls squarely into the Copyright Office's regulations barring registration of a simple combination of basic geometric shapes and mere variations of coloration. The Work essentially is a common check pattern, composed of simple squares and often used in a number of designs. The different blue and white colors do not raise the Work into copyrightability; they are de minimis and the minimum required to evoke the check pattern." The Copyright Office included a link to a Wayfair site where there was a listing of many version of this, and was described as "buffalo plaid." "Here, the Work consists of standard shapes colored in a few shades of blue, culminating in an obvious buffalo check or plaid arrangement." https://www.copyright.gov/rulings-filings/review-board/docs/hastens-sangar-fabric-pattern.pdf

Mere Copies

Mere copies are not protectable as new things. We are not surprised. The question is how much additional creative authorship is necessary to create a new copyright based on the "mere copy," or otherwise known as a derivative work. It's when the copy is indistinguishable from the new work. Exact copies of works do not gain additional protection. Examples from the Compendium:

- An exact reproduction of the Mona Lisa that cannot be distinguished from the original.
- A photocopy or scan of a photograph.
- Photocopying, scanning, or digitizing a literary work.
- A toy model that is an exact replica of an automobile, airplane, train, or other useful articles where no creative expression has been added to the existing design. Compendium, 313.4(A).

Restoring a Quilt

Restoring a work does not give it extra protection. To gain new protection, it would have to have enough creativity to qualify as a derivative work. Ann Wasserman, for example, repairs antique quilts. By putting new fabric into old quilts, the copyright is not revived. (Of course, Ann's book about repairing quilts is protectable by copyright.)

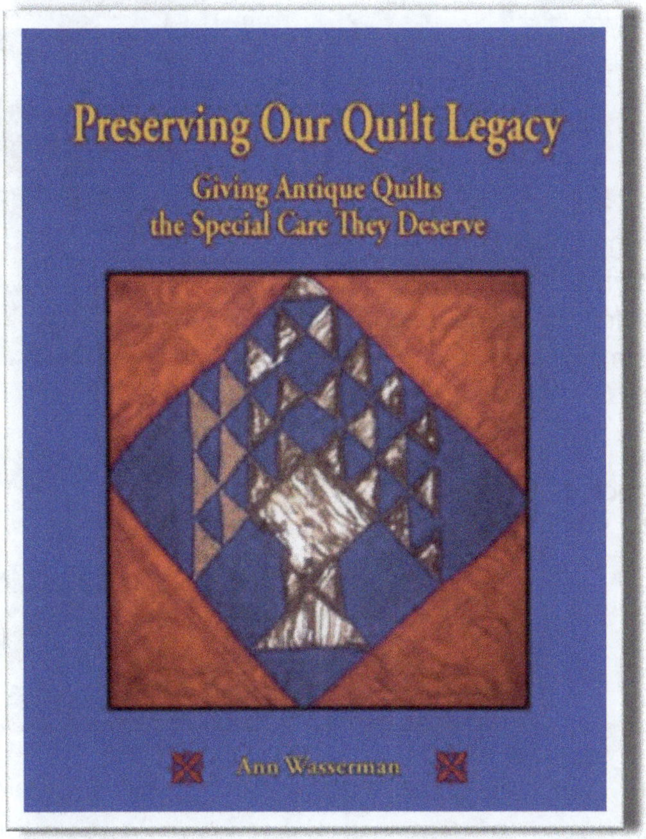

Layout or Format

"As a general rule, the Office will not accept a claim to copyright 'format' or 'layout.' The general arrangement of the specific content that is selected and arranged in a sufficiently creative manner. The claim, however, would be limited to the selection and arrangement of that specific content, not to the selection and arrangement of *any* content in that particular manner." Circular 33, U.S. Copyright Office.

2019 *Threadology* Quilt Along @ Fat Quarter Shop

So, what layouts can you think of that would *not* be protectable? Sashing and on point, of course. We all use those. What about Fat Quarter shop's use of a Spool with common blocks? The specific version would be protected, but the idea of the spool as a holder of common blocks is not a property right to be locked up.

Compare this to Sandra Hoving Engstrand's county fair award-winning quilt: *Sew Many Stitches (Right).* No one would think that the *Threadology* quilt and the *Sew Many Stitches* were substantially similar.

What about Kim Lapacek's recent Mystery block challenge that turned out to be spools?[6]

[6] https://kimlapacek.com/2020/01/clue-1-of-the-2nd-annual-project-quilting-mystery-quilt-along-3-2-2-2.html

And here's the Stealth Sewing Squad's version of the spool. The blocks were made by our Stealths. I put them into the spool. Ours could be seen as similar to Fat Quarter Shop. But the blocks are all the same size, and we added 1 inch sashing between rows. So, we will discuss infringement later. But you can see what the question is the boundary between their work and ours.

A Spool Quilt by the Quilting Army, assembled by Joel Sellers and Elizabeth Townsend Gard

Typeface and Fonts

I get this question a lot. Can I use any typeface for my commercial patterns? Are typeface or fonts protected by copyright? The Compendium says: "As a general rule, typeface, type font, lettering, calligraphy, and typographic ornamentation are not registrable." They see them as "building blocks of expression," and therefore are more like facts. Here is an example from the Compendium:

> Felicia Frost creates a font called "Pioneer Living" that evokes historical "Wanted: Dead or Alive" posters. The registration specialist will refuse to register this font because it is a building block of writing. This is true regardless of how novel and creative the shape and form of the typeface characters may be. Compendium, Section 906.4.

So, this is super interesting. Google puts out fonts that they say you can use without restrictions. Other companies claim copyright on fonts. Note, however, that this is U.S. Law; in the United Kingdom and elsewhere fonts are protectable under copyright.

But wait! Happily, for us, the Compendium has a fabric example again!

> Calliope Cash creates a textile fabric consisting of a vertically striped grass cloth and a traditional Chinese proverb. Each character is painted on a separate stripe in standard, unembellished calligraphy. The registration specialist will refuse to register this fabric design because the calligraphy consists of standard Chinese characters, and the simple arrangement of characters on vertical stripes and the choice of grass cloth does not add sufficient creativity to warrant registration. Compendium III, Section 906.4.

Wow! That seems like there was a lot of selection, arrangement, and coordination. If the Copyright Office doesn't believe there is sufficient creativity for this, what does count? This is making me rethink the protectability of fabric.

So, here's some good news for those that want copyrightable fonts. If you put bunnies or flowers into the alphabet, you are golden. And if you add extra "flourishes, swirls, vector ornaments, scrollwork, borders and frames, wreaths, and the like represent works of pictorial authorship in either their individual designs or patterned repetitions, they may be protected by copyright." Compendium III, Section 906.4. When does the extra in a font become protectable that's one question. Bad news again (for those seeking copyright protection). Texture effects in fonts (e.g. weathered-and-worn or chalk). Not protectable. You can see why. We don't want the weather-and-worn or chalk alphabet locked up with a property right. And interestingly, typeface or fonts in a computer program are protected at the source code level, but not to keep people from using the fonts themselves. Super interesting.

Jo Westfoot, the Crafty Nomad created this quilt, "Cut, Stitch, Baste, Quilt, Bind, Repeat". In the U.S. the fonts are likely not protected, but in her home country in the United Kingdom, they may be protected.

And Sandra Hoving Engstrand's quilt that she created for our first booth at Quilt Festival in 2018 (and we also used in our second book at Quilt Market in 2019), along with *Welcome to the Clubhouse* sign, made by myself and Alice Boudreaux. (You can also see other quilts made by the Stealth Sewing Squad, including Misty's dot quilts, common blocks, our books, and you will learn later, the Copyright Map quilt. And that's Gigi Baay with me at the table.)

Our booth at Houston Quilt Market 2019

Finally, we turn to Jessica Hische, a popular "lettering artist" and a children's book author (incorporating her lettering). How would her work be copyrightable/not copyrightable? Her skill is amazing. But much of her work is not copyrightable. Her books would be. Her letters with critters and flowers are. But her basic, beautiful designs are not. So why does Eventbrite and Mailchimp hire her? Not for the copyrightability of her work, but for her talent and skill. Her brand is elegance. And because many are using her services for logos, they can be protected by trademark, which does not require the same things that copyright does. http://jessicahische.is/. And this does not mean you can take her work. Other laws, including passing off, may protect her when copyright does not. And it also doesn't mean she can't sell her fonts. She provides access and convenience of the software file, and knowing that they have the goodwill and her reputation behind them.

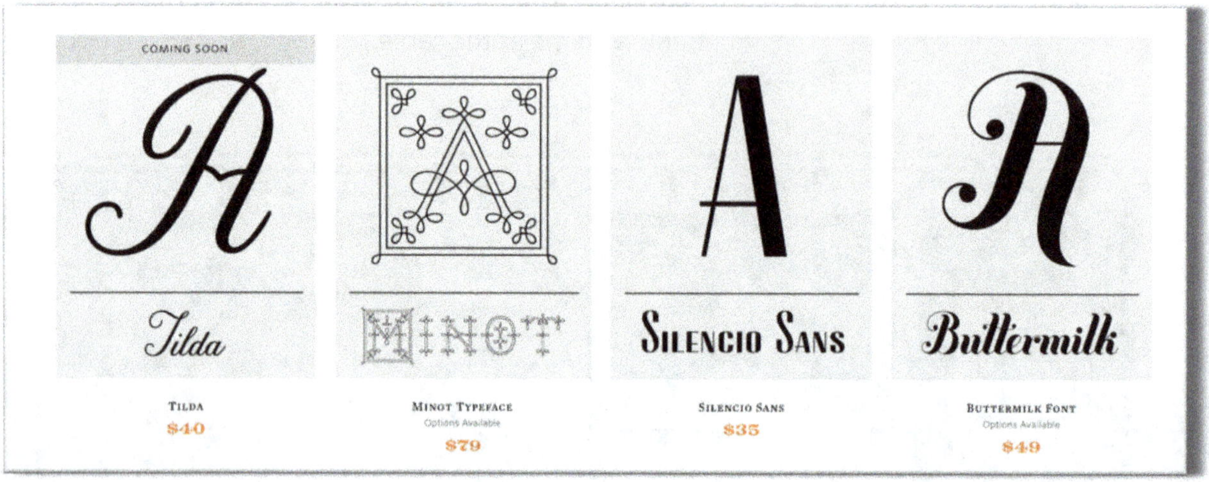

She has registered her children's books with the U.S. Copyright Office, but we did not find registrations for any fonts.

#	Name (NALL) <	Full Title	Copyright Number	Date
[1]	Hische, Jessica	Awakening and Other Stories.	TX0008755352	2019
[2]	Hische, Jessica	Drop Caps: 100 Postcards.	VA0002006213	2015
[3]	Hische, Jessica	Heart of Darkness and Other Stories (Barnes & Noble Collectible Editions)	TX0008762091	2019
[4]	Hische, Jessica	In Progress : See Inside a Lettering Artist's Sketchbook and Process, from Pencil to Vector.	TX0008201854	2015
[5]	Hische, Jessica	Made Especially For You: Labels for the Kitchen.	VA0001686935	2008
[6]	Hische, Jessica	Persuasion (Barnes & Noble Collectible Editions)	TX0008755040	2019
[7]	Hische, Jessica	Sense and Sensibility (Barnes & Noble Collectible Editions)	TX0008755042	2019
[8]	Hische, Jessica	Tale of Two Cities.	TX0008703133	2018
[9]	Hische, Jessica	TOMORROW I'LL BE BRAVE.	TX0008683486	2018

Letters, Words, Titles and Short Phrases

...are not copyrightable. If you are using the words or short phrases in commerce to identify a company, product or service, that's trademark. If you have a logo, that's logos. Logos suffer from the problem that lettering, short words, basic shapes and all the other things we've been discussing are not protectable.
What does this include?

- Title of a book or name of a company
- Domain name or URL
- Name of a character
- A catchphrase
- Mottos, slogans, or other short expressions

So, when you see adorable phrases out there, and you want to use them, you can. My favorite: "A day without quilting is like a day...just kidding. I have no idea what a day without quilting is like." Now, if someone has created an image using this short expression that may be protectable. I would have to make my own. Where did this come from? Is this like a meme that has a life beyond the creator? Is it protectable? Is there enough selection, arrangement, and coordination to be protectable? And of course, was it registered?

Ingredients or Contents

A list of ingredients or contents is not protectable. An explanation in a cookbook, crafts book, or manual can be copyrightable in the selection, arrangement, and coordination, as well as the text, photos and drawings. But the functional ingredients or directions themselves are not protectable. See why? So, how does this translate to quilting?

The image of a quilt is protectable. The directions -- the techniques to make it -- are not. The weird thing, though, which is different from cookies, is that when you follow the directions, you make a protectable work of art. I think, in some ways, the idea that the directions are functional and not protectable is outdated because the directions *are* in some ways the code. But one could argue that you can get to the artwork using different techniques or directions, and therefore, they are separable -- like we saw with useful articles. For now, the traditional view is that the directions are not protected. However, the expression of the directions ARE! I cannot copy the directions to a pattern and post it online. The expression is protected.

Stock Characters

Characters

Sometimes people want to copyright not just a novel, but want to copyright the character beyond the one story. Are characters in fabric, for instance, copyrightable? The Compendium explains: "The original, visual aspects of a character may be protected by copyright if they are sufficiently original. This may include the physical attributes of the character, such as facial features and specific body shape, as well as images of clothing and any other visual elements." Compendium III, Section 911.

Sufficiently original

Like everything in copyright, the character has to be sufficiently original and meet the copyrightable subject matter requirements.

Depiction in 2D and 3D artwork

When registering a character, you should refer to the type of art, and not the character: "2D artwork," rather than "character." Compendium III, Section 911.

Note, for visual arts, you must include the fixed characteristics in the registration; unfixed characteristics are not protected. The name is not covered either. (That would-be trademark, if it applies at all). But you can register the artwork, not the "character," which is interesting. Example in Compendium:

> Charles Crest creates a sketch of a field mouse with a straw hat and a mischievous grin. He intends to use the sketch in an animated film. He files an application that asserts a claim in "two-dimensional artwork" and "character." The registration specialist may ask Charles to limit the claim to the artwork and to remove the term "character" from the application.
>
> Chris Crow creates a series of drawings featuring a stylized flamingo in several poses and wearing different hats. He files an application to register his drawings under the title "Concept Drawings for Character Designs" and he asserts a claim in "two-dimensional artwork." The registration specialist may register the claim and may send the applicant a warning letter noting that the registration covers only the specific sketches included in the deposit.

This gets reiterated in the comic/cartoon section: "A registration for a cartoon, comic strip, or comic book only covers the specific work that is submitted to the U.S. Copyright Office. The Office does not offer so-called "blanket registrations" that cover prior or subsequent iterations of the same work. For example, a registration for a comic strip that depicts a particular character covers the expression set forth in that particular strip, but it does not cover the character per se or any other strip or other work that features the same character."

There is case law that also addresses characters. If protecting a character is something you are considering, it would be a good idea to consult an attorney that specializes in copyright.

What about Free Motion Quilting Designs?

Let's take the conversation one step further. What about free motion quilting designs? How are they more or less like fonts? In an interview with famous quilter Leah Day, she believes that the designs she creates are common motifs. She claims copyright only on her books, videos and other expressions.

Lori Kennedy also grants permission for her motifs explicitly, but not the expression—the books, the instructions, the videos, etc. So, either they are in the public domain, or she is granting you a non-exclusive right to use the motifs. But Lori Kennedy's designs look more like the bunny and less like a font. Here is an example of her lovely work:

This seems to me more than something general, that this is under copyright. But she gives us the right to use it in our work. And here is another of her designs:

While to an untrained eye, this may seem copyrightable, to many in the quilting world, we would recognize this as a common motif. But would the Copyright Office? How much do community standards play in identifying standard motifs, stock characters, and scènes à faire, our next topic. Lori Kennedy is conscious of copyright, and includes information on her website: https://lorikennedyquilts.com/about-lori-kennedy-quilts/about-lori/# . She includes specific, clear instructions regarding when copyright applies to her work.

Frequently Asked Questions

May I use the motif on my quilts?

YES—please do!

May I use the motifs on quilts I make for others?

YES–have fun adding personal touches!

May I use the motifs on quilts I sell or on quilting I do for payment?

YES–be my guest!! You do not need my permission to use any motif at any time.

May I copy the photos and step-by-step tutorials offered free here for my quilt guild?

Well, no....

The photos and the step-by-steps instructions are protected. Copying them in any form and sharing them without attribution (direct link) would be stealing. Contact me if you would like to use a photo or two–Lori@LoriKennedyQuilts.com.

In many ways, she is going beyond what copyright requires. Many of her designs likely are under copyright, but she is giving a non-exclusive license to use her work. She just doesn't want you to take her expression of those -- the images, the book and the videos.

Stock Characters and Scènes à Faire

Stock characters are not protectable. Think of Sunbonnet Sue. She's stock. Others in quilting? What makes something unprotectable? "The copyright law does not protect stock characters, settings, or events that are common to a particular subject matter or medium because they are commonplace and lack originality." Common settings and plots are called scènes à faire, which translates to "scene to be made" or "scene that must be done. What this means in copyright law are scenes in a play, novel, film, historical account, comic, or other narrative that almost obligatory for a genre of its type. The examples given in the Compendium make one think:

- the copyright for a work about the Hindenburg would not cover elements that are "indispensable, or at least standard, in the treatment of" that topic, such as scenes that take place in a German beer hall or characters who utter common greetings of the period. (citing Hoehling, 618 F.2d at 979.)

- The copyright for a work about a police station in an urban slum would not cover elements that necessarily result from the choice of that setting, such as scenes depicting drunks, prostitutes, vermin, and derelict cars, or stock themes commonly linked to the genre of police fiction, such as foot chases or the "familiar figure of the Irish cop." (citing Walker v. Time Life Films, 784 F.2d 44, 50 (2d Cir. 1986)

- "the fact "[t]hat treasure might be hidden in a cave inhabited by snakes, that fire might be used to repel the snake, that birds might frighten an intruder in the jungle, and that a weary traveler might seek solace in a tavern ... [are] simply too general to be protectable." Zambito v. Paramount Pictures Corp, 613 F. Supp. 1107, 1112 (EDNY 1985).

So, what are our Scènes à Faire in quilting, if the concept translates past narratives? Can you identify patterns, fabric, or other elements that are so common that they would not be protectable?

Let's look at an example. In 2009, the company Vollet designed the multi-layered ceramic snowman ornament consisting of a snowman's head wearing a black, stovepipe hat with a green stripe and a raised adornment on the right side of the hat's brim; the face has a curved, carrot-like nose and is painted in a cartoonish fashion with an exaggerated smile drawn from a single black line. This ornament was granted Certificate of Registration # VA 1-785-997 with effective date of registration of August 11, 2011." MUD PIE, LLC v. Clay Chick Ceramics, LLC, No. 1:12-CV-3242-CAP, 2014 WL 11820249, at *1 (N.D. Ga. Jan. 9, 2014).

Mud Pie designed a black-and-white ceramic collection of a Santa, reindeer, and snowman. Clay Chick (Vollet) sent a cease and desist letter to Mud Pie. Here, Mud Pie argued that Clay Chick had "thin" copyright at best. The court responded, "The Eleventh Circuit has recognized that "noncopyrightable material includes 'scènes à faire'—stock scenes that naturally flow from a common theme." MUD PIE, LLC v. Clay Chick Ceramics, LLC, No. 1:12-CV-3242-CAP, 2014 WL 11820249, at *3 (N.D. Ga. Jan. 9, 2014). Mud Pie contended that the Santa Claus, Snowman, and Reindeer were stock elements of a Christmas theme. The court found that you can take stock elements and add creativity to create a copyrightable work.

The Case of Sunbonnet Sue

In 1902, "Sunbonnet Babies" was published, written by Eulalie Osgood Grover and illustrated by Bertha L. Corbett, called "The Mother of the Sunbonnet Babies." The work was based on British artist Kate Greenway's children's illustrations. Now, works before 1924 are in the public domain. But it wasn't because Sunbonnet Sue's copyright had expired that it became a stock character. That happened long before the copyright expired. Between 1900 and 1930, Sunbonnet Sue quilts became a thing, as people created adaptations from adaptations, and newspapers and magazines spread the Sunbonnet Sue craze with their own versions. Over a million copies of the *Sunbonnet Babies Primer* were sold. A third artist, Bernhardt Wall, created bonneted children. The idea of bonneted children whose faces you couldn't see was widespread.

The key stock elements? Oversized hat turned to the side, with an A-line dress, and one arm and foot showing. She is usually engaged in an activity like cleaning, gardening, or baking.

What makes her a stock character? I think everyone treats her as such. Now you find adaptations of Zombie Sunbonnet Sue, Death Sunbonnet Sue, Sex Worker Sunbonnet Sue, and other parodies.

For instance, Urban Threads sells an embroidery pattern, Sinbonnet Sue - Zombie. There are so many Sunbonnet Sue zombies out there--it is its own sub-genre.

There again, the idea of a zombie Sue is not protected, but the expression is; the underlying Sue is not. And quilt historian Barbara Brackman in her blog, *Material Culture,* catalogs the Sunbonnet Sue Wrecks she finds, where the proportions or other elements are not quite right. http://barbarabrackman.blogspot.com/2010/12/sunbonnet-sue-wrecks.html

Thomas Knauer talked about his own version of Sunbonnet Sue. It is featured in his new book, *Why We Quilt: Contemporary Makers Speak Out about the Power of Art, Activism, Community, and Creativity* (Storey Publishing, 2019). One Child is Too Many, by Thomas Knauer. In his artist statement about the quilt he wrote: "Each year scores of children die in gun accidents (negligent homicides), whether as bystanders to a violent crime, by being in the wrong place when a gun accidentally fired, or through gaining access to an unsecured gun. This quilt is a protest against the pervasiveness of a gun culture that allows these deaths to occur and does nothing to prevent them."

And if you can't see the power of the public domain, and stock characters yet, look at all of the *published books* featuring Sunbonnet Sue.

Sunbonnet Sues Quilting Stencil

Can you think of other stock characters in quilting? What makes something a stock character, and transforms it from something protectable to something everyone can use?

Patterns, Stencils, How-to and Templates

What does the Compendium say about patterns, stencils, how-to and templates? It actually has a whole section about that: section 920.

Pattern books: The Compendium defines pattern books: "Pattern books contain specific instructions on how to make various items, such as knitwear and toys, while how-to books typically contain instructions on how to perform various techniques." Drawings, photographs, and text in a pattern book are copyrightable, as long as they have sufficient originality. "This may include textual instructions, technical diagrams that demonstrate cutting, stitching, weaving, or other techniques required by the pattern, as well as illustrations of the completed items."

But the registration does not extend to "individual pattern pieces that may be used to create a useful article, such as shapes that may be traced and used to make a sleeve for a dress, because they have an intrinsic utilitarian function." So, let's look at this. If you can trace it and it's a shape, it's not protected. If it is a sleeve, it's utilitarian. What parts are then protected? The text, photographs, and things that have enough creativity to be copyrightable, but not its usefulness. "Nor does the registration extend to any useful article that may be created with the pattern, such as an item of clothing." Functional aspects of bag patterns, clothing, and other useful articles *are not protected by copyright*.

A good example of this is the Mondo bag by Mattie Rhodes of Quiltsmart. She said in an interview that she put her kids through college with the sale of the Mondo bag. But it wasn't because of copyright. The bags, which are extremely popular, rely on a specially printed interfacing. While the pattern booklet is copyrightable, of course, it is the convenience of the interfacing and the ease of using her technique that made it so successful. Now what about each of our selection, arrangement, and coordination of fabric that goes into our own personal bag construction? Likely if we tried to register our version, the Copyright Office would say, no, that it would not be enough creativity to create a property right in that version. But that's just a best guess.

Celeste Poulin's sister made her this version of the Mondo bag. It's a thing.

Stencils

The Compendium defines stencils: "Stencils provide outlines and shapes that may be used for other purposes, such as a stencil of leaves that may be used for painting a border on a wall." This is fairly straightforward. If it is sufficiently creative they will register it, if it is common, they won't. The Stencil Company recognizes this, and only registers stencils that have creative artistic elements beyond basic stencils.

How-to books

"How-to books typically contain text, photographs, and technical diagrams, which may be protected by copyright law if they are sufficiently creative. However, the "project" or "craft" as a whole — even if it is original — is merely an idea that is not copyrightable. 17 U.S.C. § 102(b). The Office will reject nonspecific claims in project ideas or project design." Again, this makes sense within the copyright realm.

Most of us create "how-to books" with quilting books that include text, photographs, and technical diagrams. This is not automatic. The work must have to have sufficient originality to qualify for copyright. Magazine, patterns, and craft books would fall under "how-to books."

The Polka Dot Cases

We all want things to be both not protected (our common pool) and protected (our work). The courts have weighed in a number of times regarding polka dot cases, and so we have some insight which helps us with not only polka dots but the boundaries between protectable and not protectable. We also have a case about alphabet quilts, which we will discuss in a later chapter. The big question is: is what you are doing sufficiently original to be copyrightable? That's the question in the cases below.

Prince Group, Inc. d/b/a/ Princess Fabrics v. MTS Products and Kmart (967 F.Supp.121 SDNY 1997). The Prince Group created Mega Dot, a fabric design that they also registered with the U.S. Copyright Office. (We haven't been able to find an image of Mega Dot). MTS created similar patterns in their products. Because Prince registered the work, the burden to prove that it was unoriginal fell to the defendant, another good reason to register your work. The court begins, "The test for originality of copyright is minimal. Plaintiff must prove that its work is the result of independent creation, that is not the result of copying another's work, and it must also meet a minimum level of creativity. Feist, 488 U.S. at 245." Prince Group, Inc. v. MTS PRODUCTS, 967 F. Supp. 121, 125 (S.D.N.Y. 1997). The question was whether the particular Mega Dot design met the originality requirement.

The court found that the design was more than merely the standard polka dot: "The polka dots in this case are more than average circles. First, they are irregularly shaped, and not the perfect circles of a standard polka dot. They are "shaded," that is, there is a crescent of white around half of the perimeter of each of the dots, which is different from the standard uniformly, colored polka dot, and they consist of several different colors. Thus, the shape and the shading of the dots are sufficiently original to meet the threshold of creativity." Id. But the court goes on to say that even if one found that these polka dots were not protected, the compilation of the polka dot was (the selection, arrangement and coordination): "Here, the decision to place the polka dots in imperfect and conflicting diagonal lines at varying distances from each other giving the appearance of randomness, distinguishes this arrangement from the regularity of the generic creativity for copyright validity. Having met the tests of independent creation and creativity, the Court finds that the Plaintiff's Mega Dot design is valid." Id. The court also noted that the polka dots didn't have to be exact to be infringing. In fact, they merely had to be strikingly similar, including having the same aesthetic appeal.

Royal Printex v. Unicolors is another polka dot case, this time also with a daisy flower. The polka dots made up the background of the fabric. The pattern was registered with the U.S. Copyright Office. This one is a bit more complicated. It turned out that the daisy design was from a "forties fabric," 1949, which had stripes rather than polka dots. The court found that substituting polka dots for stripes did not constitute enough creativity and therefore a competitor could also create the same daisy/polka dot design. If something does not have copyright, then others can copy it. 2009 WL 2712055 (2009).

And here's another polka dot case, this time with boots.

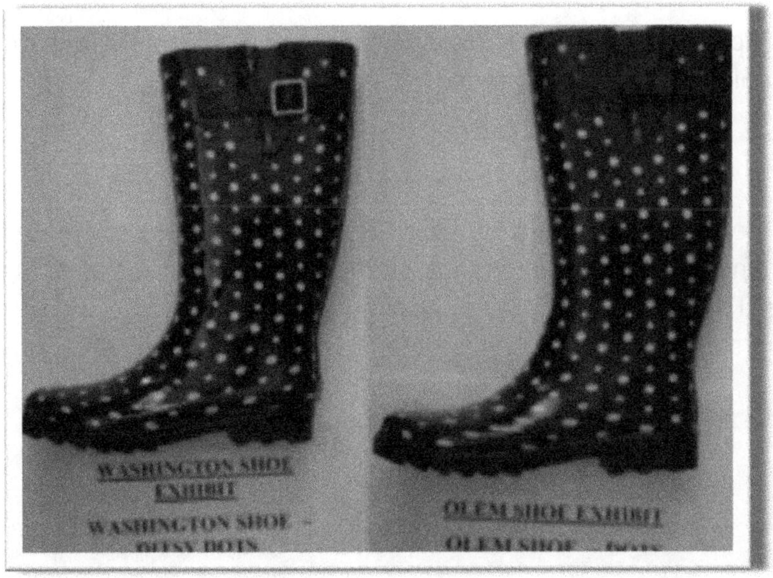

The two shoes above look very similar, don't you think? The question is whether the original one is protected by copyright. Are the dots sufficiently creative to gain copyright protection? Washington Shoe made the original Ditsy Dots design; Olem had copied. Olem argued that the design was merely a polka dot that was a "a generic, commonplace, public domain design".[7] The court decision is interesting. First, the stretchy part is seen as not protectable -- the irregular polka-dot from stretch is because of the utilitarian aspects of fitting the boot shape. "On the other hand, the particular arrangement of different sized dots at varying distances along vertical and horizontal planes, like the arrangement in *Prince Group*, is an artistic decision that distinguishes Ditsy Dots from generic polka dots—it is not merely a uniform change in dimension, size or proximity from some specifically identifiable polka-dot pattern that separately exists." 2011 WL 6202282 (S.D.Fla.), 11. Modicum of creativity.

Finally, we look at MPD Accessories v. Urban Outfitters, No. 12 Civ. 6501(LTS)(KNF), May 30, 2014 to also help us understand copyright, this time with stripes. Corrine Kamp was hired by MPD to create a design: "brightly colored block stripes, variegated color combinations and bold and small stripes, interlinking horizontal and vertical stripes and parallel and perpendicular striping" (the "Stripe Design"), from which MPD produced a scarf." *MPD Accessories B.V. v. Urban Outfitters*, No. 12 CIV. 6501 LTS KNF, 2014 WL 2440683, at *1 (S.D.N.Y. May 30, 2014). Corrine transferred her rights to MPD. The factory where the scarves were made sold strikingly similar patterns to another company, which in turn sold them to Urban Outfitters. One of the questions was whether the stripe had met the originality requirement. The court explained, "There is no genuine dispute that the color, size, arrangement and repetition of the shapes were all the aesthetic choices of the Plaintiff. Their unique combination can be protected as a whole. Accordingly, the Court concludes that both of MPD's designs are sufficiently original to merit copyright protection." *MPD Accessories B.V.*

---

[7] *Olem Shoe Corp. v. Washington Shoe Co.*, No. 09-23494-CIV, 2011 WL 6202282, at *9 (S.D. Fla. Dec. 1, 2011), aff'd sub nom. *Olem Shoe Corp. v. Washington Shoe Corp.*, 591 F. App'x 873 (11th Cir. 2015)

v. Urban Outfitters, No. 12 CIV. 6501 LTS KNF, 2014 WL 2440683, at *6 (S.D.N.Y. May 30, 2014).

These four cases help us to understand how courts are approaching the question of protectable versus not. It's complicated, and it depends.

Summary

Unprotectable elements are important for everyone. We need these to create new works. We build upon many things. This also means that when we build, we don't always create copyrighted works. They have to meet the copyrightability standards. And then, we have to assess when one person's work using unprotectable elements may infringe on another's. That's for a later chapter.

8: Old Things in the Public Domain

This is Going to Get Detailed. Sorry in Advance.

There is one more aspect that is not protected by copyright, and free for everyone to use: those things whose copyright has expired. Copyright doesn't last forever. The U.S. Constitution requires copyright last for "limited times." The length of copyright has changed over time. (And this can get complicated). We're diving in. We're looking at two aspects of old things in the public domain: the dates and how to figure out when a work is in the public domain; and the common blocks we all agree to treat as if they are in the public domain.

Robert Kaufman reproduced a number of Gustav Klimt paintings, including the famous "The Kiss" painting. Klimt's work was in the public domain. They took it, added a little bit here and there, and produced a fabric line. The fact that they reproduced it doesn't take it out of the public domain.

I purchased this panel, and decided to keep it simple. I used gold thread from Superior Thread (they sent a sample), and outlined the painting. In this chapter, we will learn why Klimt is in the public domain!

What is the public domain?

Copyright does not last forever. The U.S. Constitution dictates that right lasts for "limited Times." I.8.8. When a work is out of copyright, you can use it freely. So, the question is when is a work out of copyright? Anything published on or after March 1, 1989, is under copyright (as long as it meets the copyrightability requirements). So, we're looking at whether works before March 1,1989, are protected or in the public domain, and that depends on a number of factors. We have buckets of dates to determine the copyright status.

My specialty for most of my academic career was determining copyright duration. I wrote a great deal about duration, built a software system, started a company to help people, and was even cited by the U.S. Supreme court for the work. I spent a decade looking at the copyright laws of each country in the world. This is just a small bit of the work on that project, called the Durationator.[8] Some basics to get you started.

A note about status. The copyright term is based on the jurisdiction of *use.* The book, *Gone with the Wind*, published in 1936. The term is different in different countries. In the U.S., the term is 95 years from publication, or through 2031. In Canada, the term is life of the author plus 50 years, or 1949+50, or through 1999. The term in the United Kingdom is life of the author plus 70 years, or through 2019. So, as of 2020, Gone *with the Wind* is in the public domain in both Canada and the UK, but not the United States. (The movie is protected by a different term).

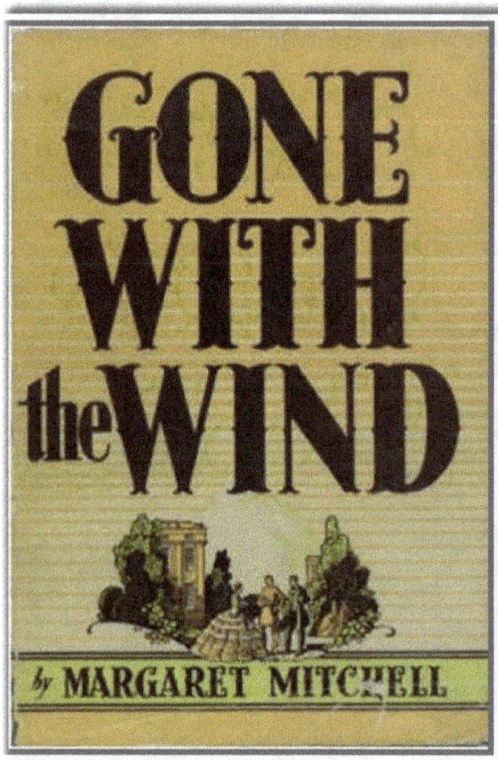

[8] For more information, see www.durationator.com.

Determining the Public Domain

Determining whether something is in the public domain is based on a number of elements: 1) whether it is published or unpublished; 2) where it was published and/or the death of the author (depending on a few factors), and 3) when it was published.

Domestic versus foreign work: The U.S. measures domestic works differently from foreign works. We will first look at domestic works, and then we will discuss foreign works.

Before 1925 (as of 2020): In the public domain

Any work published before 1925 is in the public domain. You can use it without asking permission. A lot of people know that. This date changes every year. So, as of 2020, in the United States, works published anywhere in the world are in the public domain for all works published 1924. The formula? For this period of time, the term of copyright is no longer than 95 years from publication.

Here's a chart for the next coming years.

Date of First Publication Anywhere	Enters the Public domain
1924	2020
1925	2021
1926	2022
1927	2023
1928	2024
1929	2025
1930	2026
1931	2027
1932	2028

One key element for this particular term: the work has to be published – which means anything that has been circulated without restriction. Things sold at a bookstore. A souvenir menu from a restaurant. A magazine. A flyer on the street. Anything that was sold, offered for sale, gifted, or given away without restrictions.

Domestic Works: (US works only in the US)

No Notice? For works first published between 1925 and 1989, proper notice was required in order to be under copyright. If the work was published in the U.S. before 1989 and there is no © notice, the work is also in the public domain.

Works first published between 1924-1949: These have to have been renewed in the 27th year from date of publication. To see if a work was renewed, you have to look at certain records that the U.S. Copyright Office does not still have in a searchable database. Our other company, the Durationator, built a tool. So, if you find yourself trying to figure out if something is out of copyright during these times, go to www.durationator.com. Also, they have to have proper notice. No notice, no copyright.

Works first published between 1959-1963: These have to be renewed in the 28th year starting on January 1. You can look to see if they were renewed at www.copyright.gov. Also, they have to have proper notice. No notice, no copyright.

Works first published 1964-1977: If there is proper notice, they are protected for 95 years from first publication.

Works first published 1978-1989: Needs proper notice, or in the public domain. It could have been fixed if there was no notice, but it had to be registered with the Copyright Office within five years. If notice, then under copyright for a long, long time.

Works published after Feb 1989: Under copyright. Yep. All of them. If they qualify for copyright, they are under copyright for a long, long, long time.

Foreign Works in the US

These are a little bit more complicated in some ways. The before 1924 date still applies. Anything published before 1924 (and the date moves every year) is in the public domain. The rest gets complicated. Really complicated. This is what I specialized in for my pre-tenure work, and what I got cited for by the U.S. Supreme Court in Golan v. Holder.
The U.S. treated foreign works fairly poorly until 1996. Yes, that late! In the first copyright act, 1790, only U.S. citizens and those domiciled in the U.S. were able to get copyright. This upset authors like Charles Dickens, whose works were not protected in the U.S., because he was British. Only in 1891 were foreign works allowed to obtain copyright, and then only if they had a treaty with the U.S. Some did, but they had to follow all of the formalities we've discussed above, which was difficult. As a result, most foreign works came into the public domain either because they did not have treaty relations, or because they did not follow formalities or renew the work.

The U.S.'s bad behavior caught up with us. We joined a few copyright treaties, and finally, we were forced to make it right. In January 1, 1996, millions of foreign works were restored automatically. And of course, the law is complicated. So, rule of thumb? Try not to use foreign works when you can. If you do, most are under copyright for 1925-present. Some may be out of copyright, but you have to check with a system like www.durationator.com.

Sandra's Quilt

Sandra Scheiber Johnson had an idea to take artist Robert Delaunay's "Rythme Sans Fin," or "Endless Rhythm" painting and reproduce it in a quilt. She began researching the copyright status of the work. She contacted the Legal Department at Tate Museum, where the work was located. She got a response: "As far as we are concerned, as owners of the object, you may proceed happily as planned, perhaps referencing (when possible) the underlying work is in Tate's collection. She had permission from the owners of the object. It is not clear that they also held the copyright (two separate things). But after Sandra contact me, we decided to do a Durationator analysis to determine the status *in the U.S.* Even though the painting is located in London, because Sandra would be making and displaying in the United States.

The 1934 painting was a foreign work. Robert Delaunay was a French artist, who co-founded the Orphism art movement. He died in 1941. The work is out of copyright throughout the world including Europe, Canada, and Australia. The question was whether it was out of copyright in the U.S. as well. We did a Section 104A analysis (which is a bit complicated and beyond the scope of this book). The work did not qualify for restoration. Therefore, the work is in the public domain in the United States. We provided a full Durationator report to Sandra.

Robert Delaunay, Endless Rhythm, 1934 (owned by the Tate Museum, https://www.tate.org.uk/art/artworks/delaunay-endless-rhythm-t01233)

And here is Sandra's version

Now, you may be asking, if a work is out of copyright, did she need to ask permission from the owner? Access to the object is different from copyright. It was a nice courtesy of her to reach out. But works in the public domain do not require permission. You may still need to ask permission for access, if that had been an issue. In this case, the image was on Tate's website. So, access was not an issue.

Unpublished Works

You thought we were done, right? Unpublished works, both created in the U.S. and abroad are governed by a different part of the copyright law, Section 303(a), another key topic I worked on a great deal for my promotion and tenure as a professor. This one is divided between unpublished works created before or after January 1, 1978.

Before January 1, 1978:

All unpublished works that were created before January 1, 1978, and not registered with the U.S. Copyright Office

The longer life + 70 and 2002.

If first published between 1978 and 2002, then the longer of life + 70 and December 31, 2047.

On or After January 1, 1978

Life + 70

One of my favorite examples concerns Eloise, the fictional girl who lived at the Plaza Hotel. The series was written by Kay Thompson (1909–1998). In the 1960s, she wrote *Eloise Takes a Bawth* with Hilary Knight and Mart Crowley.[9] The work was unpublished before January 1, 1978. The work was first published before December 31, 2002. So, the term? The longer of life of the author plus seventy years, and December 31, 2047.

Strangely, this book was not registered with the U.S. Copyright Office, and so we don't have official information on who is considered the author(s). But the copyright notice helps: © Estate of Kay Thompson. The Illustrations by Hilary Knight is also copyrighted by the Estate of Kay Thomson. Both list 2002 as the date--that important cut-off year. The text is likely protected for 70 + 1998, or 2068, and the illustrations for 70 years from the death of Hilary Knight (b. 1926, and 93 as of 2020). If the work had been published in 1964, the term would have been through 2059.

[9]The last page of the book reads, "To Whoever Finds this: Some say, 'Eloise Takes a Bawth' was lost at sea for forty years. Others swear it was locked up in a credenza in Venice and dried out only recently. Only Eloise knows the real story, and she's not talking. ...Even though 'Eloise Takes a Bawth' was cataloged by Harper & Row in 1964, the book was never published (artistic differences, for Lord's sake). In 2001, Miss Thompson's heirs decreed that 'Eloise Takes a Bawth' should be brought to an eager public. Ms. Knight set to work creating art from sketches he's drawn forty years ago. Mr. Crowley pieced together the many drafts of Miss Thompson's text. And Miss Thompson's niece and nephew supervised the whole, along with my colleagues at Simon & Schuster. Now Eloise's forty-year bawth is finally drawn. Soak away. -The Editor."

What about quilts? Interestingly, it's hard to know if a quilt is actually published. But we treat them like they are. Old quilts get reproduced as if they were.

What about fabric? Yes! The rules apply to fabric, too. The fact that fabric is sold means it's published. And that's how we get reproduction fabrics.

U.S. Federal Government Works

U.S. federal works are not protected by copyright. So, that's exciting. However, there is a glitch. You have to figure out what is considered a federal government work. This can get complicated. Not all work under the federal government count, because they are created by independent contractors. (Remember that stuff?) But many wonderful sites have public domain images and are free for you to use for inspiration or copying as part of your art.

State and local government works are not included; they may or may not be in the public domain. It's up to the state or local government to decide, except for cases and law. And slogans, symbols, and seals of the Federal government may be protected either by trademark law, or special laws. Two specific characters are protected: The character "Smokey Bear" is protected by 18 U.S.C. Section 711,[10] and "Woodsy Owl" character, name and slogan by 18 U.S.C. Section 711a.[11] For more, go to https://www.law.cornell.edu/uscode/text/18/part-I/chapter-33.

[10] "Whoever, except as authorized under rules and regulations issued by the Secretary of Agriculture after consultation with the Association of State Foresters and the Advertising Council, knowingly and for profit manufactures, reproduces, or uses the character "Smokey Bear", originated by the Forest Service, United States Department of Agriculture, in cooperation with the Association of State Foresters and the Advertising Council for use in public information concerning the prevention of forest fires, or any facsimile thereof, or the name "Smokey Bear" shall be fined under this title or imprisoned not more than six months, or both." https://www.law.cornell.edu/uscode/text/18/711

[11] "Whoever, except as authorized under rules and regulations issued by the Secretary, knowingly and for profit manufactures, reproduces, or uses the character "Woodsy Owl", the name "Woodsy Owl", or the associated slogan, "Give a Hoot, Don't Pollute" shall be fined under this title or imprisoned not more than six months, or both." https://www.law.cornell.edu/uscode/text/18/711a

Other Resources

There are so many resources out there with public domain images that you can include in your quilts, use for fabric design, and so much more. If you are looking for images, like Sandra Scheiber Johnson and Lyric Kinard, here are some collections to get you started. Check the copyright status information to make sure they are in the public domain.

- New York Public Library Digital Collections: https://digitalcollections.nypl.org
- Library of Congress Digital Collections: https://www.loc.gov/free-to-use/
- National Archives: https://www.archives.gov/research/alic/reference/photography
- The Met Collection: https://www.metmuseum.org/art/collection
- LACMA: https://collections.lacma.org/search/site?f%5B0%5D=bm_field_has_unrestricted_image%3Atrue
- A terrific resource on finding public domain images, maps, music, books, and other information can be found at Public Domain Sherpa. https://www.law.cornell.edu/uscode/text/18/part-I/chapter-33 (I have no affiliation with this group).

An example at LACMA https://collections.lacma.org/node/170573 litho by Paul Berthon, 1895.

A Word about Other Resources

Here are two additional resources, that while not in the public domain, can be useful, and many of the images are available under various licenses, often for free.

Creative Commons: This is a resource developed to allow you to find images and other things that tell you if you can use them in non-commercial or commercial settings, build a derivative work, or other things. We will talk more about that shortly. For more information, go to www.creativecommons.com.

Pixabay: This is a shout out to my (current) favorite site, which has works under copyright, but provides royalty-free use, even in the commercial setting, on some of their images. www.pixabay.com. There are other sites too, but I have found this site particularly lovely.

Current Term of Copyright

For those that are curious, here are the current terms for copyright in the United States for works created on or after January 1, 1978, and were published on or after March 1, 1989.

Individual: life of the author plus 70

Joint authors: life of the last surviving author plus 70 years

Work for hire/anonymous works: the shorter of 95 years from publication/120 from creation

And What about Klimt?

Let's return to Gustav Klimt. Here is a copy of the painting:

Klimt was born in Germany in 1862, and died in 1918. He painted the work sometime between 1907 and 1908, and it was exhibited in 1908. It was purchased while it was on exhibition. So, it is considered published before 1924, and is therefore in the public domain. Could it have been restored? No. The work was out of copyright in Germany as of 1988 (life plus seventy in Germany), and so was not eligible for restoration in the U.S., even if the publication date was later than 1923 (the cutoff date at the time)

Quick Quiz

1. You find a postcard at a garage sale that appears to be of New Orleans in 1920. You want to use it in a quilt. Can you?

A. Yes! It was published before 1925
B. No. That's someone's property.

Answer: A.

2. You find a pattern from 1990, and you want to reprint it. Is it out of copyright?

Answer: No. Everything after March 1, 1989 that was published is still protected by copyright.

3. You want to use a British book from the First World War, published in 1914, for your art. Can you?

Answer: Yes! Before 1925 again, even for foreign works.

4. I have a poster from 1950s France. Is it under copyright?

That is more complicated. Contact www.durationator.com for a Durationator Report.

So, that's a quick, intense introduction to copyright term, and how to determine whether a work is under copyright or in the public domain in the United States.

9: The Women Who Created the Quilting Public Domain

We Believe All Blocks are Unprotectable

There is one more aspect that is not protected by copyright, and therefore free for everyone to use: those things whose copyright has expired. Copyright doesn't last forever. The U.S. Constitution requires copyright last for "limited times." The length of copyright has changed over time, and can be complicated, as we learned from the last chapter. Date-based public domain is just half of the story. The other is a cultural public domain, where we all agree that elements are in the public domain, regardless of whether they are actually in the public domain or not. They may not qualify for copyright protection because they are merely a non-protectable element. Or we may all agree they are not protectable.

What drew me to the quilting and copyright project from the beginning was the rich pool of public domain common blocks. Here was a field (unlike poetry or film-making) where the entire community engaged in using a defined common pool of materials. They even had names for them. In 2018, we started our Common Pool Block challenge, where the Quilting Army self-identified common pool blocks, and made them in our colors. As I've already mentioned, we had over 100 sent in. It was awesome. My question was *why were these blocks in our common pool*? The answer was a mix: old blocks (published before 1924), too common (scène à faire), too basic (non-protectable), and my favorite, we all just think of them as free for all of us to use. This chapter explores this last category.

Finding the Public Domain in Quilts

> "Quilt-making is one of the most fascinating forms of needlecraft. It is occupying the attention of womankind everywhere, and every enthusiastic quilter who has one or more under construction is eagerly hunting for new patterns." Carrie Hall, 1933

We think of blocks in quilting as just always in the public domain. And it may be. But there were at least two key periods of codification. Naming blocks seems to have been important as part of quilt history -- that so many blocks--the same or nearly the same geometric shapes -- were named different things. We want and have a need to catalog, to organize blocks.

What is a block? How can we define one? It usually is of a particular size -- 6, 8, 12, 15, 18, or 36 inches square. It can be repeated in the quilt, or stand with others of different designs. Usually quilts have columns and rows of blocks. And each block contains geometric shapes. Tracing quilt block history has been a hobby for many since its beginnings. And it seems like everyone understands that this is a pool of "natural resources." No one has a lock on a Bear Paw or Log Cabin. These are common shapes and patterns shared amongst a quilting community.

A Little Bit of History

Early 20th Century Documentation

In 1915, Marie Webster wrote *Quilts: Their Story and How to Make Them*, which came out of her stories from *Ladies' Home Journal*. Others followed. Ruby McKim self-published her *101 Patchwork Patterns* in 1931. She was not the first to compile a book of well-known repeating blocks, but hers is one of the key sources, even today. She worked for the *Kansas City Star*, where she wrote a column that included patterns, and had a pattern business with her husband. Together they founded McKim Studios. She identified these blocks as part of a quilting tradition: "and the no end of fascinating patterns and tales of their history." (McKim, Introduction). I think today of similar books, the most famous, Tula Pink's City Sampler: 100 Modern Blocks. So, with my copyright hat on, I started to evaluate whether McKim's book is still under copyright. (It's not; no renewal). But that was the *wrong story*. This is a different kind of public domain.

McKim believed she was gathering blocks from history. She was telling the story of the past. She wasn't claiming copyright on the individual blocks – the book (the selection, arrangement, and coordination), likely. But only for the first 28 years. After 1959, the book was in the public domain. And it was reprinted by Dover Press (known for reprinting public domain books) in 1962. One of the things I love about this book is her commentary on various aspects of quilting that are sprinkled through the book. About cutting, she writes, "This is conceded to be the least interesting and most tedious part of quilt making; however, it is certainly not a step that can be hurried as blocks must be cut exact." (33). While methods of cutting have dramatically changed, that sentiment has not.

McKim was writing in a tradition that had begun less than 100 years earlier. Repeating blocks were a result of two things: industrialized cloth making and the rise of cheap print media (newspapers, magazines, etc.) More cloth was being made. Magazines and newspapers needed a way to get people to regularly purchase. The repeating block was perfect. You could create a column that was short and simple. People could repeat the block or make samplers. (How many have us made samplers and also repeating blocks quilts even today? These both dominate the quilt world.)

Example of repeating block (left) and example of sampler quilt, Claxton Family Guild (right), Judy Walker Collection

An example of a repeating block, the Log Cabin, by Louise Klare

My copyright hat again. If anyone owns the copyright to these columns and patterns, then, it might be the newspaper and magazine companies – the Chicago Daily Tribune, and Kansas City Star, or alternatively, depending on the employment contract, the authors. These newspapers not only published the patterns in columns, but sometimes even sold patterns, too! But we see that these newspapers are not trying to lock up the patterns. They are not claiming copyright on them. (They might on the columns, of course, or their version's expression). They instinctively knew that these blocks – even if they were more complicated than a simple hexagon or square, were common to all, and not to be property of any single individual. The repeating blocks never seem to have been thought of in that way.

There were others beside Webster and McKim, including Nancy Cabot at the *Chicago Tribune*, Prudence Penny at the *Seattle Post-Intelligencer*, Edna Maria Dunn, who took over at *Kansas City Star*, and so many others. Quilt historian Barbara Brackman, along with Joyce Gross and Cuesta Benberry had tallied 244 pattern columns during the 1930s. Ruth Finley published *Old Patchwork Quilts and the Women Who Made Them* in 1929. Carrie Hall and Rose Kretsinger wrote *The Romance of the Patchwork Quilt in America* in 1935. All of these authors were documenting blocks. All were not concerned with copyright ownership of the individual blocks. They saw these blocks, from the beginning as a common pool that had always been available. It's fascinating, really.

Carrie Hall (b. 1866) in 1933 wrote a forward to *The Romance of the Patchwork Quilt* where she explained that quilting found its groove after World War I, when knitting socks for soldiers was no longer necessary. "I found my fingers itching for some 'pick-up' work, so I turned to quilt-making, which had always interested me from the time when on my seventh birthday my pioneer mother cut the patches for a star quilt that under watchful guidance proved a masterpiece that was a nine-day wonder in the neighborhood." (7) She made some quilts, but then her attention turned to "making a collection of patches, one like every known pattern, little realizing the magnitude of the undertaking." (7) Her collection, as of 1933, included over 1000 patches, which she had "placed" at the Thayer Museum of Art at the University of Kansas. *The Romance of the Patchwork Quilt* is the book form of her journey. In the forward, she includes women who came before her:

- *Old Patchwork Quilts and the Women Who Made Them*, by Ruth Finlay
- *Quilts, Their Stories and How to Make Them* by Marie D. Webster
- *Old Fashioned Quilts* by Carlie Sexton
- And newspapers: *The Kansas City Star*, *The Seattle Post-Intelligencer*, and Prudence Penny,
- Grandmother Clark's Old Fashioned Quilt Designs
- The McKim Studios
- *The Woman's Home Companion*
- *The Ladies' Home Journal*
- *The Modern Priscilla*
- *The Household Magazine*

- *The Royal Neighbor*
- The Ladies Art Co.
- Mountain Mist Quilting Cotton
- "And many from sources unknown".

Hall indexed and retold the story from these sources. She explains: "In making the collection I found that nearly all of the better-known designs were included in every commercialized group offered for sale." (8)

Barbara Brackman

Enter the stage Barbara Brackman. As Brackman tells the story (in her book, elsewhere, and even on our podcast), she began The *Encyclopedia of Pieced Quilt Patterns* to index published pattern names. Brackman identifies Grandmother's Flower Garden as the oldest she could find, dating to 1835 in *Godey's Lady's Book*. Then, she explains, decades went by before the repeating block became a standard. "As magazines increased in the United States and technology for illustration improved, references to quilts also increased." (5).

Brackman began indexing quilt blocks in the late 1960s. She included the work of her predecessors above, and also searched local newspapers and other resources as she traveled for work. Her focus was primarily works between 1890 and 1940. This became the *Encyclopedia of Pieced Quilt Patterns* that includes over 4000 hand-drawn and cataloged patterns. She created the Brackman number system, which is standard today.

Brackman organizes her 4000+ drawings of blocks by categories of shapes: One Patch, Non-Square Blocks, Multi-Patch, Strip Quilts, Realistic, Two-Block, Sash & Block, Four Patch, Equal Nine Patch, Unequal Nine Path (two categories, One Patch-Square, Four X, Square in a Square, Maltese Cross, Nine X, Two-Patch, Three Patch, Fans, Wheels, Five & Six Point Star Blocks, Eight-pointed/45-degree Diamond Stars, Other Stars, Whole-Top Designs, and Miscellaneous. Each section is even more detailed. Let's take the first one, One Patch. One Patch is subdivided into triangles, rectangles, diamonds, four-sided figures, five-sided figures, hexagons, six-sided figures, odd shapes, curves, and three-dimensional pieces. This is accompanied by a numbering system, the Brackman system that she explains in the Introduction. Each entry has seven-digits. The Brackman numbering system helps us organize our common pool.

Brackman's work is protected by copyright. Her *Encyclopedia*—the selection, arrangement, and coordination. Not the system. Not the blocks themselves. Her work has been incorporated into Electric Quilt software, including BlockBase, likely through a licensing deal. And she has used her blocks for her books, like *Kansas City Star Quilts Sample: 60+ Blocks from 1928-1961.*

Electric Quilt

Electric Quilt, and the add-on product BlockBase, provides a means of accessing the blocks and designing quilts. Let's see what both of the products say about copyright in the blocks.

Now on its eighth version, EQ is a staple in the quilting community, costing about $200. On the back cover, EQ8 boasts: "EQ8 includes 6700 copyright-free blocks, 6200 scanned fabrics, traditional and modern layouts...." The Electric Quilt Company advertises that the blocks included are copyright free. However, under the copyright notice within the program, they are not as boastful:

> **Copyright**
>
> The Software is copyrighted 1991-2019 by The Electric Quilt Company. All rights reserved.
>
> No part of this software or its documentation may be reproduced or transmitted in any form or by any means, electronically, photocopied, recorded, translated into a machine language, or otherwise, without the written permission of the publisher.
>
> You may not sell or distribute collections or individual block designs from the EQ8 Block Library. You may not use EQ8 library blocks or other library designs in any commercial application, including software. For rights clearance, please contact The Electric Quilt Company.

Notice that legally Electric Quilt Company is not as confident about the status of the individual blocks. Are they claiming copyright on their version of the blocks? And loads of people use EQ8 to build commercial patterns and books. In fact, that is one of the most common uses I've found for the software. What Electric Quilt Company adds to the blocks to make them under copyright is not clear. The software is protected by copyright, of course, but the additional blocks themselves? Not likely.

Application: The Farmer's Wife as an Example

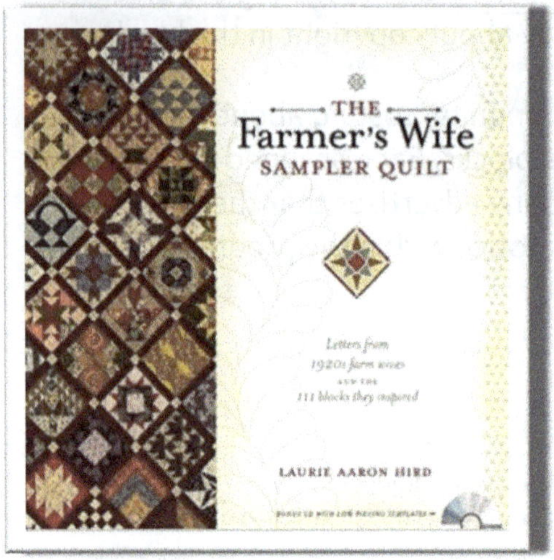

Laura Aaron Hird had an idea. She had found a book of letters from the Farmer's Wife, a magazine, and she knew what she wanted to do: pair a block she found in Brackman's *Encyclopedia* with the letter. The book had been published in 1922, and so the letters were in the public domain. *The Farmer's Wife Sampler Quilt* became a huge hit and classic, leading to two more books (with accompanying CDs of the patterns). Her selection, arrangement, and coordination of the letters, photographs of the blocks, and the block patterns are protectable by copyright.

Today, the books continue to sell like hot cakes. Paper Pieces, through a licensing deal, created English paper piecing kits to make the blocks. And there are always sew-alongs throughout the country going to make a Farmer's Wife Quilt.

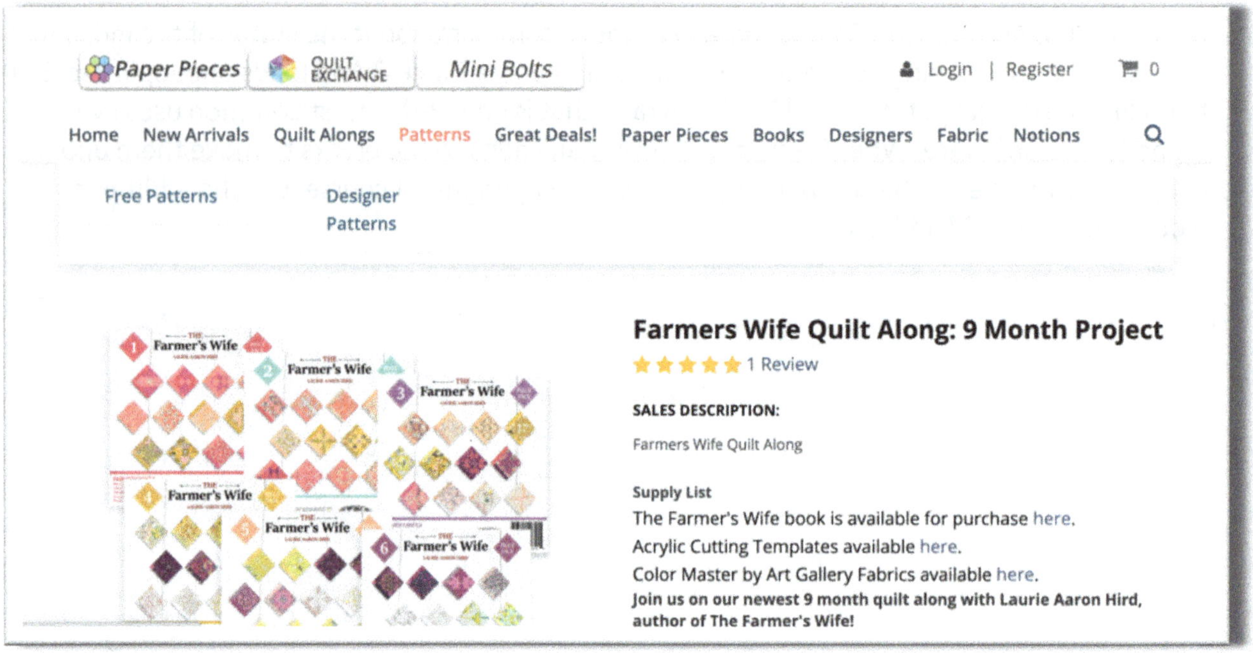

Here is Joel Seller's version, using the Paper Pieces templates and papers, and based on fabric kit. All of the pieces are hands sewn carefully. After eleven months of work, she is now ready to begin for the next step: quilting. Joel's work is amazing. There is no new copyright. But that doesn't matter. The point for Joel is the creation, not commercialization.

Here is a close-up of one of the blocks sewn by Joel.

Laura talked about the copyright issues in an interview for the Just Wanna Quilt podcast. While she had issues with the letters in the second book she was including, the blocks that she matched with the letters did not concern her, and these were obtained from EQ software. She also includes a CD of the blocks that includes foundation piecing and templates for each block.

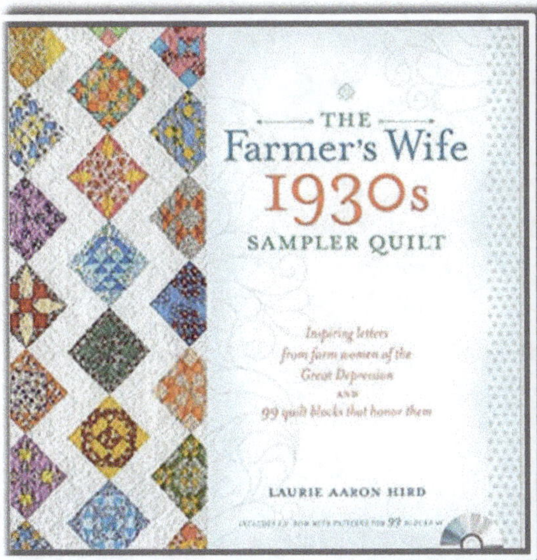

And my version of a block from the Farmer's Wife (EPP). The book itself is under copyright, and the individual letters included may still be protected, but the blocks are not. Nor is the renaming of the blocks to go with individual writers.

Laura has another book based on letters written by children that were published in 1915. Again, she matched what she liked of common blocks with the letter writers. And finally, my favorite.

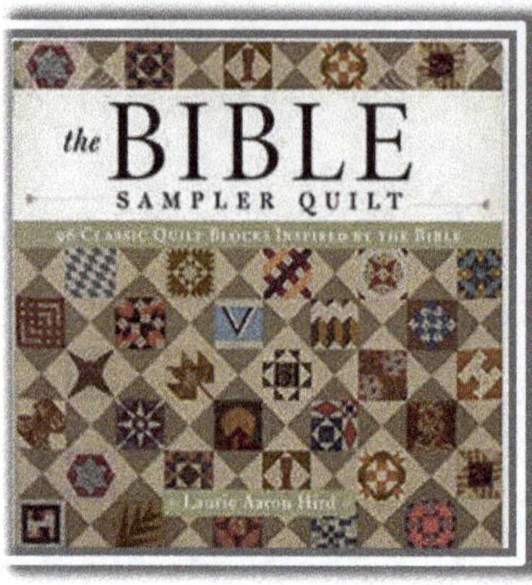

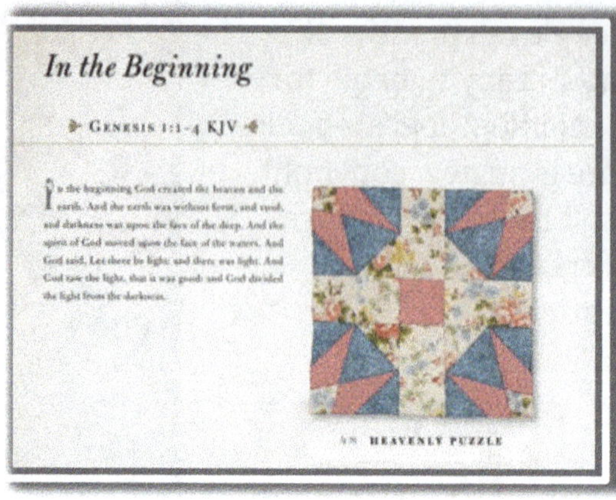

Bible quotes paired with common blocks. How could it not be awesome? It is the essence of the public domain creating a new copyrighted work by the selection, arrangement, and coordination that includes more than a modicum of creativity. Brilliant.

BlockBase

BlockBase is a separate database that can be added to EQ, which includes over 4000 blocks form 1835-1970, which can be printed for foundation pieces, templates, or rotary cutting. These are based on Barbara Brackman's work.

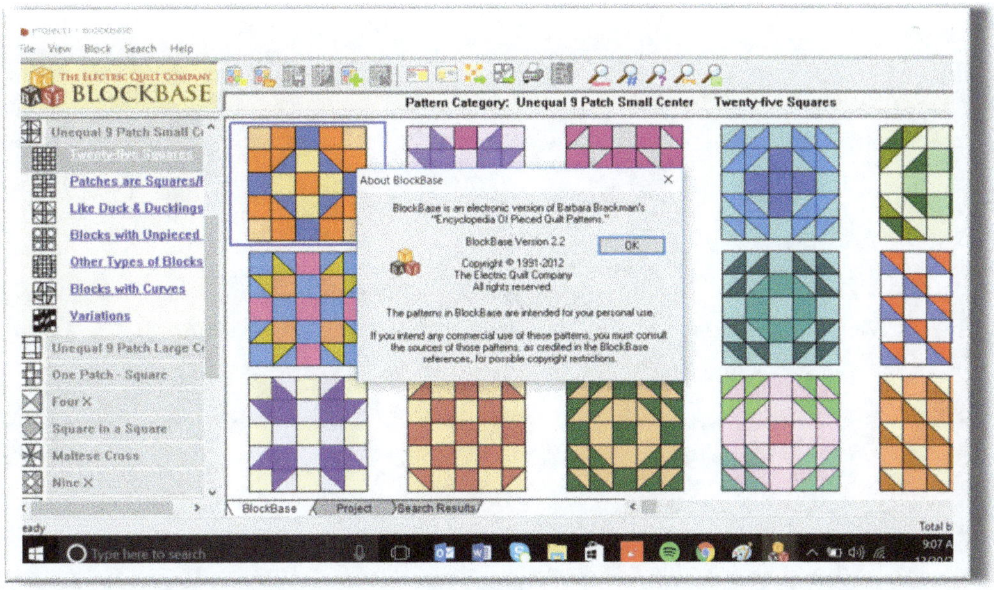

So again, we see that Electric Quilt Company has claimed "All rights reserved." We'll learn more about that in subsequent chapters. "The patterns in BlockBase are intended for your personal use." Again restrictions. "If you intend any commercial use of these patterns, you must consult the sources of those patterns, as credited in BlockBase references, for possible copyright restrictions." What? Ok. Many questions. 1) Have they gotten permission from the sources themselves to have them included in the database? 2) Are these under copyright, and were they registered? 3) How would one know? I think this is a very strange rights statement.

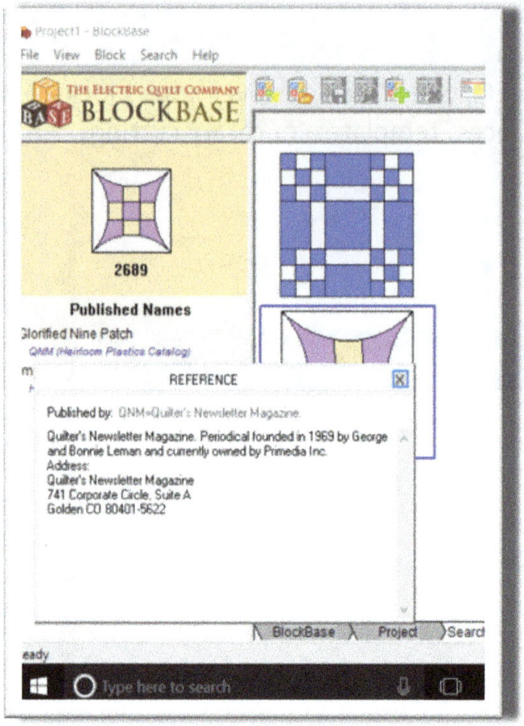

For the Glorified Nine Patch, which we will be looking at further, BlockBase credits Quilter's Newsletter Magazine in 1969 as the source and provides an address. But in fact, Glorified Nine Patch, according to Barbara Brackman, goes further back. And in reality, everyone uses the data in the system as if it is in the public domain, our common pool.[12]

Why this long tale of history? The blocks are treated as if they are in the public domain—which suggests that they have always been around. No one is checking their copyright status. And likely they would be seen as not copyrightable. And even when there is ambiguity, *who* to contact for permission is not as clear as BlockBase makes it out to seem, and whether you would have to contact them at all is also very debatable. Let's look at one block as an example, and let's stick with the Glorified Nine Patch.

[12] There are other software systems, of course, including the new entrepreneurial, Precut, which allows you to design quilts online.

The Glorified Nine Patch: An Exploration of One Block

We're going to use the Glorified Nine Patch as our way into understanding the relationship of repeating blocks, copyright and the public domain. AccuQuilt has just come out with a version of the Glorified Nine Patch. The video even credits Nancy Cabot with the original idea. This combines all kinds of elements.

Nancy Cabot, a pseudonym for Loretta Leitner Rising, wrote a daily newspaper column for the *Chicago Tribune*, beginning on January 20, 1933. Each day she featured a quilt block, and then included, for sale, the pattern for 5 cents in stamps or coins, to be mailed to the *Sunday Tribune*. She is credited with designing over 200 quilt blocks. The Tribune had a service library for hobbyists, and the Nancy Cabot Quilt pamphlets were included.

Loretta was born in 1906, and worked at the paper for 32 years, being promoted to Needlework Editor in the 1930s. The quilting patterns ran from 1933-1948. She's kind of a quilt cult figure. There was a Nancy Cabot Sew-along online that listed each pattern by the Month included in the Chicago Tribune. In 2012, a Flickr group started to pattern some of Nancy Cabot's blocks and share them. For example, Lee Heinrich of Freshly Pieced suggested directions on how she would create the Mosaic Block by Nancy Cabot, and there were over 200 people in the group all working on and sharing their version of Nancy Cabot blocks. The blocks themselves were presumed to be in the common public domain pool. And they were honoring Nancy Cabot in creating this group. Their versions -- the directions, the quilts they made, the website -- are protectable. They hold a copyright. How strong that copyright is, of course, depends on other factors. An independent creation does not preclude others from making the same quilts. Nor is the idea of creating a group to work on Nancy Cabot blocks locked up by their activities.

But back to the Glorified Nine Patch...

There are actually at least two blocks with that name in Barbara Brackman's *Encyclopedia*: Number 1611, the Five Patch, or Glorified Nine Patch, and Number 2689, the Glorified Nine Patch, otherwise known as the Inverted Nine Patch. We're going to trace the development of the second. Brackman traces this pattern to QNM (Heirloom Plastics Catalog), and the second name, to Hinson QC. No dates are given. But the Encyclopedia directs us to 306. Here we see another version of our pattern, and gives five names for the pattern:

Improved Nine Patch, Rural New York, 2/15/30
Circle upon Circle, Kansas City Star, 12/2/1933
Four Leaf Clover - Kansas City Star, 9/25/1935
Nine Patch Variation - Hall 1935
Bailey Nine Patch - Mrs. Danner 1958, where it references 2689 and 424.5

So, we also look at 424.5. There we see a variation of a diamond instead of a circle. Here it is called the Improved Nine-Patch (Nancy Cabot 2/25/1933) and the Nine Patch, also Nancy Cabot, 2/28/1933. Because we are so clever, we also know to look at what Barbara Brackman has written on her blog, Encyclopedia Quilt patterns. (Brackman actually found an earlier version from Comfort Magazine, likely from the 1920s. See http://encyclopediaquiltpatterns.blogspot.com/2018/01/improved-nine-patch.html)

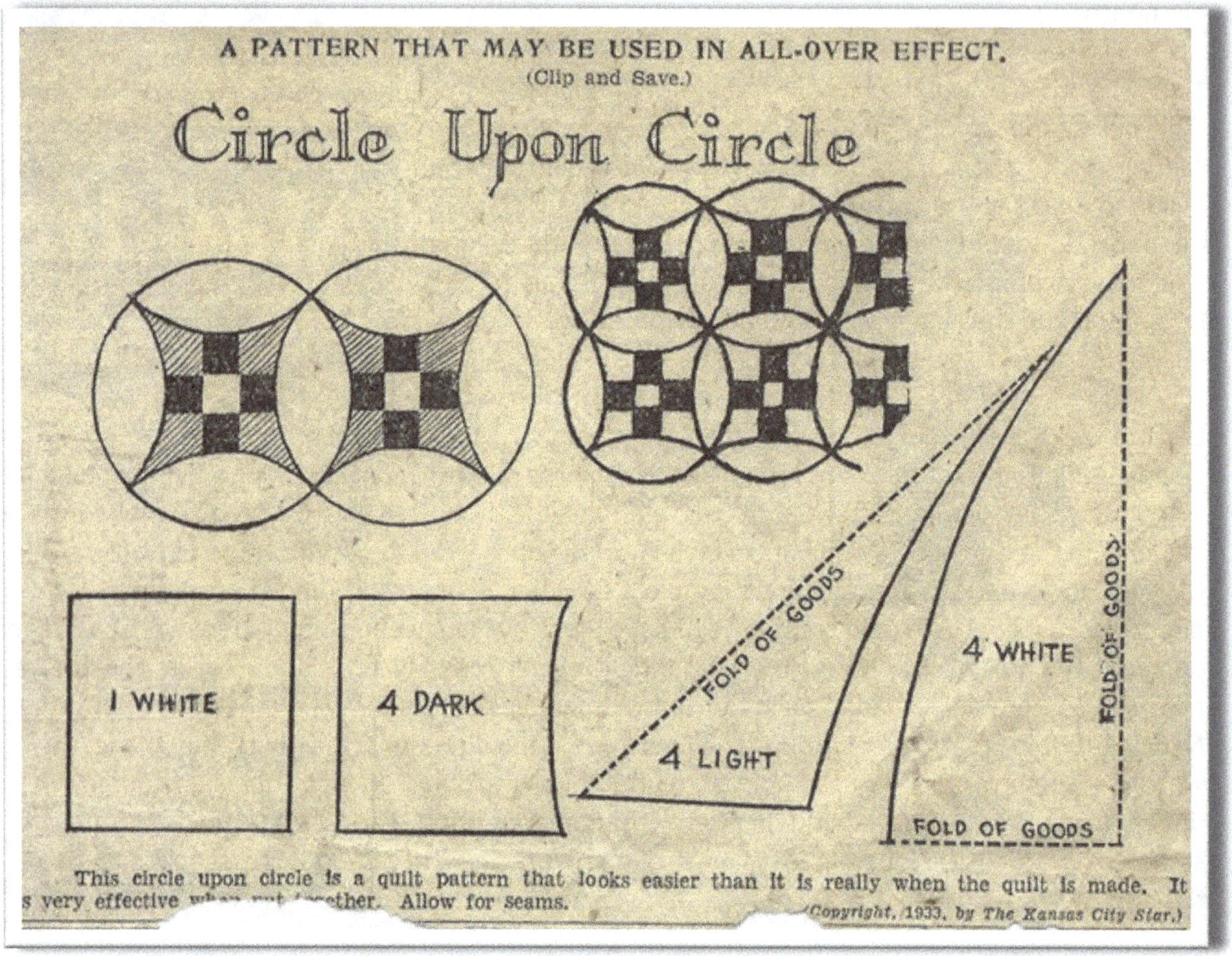

1933 *Kansas City Star* excerpt from
http://encyclopediaquiltpatterns.blogspot.com/2018/01/improved-nine-patch.html

The Glorious Nine Patch, or also called the Improved Nine Patch, has become a staple pattern in the quilting world -- one of 1000s. Note: Kansas City Star included a Copyright Notice. That means that it had protection, this version of the pattern for at least 28 years, and 95 years, if the newspaper renewed the edition.

So, as a copyright detective, we could go one of three ways. First, one could claim that the arrangement of shapes is not enough to secure copyright, that the shapes are too basic.

Second, we could assume that the arrangement of blocks is enough to gain copyright, and then investigate whether the first published source of that block had properly renewed the copyright, and therefore the block would be protected (or not) under copyright. I don't think this is the spirit in which these blocks were created or disseminated to the public. There were so many competing companies and newspapers *making the same block*, as demonstrated above with the Glorified Nine Patch, and they were not suing each other or claiming territory on the block. I don't think they saw the block itself as protectable. And this leads to the third option.

Third, we could define our common pool, our public domain works--the materials we all can draw upon, regardless of whether they are *actually* under copyright or in the public domain. We agree as a community that certain blocks and shapes, and even patterns, are in the public domain.

Terri VandenBosch's Glorified Nine Patch for the New AccuQuilt Design

What AccuQuilt is doing is making it easier to create the block. They are not even the first to create a cutting system for this block. Terri Vandenosch is the designer behind this photo. She created patterns for AccuQuilt.

An Australian company, A1 Craft and Quilting, has their own version, which can work with the AccuQuilt system.[13] What's different about AccuQuilt is that they have added special notches that if you line them up, the block turns out (except in my case) perfectly.

1A1 Craft and Quilt version

Shapes are not protectable, nor are practical things like templates. Both companies can make their own version of the Glorified Nine Patch.

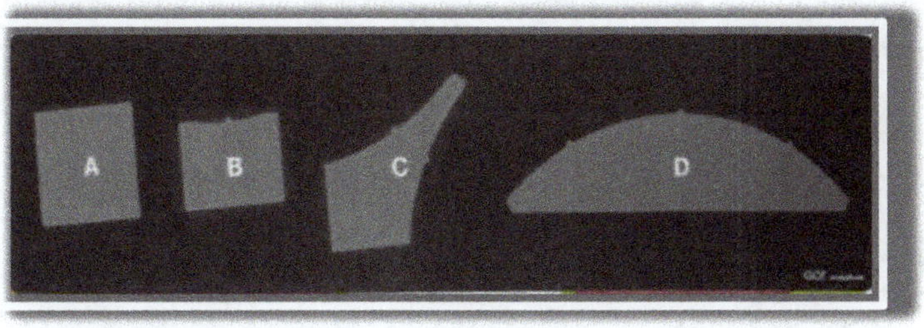

AccuQuilt's version

[13] https://www.a1craftandquilting.com.au/products/glorious-9-patch-8-finished-block-6218-mat-included

My Glorified Nine Patch using the new AccuQuilt Die I purchased, using Tula Pink and Kaffe Fassett fabric both purchased and donated to the Just Wanna Quilt project at Tulane by Jaftex/FreeSpirit.

The Case of Modern Blocks

Tula Pink, very famous in the quilt world, published *Tula Pink's City Sampler: 100 Modern Quilt Blocks* in 2013, and it has already become a classic. She divided the blocks into categories: crosses, rectangles, triangles, stripes, squares, and haiku. (Seem familiar? Think Brackman categories by shape too; does that remind you of *Feist*? Is organization by shape like organizing by the alphabet?). In the introduction, Tula talks about a new generation of quilters that may not "have a closet of full vintage quilts made by family members who have long since passed away. I know I don't have those things." (7) She wants to create blocks that will allow a new generation to tell their own story. She numbered the blocks without names. This is intentional. She is trying to get away from the Brackman history and the quilt historians. She is closer to Laura Aaron Hird's farmer's wife who also used blocks ahistorically in her Farmer's Wife projects. Tula, like McKim and Cabot before her, designed the blocks, although many of these are not "original." She writes "I may have designed the blocks and given you the instructions on what to cut and where to stitch, but I have not infused the blocks with any meaning. This is your quilt. The fabrics that you choose, the colors that you use and why you are making it are what will give the quilt a purpose." (7)

Tula Pink is communicating copyright. She says she is giving you the tools to create your own works. Mix your labor, use your creativity. "Name your blocks, write in the margins, cross out the ones you don't like, draw hearts around the ones you love." First sale doctrine. Personhood theory. "In a perfect world, everyone's book would end up looking like a journal, coffee stains and all." Tula is copyright: "I am the platform and you are the speaker, so stand on my shoulders and tell the future who you are and why you make." (7) How could you not love her?

Here is Gina Dimattia's City Sampler:

Tula Pink includes in her introduction, "The more adventurous ones might rename the book and write your own introduction." In many ways, Australian quilter Angie Wilson did just that. She calls herself the Gnome Angel, and she is famous for sew-alongs, including using Tula's book (where she requires people to purchase the book). In 2019, she created her own pattern, Kinship: 100 Blocks Fusion Sampler, and called her sew along #100blocks100days.

So, let's analyze Wilson's new pattern on three levels:

1. The blocks themselves. Are the individual blocks protectable? No.
2. The pattern. Does the pattern have enough to be protectable? Yes.
3. Could Tula hypothetically see this as infringement (this is the next chapter)?

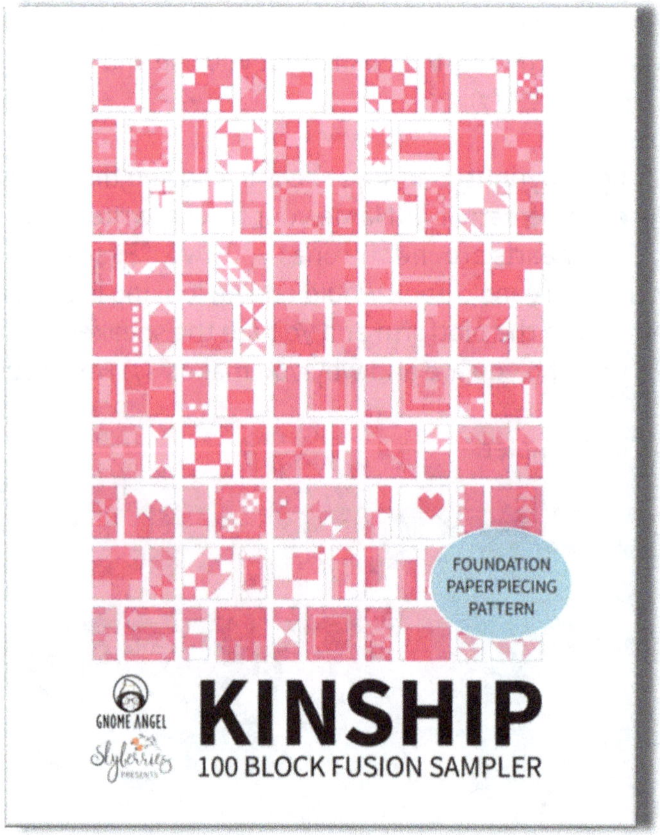

Answer:

1. I think if we are going to place the blocks from Brackman's work, and the blocks from McKim, Cabot, and others in the public domain, then any new blocks are also in the public domain, even if they are original. No double standard. And if it is considered a common block, basic geometric shapes, then it is not protected.

2. Of course, the pattern -- the directions, the images, and everything else-- is protected by copyright. We'll be discussing notice soon, and we'll come back to

this. But the basic foundation patterns of common blocks are not protectable; they can't be, right? Even if "For personal use only. Not to be reproduced for commercial purposes or classes without the express written permission of the publisher." The full pattern cannot be reproduced, and it is bad form not to have students purchase the pattern. But I can copy the foundation page of Flying Geese (it all comes back to Geese). It's not protectable by copyright.

3. So, I think that Angie Wilson did a great job of differentiating her new pattern from Tula Pink. Her *Kinship* is a different size, and a different approach. It's a good example of being inspired by something that came before and making something unique. We return to Tula Pink's sentiments at the end of her book, that we began this book with: "In the end, it all comes down to this: Making something again is easy, making something new is brave and making something personal is essential." I do think she might have a blurring problem, however, with how she is promoting her work, but that is under trademark, and not copyright.

A Few More Words

We know from the previous chapters that many things are not protectable. We know that anything published before 1924 is in the public domain. We know that anything first published in the U.S. before 1989 that does not have the © notice is in the public domain. We also know that we, as quilters, have made our own common pool of public domain blocks, as evidenced by the Brackman system. We do not check the copyright status. We use them freely and with joy. But we recognize that patterns and books created with these common blocks (created after 1989) are automatically protected by copyright given more than a modicum of creativity in the selection, arrangement, and coordination.

My hope is that you aggressively claim the public domain, non-protectable elements, and what we all see as custom-based public domain. Enjoy, share, love. And do not freak out if someone else also makes a Glorified Nine Patch. That is the whole point of the system. That we all play and enjoy. (That is different from pirating copies of your patterns, or not paying for the pattern for a class, of course.) And explore.

Part 3:
Protecting Your Work

10: Copyright Notice & Rights Statement

How to Let the World Know Your Rights

Copyright arises automatically, every time we create something, for all of us--whether we are a two-year-old making art at preschool or a famous artist whose paintings are worth millions. No registration is needed. But you can get more protection if you include a copyright notice and register the work with the U.S. Copyright Office. This chapter focuses on copyright notice, the related concept of rights statements, and how to register your work at the U.S. Copyright Office.

Copyright arises automatically, it is true. But if you do not register your work, you have much MUCH less protection. In fact, without registering your work, you cannot go to court! So, while you do hold a copyright, your protection is subpar. We'll talk more about strategies for registering your work, including costs and how to group your works to save money as well.

Everyone knows what a copyright notice looks like: © 2019 Elizabeth Townsend Gard. But what does it mean, why do you include it, and what should be included? Copyright notice is the first step to let the world know you intend to enforce your property rights. The supplemental rights statement helps navigate the property rights--no commercial use, for example, or feel free to make your own version!

Rights statements are the portion usually near or after the copyright notice that tells the world what they can and can't do with the work. The most famous one is "All rights reserved." This chapter explores what that means exactly and what alternatives there are, including, "No rights reserved," and, "Some rights reserved."

This chapter navigates through both the copyright notice and rights statement, both in learning to read what a rights statement means, and also how to create one of your own. This chapter focuses on copyright notice for works published or created on or after March 1, 1989. Let's go through the basics of copyright notice, and then turn to the rights statement.

Copyright Notice

Copyright notice tells the world who the copyright holder is and when the work was created. The date and author information helps us determine how long copyright lasts. Copyright notice is particularly important when your work is published--that is, circulating out in the public. Why? If you send something out in the world, it's a really good idea (if you care) to put your name on it and let the world know you care about the property attached to it. Now, not everyone wants this. Some want to release it out for everyone to use. Others would be happy for others to use it, but only in some instances. Before we get there, let's understand the basic components (and why) of copyright notice. **Notice should be placed on all copies that are going to be sold or distributed to the public.**

Publication

Notice is only required when a work is published, that is a work or a copy of the work is circulating out in the public without restrictions (meaning, nothing like "Draft. Do not distribute."). The legal definition has historically been complicated. Here are the basics:

- If the work is being distributed to the **public** by sale, rental, lease, lending, or transfer of ownership, the work is published. An offer to do any of these things also triggers publication. Examples: books in a bookstore or patterns sold online

- If a work is merely being displayed, this does not constitute publication, as long as there are no copies circulating to the public. So, if you have a quilt hanging in a show, that is not considered published, but if you print postcards to hand out of that quilt that would be considered published.

What about Artwork? When are works of art considered published? Sale of an original work of art (e.g. a quilt) does not constitute publication. Merely displaying the work does not constitute publication. Selling a piece of art with no intention of allowing copies doesn't seem to trigger publication. But allowing the public access to make unrestricted non-personal copies does publish the work. So, think of a one-of-a-kind art quilt. The work is still considered unpublished, and therefore would not need a copyright notice, even if it is displayed. But if patterns were made of that quilt, or the public is given unrestricted access, the work is considered published. Law scholar Deborah Gerhardt suggests the following test of whether publication has occurred:

> (1) whether the copyright owner acts in a manner reflecting an intent to share the work with the public, and
> (2) the availability of authorized copies

Unrestricted access is key. The Copyright Office and the courts have not been clear whether posting a work on a website constitutes publication.

Notice and Unpublished works: Notice is optional for unpublished works. It doesn't hurt to put it on your works. So, if you are making a label for a quilt, it doesn't hurt to add a copyright notice, if you care.

Notice and foreign works: Notice is also optional for foreign works--works first published outside of the U.S. Again, there are benefits to adding the notice, including preventing a claim of innocent infringement, which reduces statutory damages.

Elements of Copyright Notice

There are three elements to include on any copyright notice.

©, Copyright, or "Copr."

It all begins with this, although the order can be different. Any of the above words can be used, but © is considered the best, particularly if your work is going to be sold or distributed internationally. What else works? (c), CO, C, %, @, [c], and c in a square. You can also misspell copyright: copyrighted, copywrite, copyritten, copy, copyr., registered U.S. copyright office, copyright applied for, copyright pending. So, you don't have to get it exactly right to still gain protection. Interestingly, "All Rights Reserved" on its own *does not work!* It has to be accompanied by "copyright" and the other requirements below in some form.

Copyright Holder

This is the name of the owner of the copyright. It can be an abbreviation too. It is the person/company with the "rights" to the copyright at the time of publication. For example,

> *Piece and Quilt with Precuts* by Christa Watson. © 2017 by Christa Watson. Even though Martingale published Christa's book, Christa holds the copyright.
>
> *Cheerful Charm Quilts*. (Note: no author list). © 2013 by Martingale and Co.
>
> On Quiltsmart's *Mondo Bag* pattern: © 2010/2012 by Quiltsmart, Inc.

What does the name tell us? Who the copyright holder is, at least at the time of publication. It's a place to start. The copyright might have been transferred to someone else, but it is a place to begin. The name also sometimes tells us how long the copyright lasts, in combination with the date. This is important as well. When is it the author's name, and when is it the publishing company? This is based on the contractual relationship you have with your publisher, and if you are self-publishing, whether you (yourself) are the copyright holder, or you have created a company to hold the intellectual property. Sometimes copyright notices are complicated, but also help us understand which rights are held by which person. Finally, copyrights can revert back to the original owner, can be sold (assigned) or licensed. So, the copyright notice is a starting point if you want to learn more about who holds the right to grant permission.

The Departed: Deceased people cannot be named as the copyright holder, or register a copyright. It has to name the person, company or estate with rights. That's the point of copyright notice: to name and identify the person/company to contact should one need permission.

Date

The notice usually includes the year of publication. For pictorial, graphic or sculptural works, the year of publication is not required. This is important for quilting and crafting. This is a huge category of works--toys, dolls, useful articles, postcards, quilts, and fabric.

Placement of Notice

Where copyright notice should be placed is an important topic in the law of copyright. People have to be able to find it. It's a notice.

> **Literary works:** Ideally it would be on the title page or the page following the title page. At the beginning. If there are no more than 10 pages, the last page appears to be acceptable too.
>
> **Artistic works:** The notice can be a label either on the front or back, or on a mounting, matting, frame, or other materials where the work is durably attached.
>
>> **For fabric,** the Copyright Office has special rules, under "works consisting of sheet-like or strip material." The notice can be on the fabric itself; the margin or selvage; the reverse side of the fabric; or on a tag or label attached to the spool or container holding the fabric. How far apart must the notice be? We have a number of cases that give a variation on how far apart the notice must be, from once every time the pattern repeats, to 19 inches to as much as 30 inches (e.g. under a yard).

The Advantages of Copyright Notice

Since March 1, 1989, copyright notice is not required in order to be protected by the U.S. Copyright Act. Why include copyright notice when it is no longer required? There are strong advantages to including proper copyright notice on works.

> **Mine.** By putting notice on your work, it alerts the world that copyright is being claimed. In the reverse, by not putting copyright notice on your work, you are signaling that you *are not likely* to claim copyright on the work--that you are more in a sharing mood. It also helps a work from becoming an "orphan," meaning it is still under copyright but the copyright holder can't be found.
>
> **Not Innocent**. If you put a notice on a work and someone uses your work anyway, s/he is no longer an innocent infringer. They knew you claimed a property right. They used it anyway. In this case, the copyright notice has to be in proper form. Not innocent means that if there is a lawsuit, it could actually be willful infringement, and then statutory damages could be significant. Innocence or willfulness deeply impacts the amount of money a court will award. Innocent infringers can have their statutory damages reduced to $200, while willful damages can be up to $150,000 per infringed work. Putting a proper copyright notice on your work makes a difference.
>
> **Identity**. Because notice includes your name, it allows people to know who is claiming the property right and ideally can contact you (if necessary) for permission.

Copyright notice tells the world that you claim your property right. But to enforce that right in court, you need to register the work. You might also see your work being used without your permission and send a Cease-and-Desist notice. Or you might see your work on Facebook or other platforms, and file a Notice-and-Takedown with the platform.

Copyright Exclusive Rights

Copyright gives the copyright holder *rights*: to make copies, distribute the work, make derivative works, publicly display, and publicly perform the work. 17 U.S.C. Section 106. There are five basic exclusive rights the copyright holder gets *automatically upon creation* (now) *without doing anything.* A quick reminder of the exclusive rights.

Reproduction Right

Making copies of the original work is the basis of copyright: the right to copy. This includes literal copying and substantial similarity.

Distribution Right

The copyright holder has the right to decide when and how a work is distributed to the public. Once the sale occurs, however, the copyright holder does not control subsequent sales. This is called the First Sale Doctrine.

Public Display

The copyright holder decides where and when the work is displayed publicly. This makes sense. A quilter can decide which quilt shows to enter their quilt, for example.

Public Performance

Except for artwork (weird), the copyright holder controls when a work can be publicly performed during the term of the copyright.

Create Derivative Works

The copyright holder has the exclusive right to create secondary works from the original work. These are called derivative works. There are some instances (namely fair use) where others can use your work and make their own works without permission.

These are the rights of copyright. Now, let's see the choices of expressing your rights in relation to others' using your work, namely the general public. Obviously, you could also create contracts and one-on-one relationships. But when you put out a product or something to the world, it is ideal to let them know how you feel about the rights and what they can or can't do with your work and in what situations. The rights statement with the copyright notice alerts the world as to the intentions of the copyright holder on what others can do. Sometimes there are additional words that communicate to the world permissible uses and restrictions on the use of the work. There are three basic kinds:

All Rights Reserved. Copyright holder wants to control as much as possible. This is the default, even if you don't include the rights statement.

No Rights Reserved. Copyright holder sends its work out into the world.

Some Rights Reserved, or a Creative Commons License. This tells anyone that comes to the work what they can and can't do, without having to ask direct permission.

What is a Creative Commons License?

In the 21st century, with the rise of the Internet, people found that "All rights reserved" was a bit too restrictive--that there were many times where the copyright holder was okay with people further distributing/sharing the work, using the work to build new things (derivative work), and even using the work commercially. Creative Commons transformed how we think about rights statements. They allow a license from the copyright holder to be placed on the work--tagged, embedded--and so anyone coming to the work already knows the permission and limitations in using the work.

- **Attribution**: your name/company is included when someone else uses (posts, remixes, etc.) the work.
- **ShareAlike:** you allow people to use your work, but only if they share what they make, too.
- **No Derivatives:** you allow people to use your work, but they can't make different versions - they can't change or add anything to your work.
- **NonCommercial**: they can't sell your work or anything they make using your work, and they can't use it in a commercial context.
- **CCO "No Rights Reserved":** you disclaim all rights in the copyright and send it out into the world. No restrictions on how other people use the work.

You can create a Creative Commons license at their website and make a combination of these terms, or you can put them on your own works. www.creativecommons.com These tell the world what kind of license to the work you are giving them. You should still put the copyright notice in addition to these terms.

Creative Commons licenses are really great when you are OK with people further distributing and using your work. Free patterns, for example, would be great--they would include the right of attribution, would require others to share in the same manner (free) if they create a derivative work, and can even be used in a commercial context. But CC licenses are not for everyone, and that's okay.

Searching for Creative Common Images

Not only can you add a Creative Commons license to you work, you can also search and use Creative Commons works as inspiration or within your work, depending on the license. Here are ways to look for Creative Commons images, both at www.creativecommons.org, and also through Google, Flickr and other platforms. For instance, I did a Google image search for "butterfly quilts." I chose the dropdown option "Usage rights" under the "Tools" tab to limit my search.

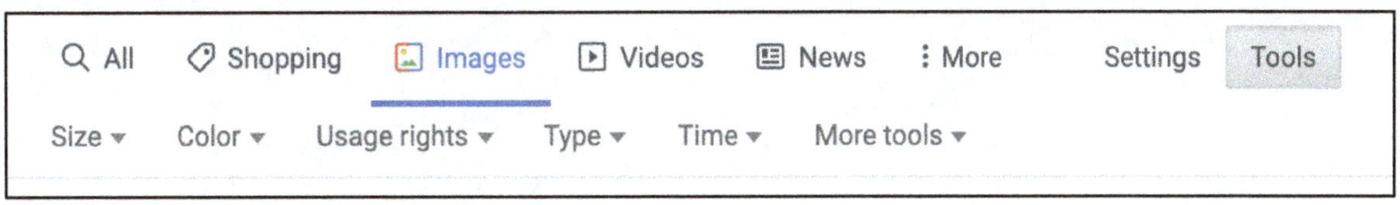

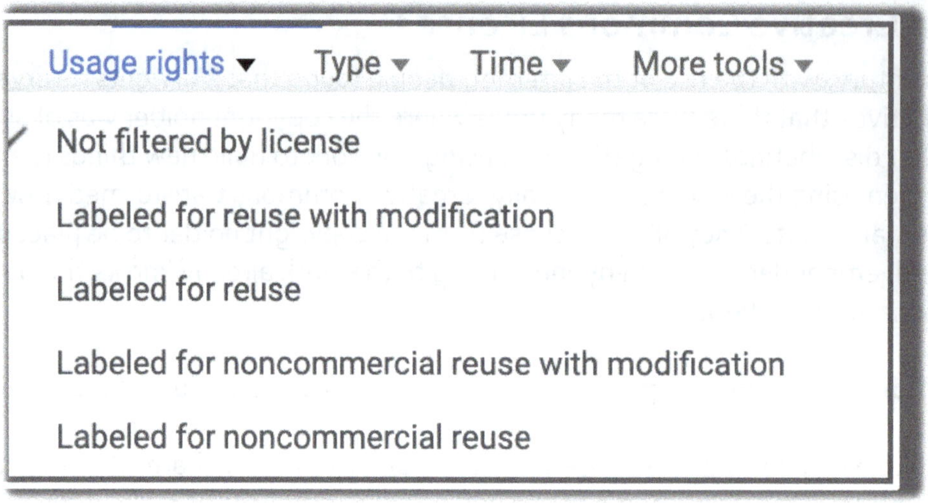

See how Creative Commons licenses are embedded. I chose "Labeled for reuse with modification." And I found this: Olga Kuba, Butterfly of Love on Flickr. https://www.flickr.com/photos/olgakuba/16333734340.

On the right-hand side, there is information about the license.

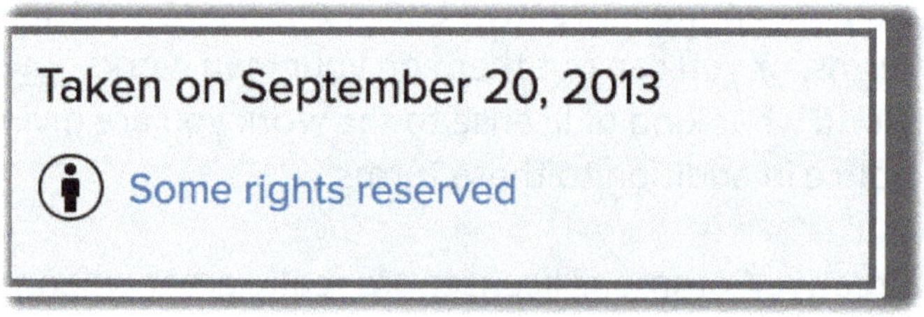

I clicked on the link. It took me to the CC License the creator had chosen.

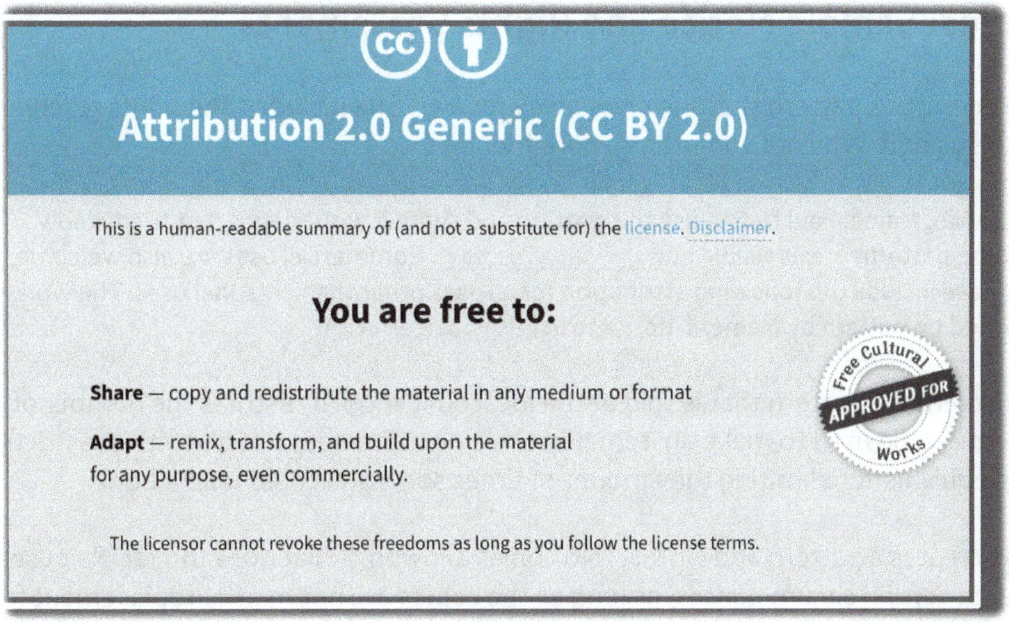

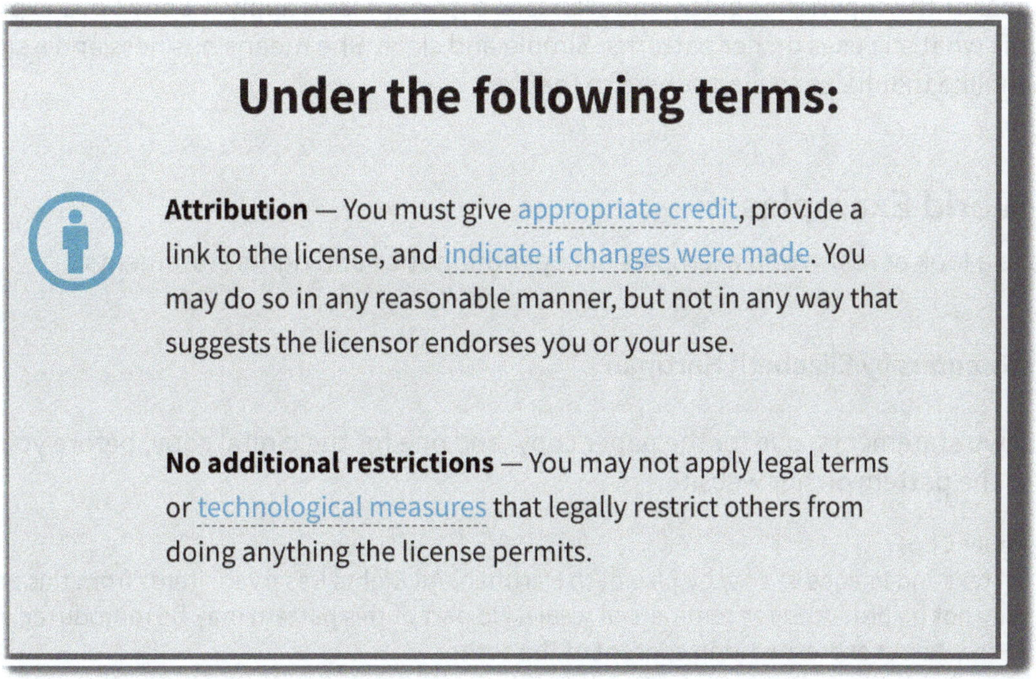

Using Creative Commons works is an awesome way to add resources, and the rights statements are very helpful. In part 2 of this chapter, we will look at how to choose a CC license for your own works.

Scenarios: Sample Notice and Rights Statements

Someone creates a pattern that she *gives away for free*. She includes "All rights reserved." This always seems odd. Why not something more friendly?

> © 2010, Name. Feel free to use this pattern and share it with friends. Let them know more patterns are available at www.patterns.com. Commercial uses are also welcome. Please include the following attribution for all uses other than personal uses: The work based on pattern by Name, Title, © 2010, www.pattern.com.

Someone creates a pattern that is sold at the local quilt shop. It restricts the number of times the pattern can be used to make an item. First sale doctrine does not allow this restriction. This would be equivalent to limiting the amount of times someone could read a book.

Someone creates a pattern and writes, "No copies allowed." That goes too far. Fair use allows for copies in certain circumstances, as long as the copies are not market replacement for purchasing the pattern.

Someone creates a pattern for sale and uses "All Rights Reserved." This alerts the user of the seriousness of the copyright holder, and standard copyright laws apply. Ebony Love explained that this is what she uses on her patterns. Simple and clear. She means business and a simple statement like that helps to alert others to that fact.

Real-World Examples

Let's take a look at real-world examples of copyright notice and rights statements.

Dogs in Sweaters by Elizabeth Hartman

She has two statements, one for the paper copy, and one for the digital copy, before you purchase the pattern on her website.

> Paper Copy:
> All text and images © 2017 by Elizabeth Hartman. All Rights Reserved. Items from this pattern may not be produced for commercial resale. No part of this pattern may be reproduced in any form without express written consent of the author.
>
> Digital Copy on her website before you purchase the pattern:
> Please note that my patterns are intended for non-commercial use by home sewers. They are not intended for making items to sell." This is not a copyright notice per se. It's a warning before you download the pattern. This seems to make a good deal of sense.

The copyright notice is proper. All rights reserved means that Hartman is claiming all of the rights under copyright - including the right to copy, distribute, create derivative works, publicly display, and publicly perform. The last portion regarding reproduction is a reach. There are instances where copyright law allows for reproduction, including fair use and other instances.

What Hartman is likely trying to do is to keep people from reproducing the work as a market replacement for paying for another pattern. That makes sense. But she does not control all reproductions in any form. Moreover, *making the pattern* is a reproduction of the pattern, and by purchasing a pattern, she gives users an implied license to make a copy of the work, and even a limited derivative right to change it as the sewist wishes, even if it is for personal use.

I looked to see if there was a copyright registration for Hartman's Dogs in Sweaters. I found one for 2010 for "Dogs in Sweaters," and they were described even as dachshunds in sweaters, but it doesn't seem to be Elizabeth Hartman's dachshunds in sweaters. So, she has not registered the work, even though it is incredibly popular. Any damages for infringement of her pattern would be appraised only *after* registration. This exercise also indicates that the idea of dachshunds in sweaters was not Elizabeth's original idea. Others had done it before her. Others can do it after her. The question is how close one can get to her design before it is infringing. The spectrum of infringement.

Modern Simplicity: Machine Quilting Design for Modern Quilts by Jodi Robinson

This is a self-published (photocopied) book. On the cover, the copyright notice is included: © JR Designs 2013. The first page is sort of a letter to users, which includes encouragement to contact Jodi if there are any questions or comments. Her contact information is included at the back of the book, along with a longer statement.

> All rights reserved. No part of the work, covered by the copyright, may be reproduced in any form or by any means, electronic or mechanical (including photocopying) and/or used in conjunction with teaching, without written permission from the author. Purchase of this book only grants permission to the purchaser to use the designs or likeness thereof for their individual use or use in their business on clients' quilts. Use on mass-produced quilts is prohibited without written author's permission.

Hmmm.... There's a lot to unpack here. First, again, the law does not allow the prohibition of all copying. It even allows it for classroom use. It just can't be a market replacement. We know that. And the techniques of the book are not protectable. The question is are the designs in the work sufficiently original to be protected by copyright? It seems that Jodi wants to keep her quilting designs from being used in a commercial setting. The question becomes does she hold a property right to do so? Are the designs original or are they more like blocks? What is protected is the *book* itself--the images, the selection, arrangement, and coordination, and the text. Not the techniques. It is unlikely that a commercial entity would be copying the book. She's concerned with them copying her designs. And again, there is no registration record at the U.S. Copyright Office.

June Tailor's Quilt as you Go Pet Placemat

We have a number of kits from June Tailor--quilt as you go kits. We did not find any copyright information on them. I think this is because you buy the materials–and it is the printing on the materials that is valuable, not the pattern. There was no copyright on the printed batting either. June Tailor is a sophisticated company with lots of patents. One imagines that the focus of the business is not, at least on these patterns, to copyright them. The brand and the ability to print on batting gives them the competitive edge, and not whether they are protected by copyright or not. The usefulness is also a factor, which we know is not protectable under copyright either.

The Whole Country Caboodle's Siberian Bowtie Cat

This is an applique kit of a cat, created by laser cutting. A simple © Leanne Anderson 2017. That's enough. All rights reserved is implied.

Crafty Nomad's London Calling Quilt

This Jo Westfoot's pattern from the UK. And it has the copyright notice:

> All text & images © 2018 by Jo Westfoot at the Crafty Nomad. All rights reserved. No part of this pattern may be reproduced in any form without written consent from the author.

Pretty standard, albeit a little overreaching. Her work is protected here in the U.S. automatically, as well as around the world. That's true for U.S. authors too. Still, it's never a bad idea to register your copyright in the U.S., even if you are foreign, because if you went to court, you can't obtain attorney's fees or statutory damages without registering your work, even if you are foreign.

Quilt in a Day - Homestead Stars Quilt by Eleanor Burns

This appears to be connected to the promotion of a particular fabric line. It's a pamphlet. The copyright information is simple: © 2017 Quilt in a Day®That's really all that has to be part of a copyright notice. No additional information about the rights is necessary.

Quiltworx's Tea Leaf Table Runner

Quiltworx's Tea Leaf Table Runner for Hoffman Fabrics is a kit for paper piecing one of Judy Niemeyer's famous foundation piecing patterns. It includes a long copyright notice:

> © Copyright April 2014 Pattern: Tea Leaf Table Runner. All rights reserved. No part of this pattern can be reproduced in any form for any commercial purpose without the expressed written permission of Judy Niemeyer Quilting. The written instructions, foundation papers, graphics, and photographs for this pattern were designed as a package for the purpose of retail sales and as a result, fall under the protection of federal copyright laws of the United States of America. Extra materials may be obtained from local quilt shops or directly from Judy Niemeyer Quilting aka Quiltworx.com.

So, they seem to realize that parts of what they produce may be seen as useful articles and not protected, but they claim copyright on the whole set, the package. The rights statement limits use to non-commercial as well.

Orange Dot Quilts. Split Pinwheels - Pattern Design by Dora Cary

This is a PDF pattern that was downloadable. The copyright notice is included on the last page of the pattern. "Copyright 2016 Dora Cary." Under the copyright notice, the rights statement:

> All images and artwork are property of the author and the author retains copyright after sale. All rights reserved. For more insights, coupons, and giveaways follow Orange Dot Quilts on Facebook and on Instagram (@orangedoquilts.)

So, she retains all rights under copyright. She seems to focus on the artwork and the images, rather than the directions, which is terrific. If she does not want the digital pattern sold, I would encourage including something like that to make it clear to the general public, even though copyright experts would know this: "Digital pattern downloads are not for resale or transfer, and are a license to use the pattern for personal use only."

Flying Parrot Quilts – Spooky Spider

The copyright on this one, "designed by Sylvia Schaefer @ 2016" has all the parts necessary. The rights statement: "All rights reserved. This pattern is for the use of the person and may not be reproduced or distributed without express written permission. For personal use only."

So, this is a paper pattern. I can re-distribute it. First Sale Doctrine allows me to resell, give it away, do anything I want with my physical copy, except make copies of the pattern and sell/give away those copies. Regarding making copies, the pattern itself is foundation piecing. The preparation directions. "With the copier set to 100% or Actual Size, make copies of the paper piecing templates...." So, what the rights statement is trying to say is that you can use and copy the pattern for personal use. She doesn't want you to take away her potential sale by making copies for your friends.

Explore Walking Foot Quilting with Leah Day

This is a self-published book by a very famous quilter. Her copyright notice and rights statement are worth looking at.

> Published in 2017 by Day Style Designs, Inc.
> All rights reserved. Apart from any fair dealing for the purpose of private study, research, criticism or review, no part of this publication may be reproduced, stored in a retrieval system in any form or in any means, electronic, electrical, chemical, mechanical, optical, photocopying, recording, or otherwise without the prior written permission of the copyright owner. Inquiries should be addressed to the publisher.
>
> We have taken great care to ensure that the information included in this book is accurate and presented in good faith, but no warranty is provided nor results guaranteed. Having no control over the choices of materials or procedures used, neither the author nor Day Style Designs shall have any liability to any person or entity with respect to any loss or damage caused directly or indirectly by the information contained in this book.
>
> Any similarities to existing designs, graphics or patterns are purely coincidental.
>
> Text, photographs and illustrations, Copyright © 2017 Leah Day.

Ok. Let's break this down. Leah is recognizing fair use (she uses the Canadian and British version, "fair dealings"), and she recognizes that some fair uses are permitted under the law. Fair use is broader than what she includes, but it is one of the few rights statements that does recognize fair use. The next sentence about reproduction is pretty broad, including "chemical" copies. Like other books, some of the pages in the book require you to make copies, and so I would have preferred her to include, "Copying for personal use at the direction of the author is permitted." It's also interesting that the book seems to be copyrighted by her company, but the specific text, images, and photographs remain under her personal copyright. That's interesting. I'm curious about that split.

Martingale Books

Martingale books all have the same pattern of copyright notice and rights information. First, the copyright is in the author's name, or in Martingale's. Second, two significant paragraphs are included in each book. Let's begin with **180 Doodle Quilting Designs by Karen M. Burns.** This book was published by That Patchwork Place, a Martingale publication and a big player in the quilt world.

> © 2016 by Martingale and Company.

Karen Burns, in this case, does not hold the copyright; Martingale does. She is the editor, or in this case the compiler. The selection, arrangement, and coordination of the book was done by

Burns, but there were other contributors. The authors likely signed a contract that assigned their copyright to Martingale in their individual pieces. Each of the 180 patterns is designed by one of nine designers that include Angela Walters, Christa Watson, and others. The rights statement: "No part of this product may be reproduced in any form, unless otherwise stated, in which case reproduction is limited to the use of the purchaser."

Ok. So, a bit too broad for copyright, but trying to protect from wholesale copying. If I need to copy a page, then it is limited to me copying it for my use. That is what it seems to say. It continues...

> The written instructions, photographs, designs, projects, and patterns are intended for personal noncommercial use of the retail purchaser and are under federal copyright laws, they are not to be reproduced by any electronic, mechanical, or other means, including informational storage or retrieval systems, for commercial use.

So, you can't copy and put these into a commercial database, among other things. And it continues.... "Permission is granted to photocopy patterns for the personal use of the retail purchaser." They said that already. But it's good to have it explicit. I can make a copy.

And they continue: "Attention teachers: Martingale encourages you to use this book for teaching, subject to the restrictions stated above." I'm not exactly sure what that means. I think they want teachers to have their students purchase a copy of the book. But let's say I bring 20 books to a FMQ class, and the students can use books there. That is totally acceptable; I purchased the books--the sale was made. They can't photocopy the books. Or let's say, I'm teaching a class and I want to compare half-square triangle methods, and I make copies from five different books to compare and hand it out to the class. That is totally okay too under Section 107 of the copyright act. I'm teaching. Now, if I'm using this book and we are working through it –then the students should purchase it. And if they liked it in class when I brought the 20 books, they should purchase it.

There's more:

> The information in this book is presented in good faith but no warranty is given nor results guaranteed. Since Martingale has no control over choice of materials or procedures, the company assumes no responsibility for the use of this information.

So, a disclaimer. What is interesting about the book is like Leah Day's book, the book focuses on motifs you can use in your quilts. So, the concern is likely not copying the book, not the directions and techniques taught in the book, right?

We looked at other Martingale books: Fast and Fun Baby Quilts; Piece and Quilt with Precuts by Christa Watson (This time, © 2017 By Christa Watson); Cheerful Charm Quilts; and The Splendid Sampler by Pat Sloan and Jane Davidson (© 2017 by Pat Sloan and Jane Davidson); and The New Hexagon by Katja Marek (Copyright: © 2014 by Katja Marek). The copyright notice and rights statement is the same.

Adding Copyright Notice to Your Quilts?

If you add copyright notice © Name Year, that means that no one can be an "innocent infringer." If you care about that quilt, do what Paula Nadelstern does, and register those quilts with the U.S. Copyright Office. You can register up to 10 quilts (in the unpublished category) at the U.S. Copyright Office. This is a great opportunity. It costs $55 to register ten works. For more information on fees, go to https://www.copyright.gov/about/fees.html.

Scott Murkin has included the name of the quilt, his address, phone number, email and domain name, along with the month, year and ©. (No photo included for privacy reasons.)

And here is Carla Zahl Jolman. Again, exactly what needs to be included, and I would encourage just adding a © to that date. But the custom has not necessarily been to do that. How important is this? It depends on how a court would respond. The © alerts the world that you are asserting your automatic copyright.

Thinking Like an Entrepreneur

When thinking about your rights statements, put on your entrepreneur hat and ask yourself, what is the purpose of the work I am offering to the public, and what do I have to communicate in its use.

Free patterns: you want them to circulate so that people come to your site to pay for patterns (or get more free ones). That's what big fabric companies are doing. They are using the free patterns as bait to get you to buy fabric. You may have the same idea. Sometimes patterns are free for a time –e.g. Bonnie Hunter's Mystery Quilt or Pat Sloan's Splendid Sampler. They start out to invite the public to use the pattern, often distributing one bit at a time over a number of weeks or months. Then once the pattern is out there, they pull the free version and offer a full paid version.

Form:

> **Digital Copies**: Digital copies are considered licensed works, and therefore not for sale. First Sale Doctrine doesn't apply. You can't share or resell digital copies. But they are so much easier to transfer. You might think of putting a username/password on digital copies so that they are not easily transferable.
>
> **Paper copies:** These can be resold, given to a friend, and even shared. Think of a novel. You can read it, let a friend borrow it, sell it at a used bookshop, and even tear it up or burn it. The physical copy is yours. So, as an entrepreneur, why not encourage this? Be creative. Create an email bank. "If you share this with a friend, let us know! We'd love to get to know them. Go to our website and register. We'll send you and your friend updates and a free pattern."

Allow commercial uses? So many pattern makers and others shy away from commercial uses. They are afraid someone else will make money off of their pattern. Why not? Allow licenses for commercial uses, but decide what kind: micro commercial uses (like Etsy sales or local sales) or even large-scale commercial uses by manufacturers. Put that information in the rights statement. Provide license opportunities. Allow sewists to make versions of your patterns to sell. Even suggest ways to help them in their endeavor. You become a hero instead of a policing agent. You could even have a subscription service for patterns that could be used commercially.

Register your Works. Defend your property. If you are serious about defending your patterns, register your work with the U.S. Copyright Office. Without registration, you cannot enforce your copyright in court. You can also include that you have registered the work in a cease and desist letter, and threaten that any infringement is considered willful and could cost up to $150,000 plus the costs of litigating. It gives you teeth. And if you do so, potentially payment of attorney's fees and the statutory damages described above. Litigation is hard. But as a weapon, registration helps deter infringers. They will get to know that yours are not patterns they should copy.

Idea/Expression. Make sure that what they have taken is more than merely the idea and not expression, and be careful yourself to recognize whether you have taken others' expressions (even subconsciously) yourself.

Value. You also have to think about what is of value. Martingale (a huge publisher) offered free downloads on a number of pages of its Splendid Sampler 2 book. It knows that it is out there. Are they going to go out and police uses after the book comes out in October? Only those really egregious uses: those selling them, likely, or doing something that catches their attention. Their goal is to get more sales of the book and putting out bits of the pattern seems to increase sales. That's why they are doing it again.

Classes, Groups, and Guilds. Create special packets, including special teacher's instructions for classes, groups, and guilds, with pricing that includes packets of materials. You could do guild-only packets too, where the pattern is only available for guilds or groups. An exclusive-only pattern. ByAnnie does packages of 25 for their instructions, for example.

The Package. Make the pattern in a way that you want the original pattern and not a copy. The beauty of the pattern is coveted. Make collecting the pattern itself something people want to do. Quiltfolk magazine is a great example.

Trademark, Not Copyright. Copyright does not protect the math of patterns or directions. What's a pattern maker to do? Trademark. If people come to know your brand because your directions are wonderful, or because they love your designs, they will come back. That's ByAnnie again. People love them. That's Leah Day's teaching. They love her. Make your brand something people want again and again. That's Tula Pink.

Super Fans v. Freeloaders. Quilters purchase a lot of things. Some quilters purchase more than others. Recognize there will always be freeloaders. But there will potentially be fans, even super fans that buy everything you do. Focus on those fans.

Don't be Buffy. The stories of Buffy the Vampire Slayer may not even be true. When fans first started to use the Internet to upload pictures, the owners of Buffy wanted to stop them from copyright infringement. Don't mess with your fans. Think about what your fans need, how to build your brand and encourage sharing while at the same time bringing in revenue.

Readings Rights Statement: To Consumers (all of us) of Patterns

So, when you see a copyright notice on a pattern, understand what that means.

- The copyright holder *cares* about their intellectual property in that pattern.
- See if there are restrictions on the use. You should be able to do that before you purchase the pattern.
- Contact the copyright holder (even if they haven't said so) if you are going to use it in a commercial manner, or for more than just your own personal use.

Creating Rights Statements

If you are a pattern or other craft-maker, make sure to make it clear and helpful on what you want:

- Did you put © or "copyright", your name and the date on the work?
- Rights Statement. Choose what you feel most comfortable. Remember the option of Creative Commons or commons-like license to help people know the parameters of the use of the work.
- Did you include whether the work could be used commercially, or only for non-commercial purposes?
- Did you include information for guilds and groups?
- Did you include whether you require the use of attribution?
- Did you include whether you permit derivative works to be made?
- Did you include a way for people to contact you to ask permission to use the work?

We've included a checklist for creating a notice next. You always have the option of just putting © Elizabeth Townsend Gard 2020. All rights Reserved. But you can let the world know that you will let them do other things, without giving up your rights as a copyright holder.

The © Notice Checklist

Making A Copyright Notice and Rights Statement

Mandatory Parts:

- [ ] Copyright or ©
- [ ] Name of Copyright Proprietor (person or company that holds the "rights" to the copyright holder at the time of publication.
- [ ] Year of first publication (and sometimes revisions)

Why include this?

- Puts the world on notice that you are planning to enforce your rights
- No "innocent infringer" defense available if there is a notice included

Rights Statement Choices

Rights statements help tell the world how you feel about your copyright. These are not mandatory. The default without a rights statement is that the copyright holder retains all the rights under Section 106 (reproduction, distribution, derivative work, public display, public performance). Note: these are not absolute rights, and a quilt show is not necessarily considered public display (according to one court). Including a rights statement is encouraged.

- [ ] **All rights reserved.** You want to control as many uses as possible.

This is the default protection. Any uses other than permitted and fair uses, including library exceptions, first sale, etc.) are under the authority of the copyright holder. This means usually permission in the form of an exclusive license, a non-exclusive license or an assignment is needed for further uses.

- [ ] **No Rights Reserved.** The least control. You claim ownership but you don't care how people use it, even in a commercial context. This is also sometimes called CCo (Creative Commons Zero).

    - [ ] Feel free to use this pattern, even for commercial purposes, without asking permission. You may make derivative works, make copies and distribute freely.

    - [ ] Option: right of attribution. Please include "Original pattern by ______." when you use this pattern.

- [ ] **Creative Commons License**

    - [ ] **Attribution**. Please include the following for any use of the pattern: "Original pattern created by Elizabeth Townsend Gard, Copyright 2019.

- ☐ **Derivatives Allowed.** You may create derivative works (your own version) of this pattern.

- ☐ **Sharealike.** You may use this pattern but are required to share your versions with others freely as well.

- ☐ **Commercial Uses.**

    - ☐ **Commercial Uses.** You may use this pattern for commercial use without additional fees.

    - ☐ **Noncommercial Uses.** You may only use this for non-commercial and/or personal uses. No commercial activity is allowed. Please write for permission to any retail sale of the products created from or copies of the pattern itself.

    - ☐ **Guilds or Groups.**

        - ☐ **Permission Required.** If you are a group or guild and would like to use this pattern, please email the copyright holder, [name] [email].

        - ☐ **Permission Granted.** Guilds and quilting groups may use this pattern without additional permission, even for fundraisers and charity events.

    - ☐ **Registered.** This pattern has been registered with the U.S. Copyright Office, and any infringement could be up to $150,000 in damages.

    - ☐ Nothing in the rights statement is meant to interfere with any exceptions or limitations under the U.S. Copyright law, including fair use, library exceptions, and the first sale doctrine.

Other options:

- ☐ **Charity Quilts.** Feel free to use the pattern for charity purposes.

- ☐ **Low Commercial uses.** You may obtain a license for commercial uses of the pattern on Etsy, your own website, and in situations where you are making less than $50,000 year as a business. Please email ___________.

- ☐ **Elements in the Public Domain.** Some elements used are in the public domain, as are the techniques. The expression of those elements took time and energy to create this pattern. Please respect the expression and make sure to purchase a pattern. Your purchase supports pattern-makers.

☐ **Underlying Work.** This work is based on a work by ________, Title, year.

> ☐ Permission by the copyright holder has been granted to use the underlying work within this new, derivative work. 17 U.S.C. Section 106.

☐ **No Warranty**: The author has in good faith believes the information is accurate, but no warranty is given for the results or information.

☐ **Digital Download.** "Digital pattern downloads are not for resale or transfer, and are a license to use the pattern for personal use only."

11: Registering Your Work

Get to Know the Copyright Office – www.copyright.gov

Copyright arises automatically upon fixation; when you make, write, or draw something, it has copyright. To have power, registration at the U.S. Copyright Office is necessary. Registration allows you to sue in court, and if you win a lawsuit, you may elect statutory damages (up to $150,000 for willful infringement) and attorney's fees may even be awarded in some cases. But more importantly, registration tells others in the world how to find you, in case they want to seek a license from you. And of course, registration allows the U.S. Customs to seize illegal copies of your work for you, too! Registration is important. It lets the world know that you care about your work –that you took the time to make a public record of its existence, and provide information about the work, including authorship.

A Short, Important Story

Paula Nadelstern is an important, famous quilter. She is also famous for a lawsuit she brought for copyright infringement, which she won in settlement! I interviewed her recently. She said the only reason she could even bring a lawsuit is that her publisher, C & T, had registered her book, which gave her the ability to file a lawsuit and attract an attorney to take her case. Now, she religiously registers each of her major quilts after she completes them. She said she gets them appraised and she registers them. Hers is the story about the importance of registration. We'll look at Paula's copyright infringement story in the next chapter. For now, the lesson is: if you care that someone might swipe your work, register it now.

Return on Investment: Set up a System

Another way to think about registration is the return on investment. A new decision from the U.S. Supreme Court, *Fourth Estate Public Benefit Corp. v. Wall-Street.com*, 586 U.S. ___ (2019), has confirmed how important registration is. First, a work must have a registration certificate, and not merely an application to file a complaint in court. Registration takes up to 18 months. So, think about registering *before the problem occurs.* You cannot file a lawsuit, have teeth related to sending a cease and desist letter or follow through on a notice-and-takedown through Internet Service Providers (ISPs) without registering your copyright. If you register within three months of publication, registration allows you to reach back to any infringement that occurred even before registration. Alternatively, you can do an expedited registration once there is trouble. You do not get the benefit of statutory damages applying to infringement prior to registration, and only actual damages (which is harder to determine) for infringement occurring before registration. You are gambling on the need for registration. You will have to wait until the registration certificate is complete before filing a lawsuit.

Strategy

So, deciding when and how to register your copyrighted works is a strategy. And we see interesting trends. Book publishers consistently register works. Photographers often don't, but are doing so more in recent years. The recording industry regularly registers their works, as do content owners. Two very different approaches can be seen from different fabric companies: Jaftex and Michael Miller. Jaftex relies on expedited registrations. They have 50 to 60 lines of fabric, and so they find registering each design as unworkable. It's just not practical, said president Scott Fortunoff, for them to register each collection or each item in a collection. In contrast, fabric company Michael Miller registers *all of their designs*. So, think of the Copyright Registration as part of your business. Either keep it as part of your process (once you finish a work, you register it before you put it on sale), or you have a time that you regularly register (once a year, the 21st of every month, etc.) Or, expedite the registration (and pay more) when there is a problem. You do not need an attorney to register your works. You can learn to register them yourself.

Do you need to register everything? No. You are registering works you feel are valuable -- the ones that if someone swiped them you would be very unhappy about. The blog post you wrote this morning? Well, probably not. But maybe if that is really important to you, you will.

If you think you are going to pursue someone if they infringe, then you should register. If you are going to be a "let the chips fall where they may" kind of person, then you really don't need to register. But again, take note: the big companies register their works. They know that without registration, the copyright isn't very strong.

Choosing the Form

Once you choose the form, you will be asked for the type of work.

TX: literary
VA: visual arts
PA: performing arts
SR: sound recording

You choose the one that makes the most sense for the work.

So how do you register a work?

It's easy. You go to the Copyright Office's website: www.copyright.gov. You have to choose a category to register the works: literary, visual, performing arts, or sound recording. Once your application is submitted, the full registration process takes around seven months.

The Deposit Requirement

The deposit requirement varies depending on what type of work is being registered.

> Published work: two copies
> Unpublished and foreign works: one copy

For artwork that is unpublished, has a limited edition, only one version, or it is an expensive item, you can send in a photograph.

Published artworks with circulating copies require a deposit of the object, and not a photograph.

Disclaiming pre-existing work

As part of the registration application, make sure to disclaim work that is not part of the copyright, that is public domain works, pre-existing works, etc. Here is an example from the Compendium:

> Theresa Tell creates a collage that combines her own artwork with logos from a number of famous companies. She files an application to register her "two-dimensional artwork." Depending on the facts presented, the registration specialist may ask the applicant to exclude the logos from the claim by stating, "preexisting logos incorporated" in the Material Excluded field. In addition, the specialist may ask Theresa to limit her claim by stating, "selection and arrangement of preexisting logos with new two-dimensional artwork added" in the New Material Included field.

Filling Out the Registration Form

Once you are ready to file your own copyright registration, create an account at the U.S. Copyright Office.

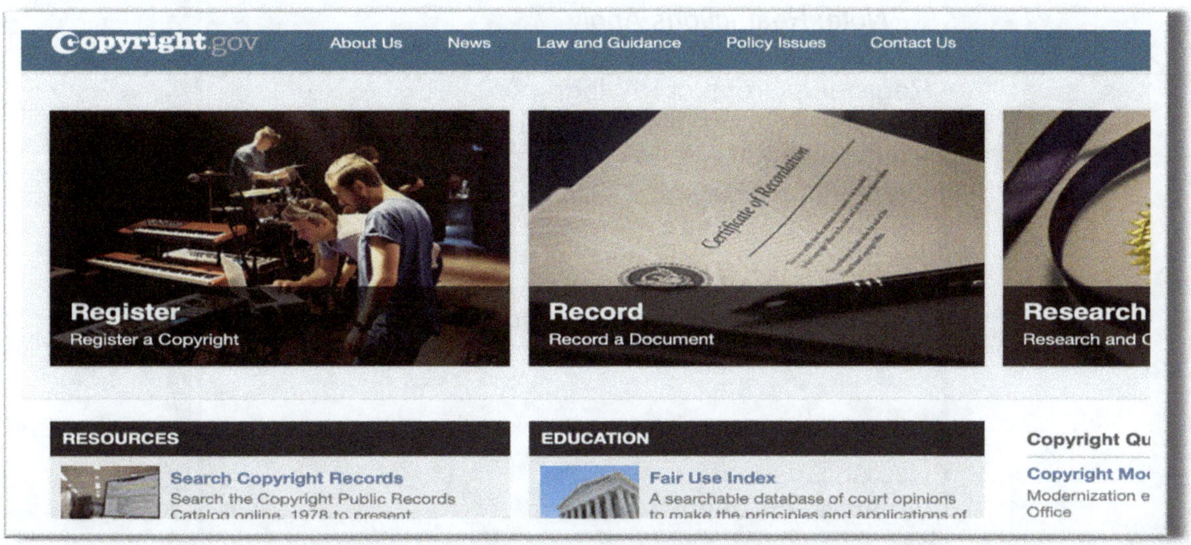

This screen (below) looks a bit intimidating. Never fear. We are here. The registration filing is based on both the type of work and also a few other factors. Let's walk through the choices.

Look at the left-hand column. You have some choices:

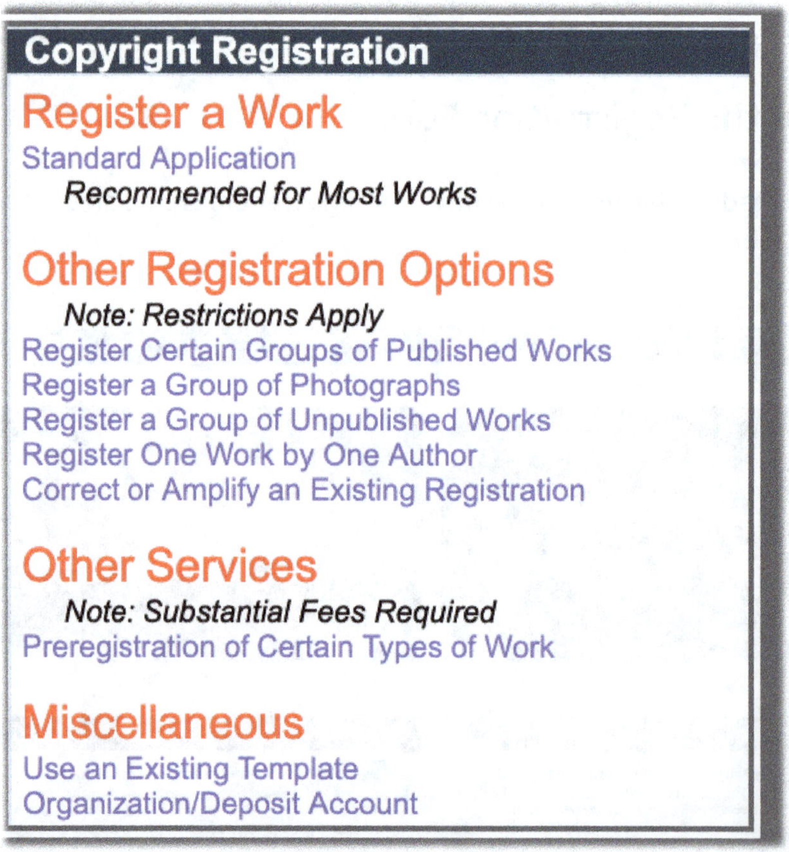

1. Standard Application:

Most works fall under this application. The author can be a single author, a joint author, a work for hire, and even an anonymous or pseudonymous author. You can also use this form to register a collective work authorship (see below), and an individual component work of a collective work (again, see below). There are certain works that cannot use this standard application: groups of unpublished works, groups of photographs, groups of serials, newspapers, or newsletters, or groups of contributions published in a periodical.

Collective Works: where a number of separate and independent contributors are assembled into a collective whole. "A registration for a collective work covers the collective work as a whole and may cover the individual works contained in it if (1) the collective work and the individual works are owned by the same party, (2) the individual works have not been previously published or previously registered, and (3) the individual works are not in the public domain." Circular 34, Multiple Works, https://www.copyright.gov/circs/circ34.pdf.

The Copyright Office provides a list of what counts and does not count as a Collective Work for registration purposes.

For purposes of registration, representative examples of collective works include:

• A newspaper, magazine, or other periodical containing multiple articles, illustrations, and photographs
• An anthology containing multiple poems, short stories, or essays
• An online encyclopedia containing multiple articles, entries, or postings on various topics
• An album containing multiple sound recordings that embody multiple musical works
• A DVD containing a motion picture, theatrical trailers, deleted scenes, and audio commentary from the director

A collective work is not[14]

- a single unified work that contains separate parts or elements, such as
- a novel consisting of multiple chapters
- a song with melody, harmony, and rhythm
- a drawing in pencil and ink
- a carpet design of overlapping figures and colors
- an architectural work or technical drawing with multiple illustrations of the same object
- an illustrated children's book created by one author
- a unified work created by multiple authors, such as
- a musical work created by a singer and songwriter in collaboration with each other
- a musical with script, music, and lyrics by two or more authors
- a motion picture with screenplay, soundtrack, directing, acting, cinematography, costume design,
- visual effects, or other production elements contributed by multiple authors

[14] Circular 34, Multiple Works, U.S. Copyright Office, https://www.copyright.gov/circs/circ34.pdf

- a children's book created by a writer and illustrator in collaboration with each other
- a textbook
- a single contribution to a collective work

Contribution to a Collective Work

You can register your contribution to a collective work separately. This includes an article within a periodical, a song on an album, or a photograph that appears in a newspaper or magazine.

Registration Options for Collective Works and Contributions to Collective Works:

You can register the collective work and the individual works under one application, but the individual works must also be from the author of the collective work, and the individual works cannot have been previously published or previously registered.

Damages consideration: If you register a collective work, it is considered one work for the purposes of damages.[15] If you register individual works within the collective work, each of those registrations is calculated separately, and so potentially more damages could be awarded.

2. One Work by One Author

This application is for **one work**, by **one individual, an**d the work is not a **work for hire** and **does not include pre-existing materials.** For example, one poem, one song or one photograph. For instance, Ricardo Gonzalez's *Just Wanna Patent* qualifies as a single application. The current cost is $35, but will likely be raised to $45 in Spring 2020. The Copyright Office has a video to explain the process. See https://www.copyright.gov/eco/single.mp4. This video takes you step by step through the registration application. Note: you cannot use this application if the work contains pre-existing material, including materials created and included by others that you are excluding from the application.

---

[15] "Section 504(c)(1) of the Copyright Act states that a copyright owner may be entitled to recover "an award of statutory damages for all infringements involved in the [infringement] action, with respect to any one work," and "[f]or the purposes of this subsection, all the parts of a compilation . . . constitute one work." Circular 34, Multiple Works, U.S. Copyright Office, https://www.copyright.gov/circs/circ34.pdf.

3. Group Registration

"Generally, you may only register one work per application but there are several exceptions to this rule." FAQ, Copyright Office, https://www.copyright.gov/help/faq/faq-register.html Some works can be registered in groups, which make it more affordable to register works. But be aware, it impacts on potential statutory damages. The collection, for award purposes, is treated as one work. So, what do people do? These are a group of related works that can be registered under one application and one filing fee. There are only a few types of works that qualify:

- Unpublished works
- Serials
- Newspapers
- Newsletters
- Contributions to periodicals
- Published photographs
- Unpublished photographs
- Database updates and revisions
- Questions, answers, and other items prepared for use in a secure test.

Unpublished Works: Unpublished works can be registered as a group of up to ten works. There are restrictions. They must all be unpublished, and created by the same author or joint authors, with the authors being the named copyright claimants, with the works being the same type (e.g. "unpublished illustrations," "unpublished musical compositions," or "unpublished jewelry designs"). Each work must have a title. You cannot register different types of works on the same application. The Copyright Office has provided a tutorial to walk you through the application of a group of unpublished works. Tip: if you are planning to publish works, you might think of registering them as unpublished under this grouping to save money. You do not need to re-register them when they are published to get the statutory benefits of registration. See the tutorial from the U.S. Copyright Office: https://stream-media.loc.gov/copyright/gruw.mp4. What is cool about this is you can file up to 10 unpublished works under one registration record. If you make substantial changes or want to re-register it when it is published, you can do that, too. The works are treated as individual works, not as a collection of works. Ten short stories, not an anthology of stories, UNLESS you claim the unpublished as an unpublished collective work, rather than a collection of works.

Bundled Physical Packages: this is a really interesting option. If you have a physical package that contains separately fixed works that have been bundled together for distribution to the public as a single, integrated unit, you can register it as a group registration. Here are the examples the U.S. Copyright Office gives:[16]

- A board game with playing pieces, game board, and written instructions
- A bound volume published with a dust jacket
- A book published with a CD-ROM
- A multimedia kit containing a book, a compact disc, and a set of stickers

---

[16] Circular 34, "Multiple Works," U.S. Copyright Office, https://www.copyright.gov/circs/circ34.pdf

- A compact disc containing multiple sound recordings packaged together with liner notes and cover artwork
- A box set containing multiple compact discs containing multiple sound recordings, packaged together with a booklet containing liner notes and photographs
- A multi-DVD package with a disc containing a motion picture, a disc containing trailers and deleted scenes from the motion picture, and a disc containing interviews with the director and the cast
- A physical package containing a computer program and a user's manual
- A physical package containing a video game, cover artwork, and written instructions for installing the game
- A package of greeting cards
- A jewelry set of a necklace and earrings that are sold to the public as a single unit.

What are the requirements? Each element must be a self-contained work, and must be first published as a single unit on the same date. The Copyright claimant must be the same on all units. It must be a physical copy and must be distributed to the general public. Important: "[The work] cannot be created solely for the purpose of registering the work with the Copyright Office."[17]

Contributions of periodicals: if you have created separate and independent work that has been published in a periodical, you can register your work as a contribution to a periodical. This includes newspapers, magazines, and journals.[18] You use the group registration form. This is called "GRCP". You will need to list the contributions in chronological order. The works can be in different periodicals and on different dates, with no limit on number of contributions. You have to have a least two contributions to use this form. All contributions must have been created by the author; the works must not be work for hire, the copyright claimant is the same person/entity for all contributions, and *each contribution was published within a twelve-month period, Jan-Dec of the particular year.* Here is a walkthrough tutorial for contributions to periodicals: *https://www.copyright.gov/eco/cp-transcript.pdf* and the accompanying video: https://www.copyright.gov/eco/grcp.mp4.

Newsletters: Newsletters can be registered with the U.S. Copyright office, as long as there are at least two issues, and neither of them have been previously published. They must be "fixed and distributed as a discrete, self-contained work."[19] The issues have to be published in the same time, with the same claimant. Issues must be published within the same calendar month, and must bear issue dates within the month. You submit one complete copy of each issue. This is a huge limitation. Ideally, it has an ISSN number for the newsletter.

Published photographs: You can register up to 750 photographs that have been published within the same calendar year created by the same author. Make up a title for the group, and sequentially number them, and you are good to go. You use a template that the U.S. Copyright

---

[17] Id.

[18] Definition: periodicals are published on an established schedule (daily, weekly monthly). See https://www.copyright.gov/eco/grcp.mp4.

[19] Help: Daily Newsletters, U.S. Copyright Office, https://www.copyright.gov/eco/help-newsletters.html.

Office provides. For more information, go to:
https://www.copyright.gov/eco/help/group/grpph.html

Unpublished photographs: this is up to 750 photographs in one application. Like published photographs, they must be by the same author, but there doesn't seem to be the one-year requirement.

Here is a handy table created by the U.S. Copyright Office.[20]

Registration Requirements	*Group Registration of Published or Unpublished Photographs*	*Group Registration of Contributions to Periodicals*	*Group Registration of Unpublished Works*
Type of work	Each work must be a photograph	Each work must be a visual arts or literary work	The application may be used for any type of work; however, each work in the group must be the same type
Application requirements	The applicant must use the online application	The applicant must use the online application	The applicant must use the online application
Number of photographs in the application	The applicant may include up to 750 photographs in the group	No limit on the number of works that may be included in the application	The applicant may include up to ten works in the group
Author	All the photographs must be taken by the same author	All the works must be created by the same author	All the works must be created by the same author or authors
Claimant	The claimant for all the photographs must be the same person or organization	The claimant for all the works must be the same person or organization	All of the authors must be listed as copyright claimant
Work made for hire	The photographs may be created as works made for hire	The works cannot be created as works made for hire	The works may be created as works made for hire
Publication	All the photographs in the group must be either published or unpublished. Unpublished and published works may not be combined on the same application.	All the works must be published	All the works must be unpublished

[20] Circular 62C, "Copyright Registration of Contributions to Periodicals,' U.S. Copyright Office, https://www.copyright.gov/circs/circ62c.pdf, p. 4.

As you work your way through the registration process, here are a few things to consider:

Author: Unless you are filling this out for someone else, or you have created the works in the course of your employment (and you are not for tax purposes an independent contractor), you are likely the author. You have to be either creating the work within the course of your employment, or it is a commissioned work that falls under the nine enumerated categories in 17 U.S.C Section 101.

Claimant: Unless you have assigned, transferred, sold, or licensed your rights to someone else, you are likely the claimant. If you have done any of the above, then the person controlling the copyright is the claimant.

Limitation of Claim: Here is where you disclaim anything for which you are not claiming copyright. So, if you recognize that some parts of what you are doing are in the public domain, for instance, or are based on another's work, you can place that info here.

Rights and Permissions: Who is allowed to give out rights and permissions? Usually this would be you, but you could put someone else down.

Correspondent: Who does the Copyright Office contact if they have questions?

Special Handling: If you check this box, you are expediting your application (in expectation of litigation), and you will pay a hefty fee. You would do this if you believe there has been infringement of your non-registered work, and you are planning to go to court. This would allow you to register the work quickly. It would not cover you for any infringement before the registration certificate issues. But it will quickly allow you to be able to go to court and collect (if you win) statutory damages. Special handling usually takes around five business working days and has an extra $800 cost.

You then pay the fees, and you also have to submit copies of the work. You can either upload them or mail them. You can upload lots of file types including .jpg, .gif, .pdf, .tif, .psd., and .bmp.

Costs

U.S. Copyright Office fees to register a work vary:

Basic registration: $35 (single author, same claimant, one work, not for hire)
Standard: $55
Preregistration for certain unpublished works: $140

There are a bunch of different types of group registration:

$25 Serials, per issue, minimum two issues.
$80 Newspapers (online) or newsletters
$85 Contributions to periodicals
$55 Published or unpublished photographs
$85 GATT form (for older foreign works)
$55 Ten unpublished works

Here is a link to the fee rates: https://www.copyright.gov/about/fees.html. **Note: the fees are expected to rise in Spring 2020, but at the time of writing the official fee schedule has not been published.** [21]

Special Handling/Expedited service. Special handling is an expedited method of obtaining a copyright registration from the U.S. Copyright Office. You can only request special handling if there is "[a] pending or prospective litigation, [b] customs matter, or [c] contract or publishing deadline that necessitates the expedited issuance of a certificate." With special handling, the registration process takes about five business days. The fee for special handling starts at $800, as of 2020, but may change in the Spring.

What is the difference between registration or pre-registration? Most works are registered as either published or unpublished. The pre-registration category was designed for films, music, literary works, and other popular items that might get stolen before the release date, and so needed extra protection. If you are creating patterns and/or books, and want this extra protection, you qualify. However, pre-registration comes at a price: $140 along with the additional fee for actual registration fees. So, if you are not afraid of pirates on the Internet stealing your work before it is released to the public, you really don't need to do pre-registration.

---

[21] Note: there is a proposal for fees to go up in Spring 2020, but they have not yet been implemented at the time of writing. Many of the fees remain the same, or increase by $10: Basic registration would go up $10 to $45; a55 to $65; registration of a group of photographs remains at $55; series goes from $25 to $35; newspapers increase from $85 to $90, registration of a claim in a restored copyright goes from $85 to $100, A group of up to 10 unpublished works goes from $55 to $85, which is concerning. The very big jump is for updates and revisions to a photographic database, which goes from $55 to $250, among a few other database-related categories. Two new categories are being proposed: registration of a group of short online literary works at $65, and a group for musical works, sound recordings, and associated literary, pictorial, and graphic works contained on an album for $65.

The New Proposed Category: Group for Short Online Literary Works

The Copyright Office has proposed a new category "group of short online literary works," which would cost $65. If it becomes an option, it will likely be defined as works that are 100 words to 17,500 words. Think poems, articles, blog entries, and social media posts. You would designate it a "literary work," and can upload 50 works with one application and filing fee. But each application is for a three-month period.

Regroup and Strategize

That was a lot to take in. Registration is important, in certain circumstances. And there are ways to strategize.[22]

1. **Single Work**. A less expensive way than a standard application, and you are the only author, and it is not a work for hire.
2. **Unpublished works.** This is a great deal. Register up to ten of your works before you put them out, and they are protected even after they are published as individual works.
3. **Contributions published in a periodical.** This is a way to register a number of patterns and articles that were published in a periodical in the same year. Then, you could release them individually as patterns.
4. **Newsletters.** If your newsletters have material that you would like to protect, you can register them as a group every three months.
5. **Photographs:** unpublished allow you to register 750 at a time, but it protects the photograph and not the underlying work.
6. **Collective work.** You can register your works as a collective work -- register the patterns as a book, and then all of them are protected.
7. **Physical Bundle.** If you sell separately copyrightable works as a bundle, you can register them under one application.
8. **Short Online Literary Works.** We'll have to see if this becomes a choice!

What saved Paula Nadelstern is that the quilts that were infringed had been registered in the book, and the book is what was used to infringe. She had not registered the individual quilts. Now she does. If the quilts matter to you, register them. If the book about the quilt matters, register that. Think about what you need protected. There are lots of ways to register your works. Be clever. Protect your works.

[22] And what does the Compendium have to say? "As a general rule, it is not possible to register a group of pictorial, graphic, or sculptural works with one application, one filing fee, and a submission of identifying material. Instead, the applicant generally must submit a separate claim for each work. However, there are two limited exceptions to this rule. • If the works are unpublished it may be possible to register them as an unpublished collection. Photographs or illustrations of the two- or three-dimensional works may be used as identifying material in this situation, provided that the applicant asserts a claim in the works depicted in those images rather than the authorship involved in creating the images themselves. • If the works were physically bundled together for distribution to the public as a single, integrated unit and if all the works were first published in that integrated unit, it may be possible to register them using the unit of publication option. When a group of photographs are published in a catalog the works depicted therein are considered published, regardless of whether they are two- or three-dimensional. However, the fact that a group of works were published in the same catalog does not necessarily mean that the catalog constitutes a unit of publication or that the works may be registered together with the unit of publication option." Compendium III, Section 914

12: Exclusive Rights and Infringement

Rights of the Copyright Holder

We discussed briefly a couple of time the five-exclusive rights copyright bestows upon an author when we discussed rights statements. Let's look again at these rights more in depth, and in the context of infringement. To refresh, upon fixation and meeting the minimum requirements of independent creation plus a modicum of creativity, the author of a copyrightable work automatically gains the following exclusive rights for "limited times":

1. Right to reproduce (make copies)
2. Right to create derivative works (make new things based on the old thing)
3. Right to distribute copies (post, sell, etc.)
4. Right to publicly perform (show a movie, perform a play)
5. Right to publicly display

We want to understand what the rights are, and what happens when someone infringes those rights. Infringement occurs when someone uses a copyrighted work without permission. The question is what qualifies as infringement. Copyright has developed tests for this. These exclusive rights are not absolute. There are permissible uses of a copyrighted work by a third party, even without permission of the copyright holder and even before the work goes into the public domain.

Now, with every exclusive right, there are exceptions. We'll talk more about this soon. Property does not give one an absolute property right to an object. We teach our law students that there may be times that even when you own a house, there may be reasons that others can enter the property—someone happens upon a cabin when it is snowing and they are lost, they can enter the property, for example. So, too, with copyright. Fair use and library exceptions are the most well-known. And, the most prevalent version of exact copying is something we all do every day: the copies made on to our computers as we use the Internet! Copyright law had to come up with a way to say that the copies stored in our RAM as a temporary copy, for instance, was not a copyright violation. But for now, we are talking about copies made on purpose by humans. When is it a violation of copyright to make a copy of a work? Section Four will look at the permissible uses of a work while it is still under copyright, including fair use.

Let's look at the 106 rights of a copyright holder.

#1 - The Right to Reproduce

This is in the name of the right--to make a "copy." The copyright holder has the exclusive right to make copies. What does making a copy mean? It can mean an exact copy. You take a pattern and make a copy in the photocopy machine or scan it into a PDF. Or it can be a not-exact copy, a substantially similar copy. You are a little too inspired by a Georgia O'Keeffe painting, your quilt is now being reproduced by a company in China, and the O'Keeffe estate is not too happy. You may not have even realized that your painting was a subconscious copy—you copied but you didn't even remember seeing the original (scary, right?). When do you know when you have crossed the line from inspired to infringing? That's the big question. And the reverse, when do you know when someone has crossed that infringing line with your work? 17 U.S.C. Section 106(1).

2 Derivative Right

The right to create derivatives works allows you to control that make things based on your work. When does something have enough difference/new materials from the original to be a derivative work? 17 U.S.C. Section 106(2).

#3 Right of Distribution

The right to distribute often connects to right to copy. Someone pirates your work, and they copy it. Now, they want to sell or put it on the Internet. That's the right of distribution. The full right is: "the right to distribute copies...of the copyrighted work to the public by sale or other transfer of ownership, or by rental, lease, or lending." 17 U.S.C. Section 106(3).

#4 Right of Public Performance

Interestingly, the right to publicly perform a copyrighted work is limited to literary, musical, dramatic, choreography, pantomimes, motion pictures and other audiovisual works. Visual works of art do not have a right of public performance. How odd is that!

#5 Public Display

The copyright holder gets to decide where a work is shown. This right stay with the copyright holder unless it is transferred in writing. You can have an implied non-exclusive right without writing.

Right of Reproduction and Infringement

Your right of reproduction: you decide when, and in what manner, someone can make copies of your work. You can license the right to copy and you can sell that right. Faith Ringgold, famous quilter, licensed the right to make posters of her famous quilts to High Museum of Art. A pattern maker licenses the right to use a pattern and images to a magazine. The right to copy is fundamental to copyright.

Cheryl Quilter creates a pattern. Someone else takes that pattern, scans it, and posts it online in a Facebook group. That person has made an exact copy. We talk about this being "piracy." Pirates steal exact copies and then either try to sell the unauthorized copies, or sometimes, just post them on the Internet. Pirates posting for free are very dangerous, too. Now, the problem is, that by doing *either* of these activities, the "pirate" has stolen from Cheryl the potential from charging for and making money from those versions of the pattern. They might even be a market replacement, where someone that would have bought the pattern now does not need to because they already have an exact copy. (Note by making the copy and posting it, the pirate has not only violated Cheryl's 106(a) right to reproduce, but also 106(c) right to distribute.)

Courts are often concerned with how much is taken from the original—the amount, both qualitatively and quantitatively. (We will see this again with fair use.) We want to understand how much is okay to copy. It's easy to see when the whole work is copied. But what about other situations?

De Minimis Copying

When is copying bits of something enough to infringe on the Section 106(1) reproduction right? We talk in copyright about *de minimis copying*--so small that it doesn't really impact on the economics of the original work. The full Latin phrase is "de minimis non curat lex," meaning "the law does not concern itself with trifles."

De minimis copying became particularly prickly when things were filmed in the background in movies or documentaries and then the copyright holders were claiming "copyright infringement." A pinball machine in the film "What Women Want," a baseball game playing in the distance when an interview was taking place, and a baby dancing to a faintly heard Prince song in the background are all real-world examples. The focus of each of these was not the copyrightable work, but somehow parts of them were now part of a new work.

Film "What Woman Want"

The pinball machine in the background in the film *What Women Want*

How does a court determine (and us before it reaches the court stage) when something is *de minimis?* Is Paramount allowed to have a pinball machine in the background of a shot without getting permission from the owners of "Silver Slugger?" To have an infringement suit, the copying, explains the court must be "more than *de minimis*." In the case of films, courts will look to "the length of time the copyrighted work is observable as well as factors such as focus, lighting, camera angles, and prominence." In this case, the court found that the copyrighted work, the pinball machine, was not the focus of the scene, and that it was only on screen for a very short period of time. None of the characters talk about the pinball machine, and the pinball machine is not even fully viewed. *Gottlieb Development LLC v. Paramount Pictures Corp*. 590 F. Supp. 2d 625 (S.D.N.Y. 2008)

A 2018 case involved graffiti. In Gayle v. Home Box Office, HBO won a case involving a scene from the TV series, Vinyl, where a woman walks by a dumpster tagged with graffiti that says, "art we all." The court found two kinds of *de minimis*: "In the copyright arena, *de minimis* can mean a technical violation of a right so trivial that the law will not impose legal consequences, or it can mean that copying has occurred to such a trivial extent as to fall below the quantitative threshold of substantial similarity, which is always a required element of actionable copying." Here the graffiti was barely visible for less than three seconds, was not the focus of the scene, and one would barely have noticed it at all. Fleeting uses, the court explains, are *de* minimis. *Gayle v. Home Box Office, Inc.*, 2018 BL 154554, (S.D.N.Y 2018).

Compare *Gayle* to a decision by the Second Circuit two decades earlier involving a poster of Faith Ringgold's "Church Picnic Story Quilt," which had been a key case in the *de minimis* conversation. Faith Ringgold v. Black Entertainment Television, 26 F. 3d 70 (2d Cir 1997). Faith Ringgold is a famous artist that is best known for her narrative quilts. She began as a painter, but switched to fabric, where she began writing stories into her quilts, with her first one *Who's*

Afraid of Aunt Jemima? (1983). Ringgold also writes children's books, including *Tar Beach* (1991), which is based on her quilt of the same name and has become very famous.

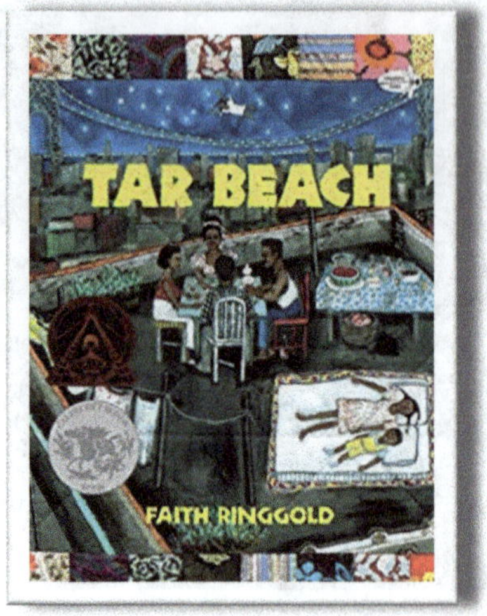

Faith Ringgold's "Church Picnic Story Quilt"

Faith Ringgold's children book

The High Museum had a license to sell poster reproductions of the quilt. In the television series *Roc*, a poster of Ringgold's quilt was used on nine different occasions for a total of 26.75 seconds *without permission from Ringgold*. HBO and BET raised the *de minimis* defense. The court rejected it.

To determine whether *de minimis* applied in this case, the court turned to the Library of Congress' royalty rates to be paid by public broadcasting entities for the use of published pictorial and visual works, which distinguishes between a "featured" and "background" display, setting a higher royalty rate for featured. Featured is defined as "a full-screen or substantially full-screen display for more than three seconds." The court cites to 37 C.F.R. Section 253.8(b)92). Background requires less than full-screen, or full-screen for less than three seconds. The court applied this to the case, finding that the poster was visible for a total of 26 to 27 seconds. Moreover, the poster was chosen because of its significance as recognizable, and well suited for set decoration as an African-American church scene. "The *de minimis* threshold for actionable copying of protected expression has been crossed."

One commentator, Mitchell Zimmerman, suggested that to be *de minimis* a work must not be observable–that the time you see the work is short (under 3 seconds) or that it is blurred and unidentifiable. The pinball case would suggest inconsequential as well. Here again, the pinball machine was not in focus, and not very visible. *De minimis* require the use to be incidental and brief, preferably out of focus, in the background, not significant to the plot, and not readily discernible.[23] *De minimis* has been a significant topic of conversation with music sampling–how much can you take, and does *de minimis* apply? That is beyond the scope of this book, but it is an important issue.

---

[23] "All the world's a stage, and some players are de minimis under copyright law, Fenwick and West LLP, July 10, 2018, https://www.lexology.com/library/detail.aspx?g=629ab392-b698-4f88-ada4-ac6ef49f2a9f.

Independent Creation versus Subconscious Copying

Copyright allows for different creators to create the same work independent of each other. When Victoria Findlay Wolfe says that she doesn't look at other people's work, she is signaling that she creates her works independently. So, we can both create a rainbow quilt. I didn't know about yours. You didn't know about mine. But let's say you want to prove that I *did* know about yours. You would have to prove that I had access to your work and that in fact there was copying. (We'll go over those elements a bit more.) But in short, copyright allows for us both to create rainbow quilts, even using the same idea, and in some cases, if there is independent creation, neither will be infringing of the other. This creates a need for documentation: document your work so you can prove independent creation. This is super, super, super important.

There was a recent discussion on Quilt Pattern Designers about this very subject. Professional quilter and designer Melissa Marginet (www.melissamarginet.ca) writes, "I have designed quilts that I have later seen very similar versions of. I know I didn't copy anyone, and I don't believe they copied me either. ... I like simple geometric designs and the chance of someone else coming up with something similar is a definite possibility. My pattern was in the most recent McCalls quilting and then I saw someone post a quilt they had made that was almost identical. I went searching and found a free pattern by someone else. Hers is a two-color quilt, mine has a 3rd color and the focus is on the quilting. If you have a more complicated pattern it is less likely that someone could come up with the same thing. ... I also wonder with the vast amount of images we see on social media if sometimes we think we have an original design and we had actually had seen something similar and just didn't remember. ... I'm not trying to make excuses just saying that it can happen." In many ways, this is the essence of the world in which we live.

There is another side of that coin. Let's say I see a very cool quilt in Toronto at a Quilt Show in 2004. In 2018, I make a quilt that turns out to be nearly identical to the quilt. I didn't remember the quilt. I post it, and it becomes the cover of my new book, which sells millions of copies. The original copyright holder of the quilt sees it and gets very angry. The court will likely see this as subconscious copying. I had access to it. I copied it. It will then come down to degree. We see cases regarding subconscious copying in music all the time. Sam Smith, for example, didn't realize that his song "Stay with Me" was a lot like Tom Petty's "I Won't Back Down". When brought to his attention, a licensing deal with created and Tom Petty was added as a co-writer.

Subconscious copying is probably the scariest part of copyright for the artist, because how do you know what your subconscious remembers? The courts will look again to how available the image was and how likely you copied it, even if you don't remember, meaning that even though Victoria Findlay Wolfe says she never looks at things on the Internet, if it is popular and widely available her personal experience will not matter. If it is well-known enough, the court will assume access, and then look to see how similar the two works are.

Public Domain and Other Non-Protectable Elements

Finally, two quilts may look the same because the underlying reference is in the public domain. Alternatively, a technique, font, shape, or other element that is used in both may be in the non-protectable elements. Now, it will come to whether the expression of those non-protectable elements is infringing. Improv quilting, for instance, is a technique. That can't be protected. But books about improv quilting, and the quilts produced by this technique are protected. The same with basic blocks. A Churn Dash is a familiar block to many. The block itself is not protectable, but quilts made from this block may have enough protection to garner copyright.

A Note on not so Innocent Infringers: If a work has a copyright notice attached, there is no defense of innocent infringement. It is also not a defense that you just didn't know it was under copyright. Copyright applies a strict liability approach; copyright doesn't care about whether you knew or not. In the reverse, the court can reduce damages to $200 if there someone claims to be an innocent infringer and there was no copyright notice. 17 U.S.C. Section 504(c)(2); Section 401(d); Section 402(d).

Substantially Similar Copying

Not all copying is exact copying. The courts have developed tests to determine if things that seem substantially similar are in fact infringing. As we talk about this, we are going to use legal language: plaintiff for the person with the original work who believes that their work has been infringed. In this case, this is the person bringing the lawsuit. And the defendant is the person with the work that looks similar to the original work, and may or may not have infringed the plaintiff's work.

Step 1: Was there copying in fact? Either it is an exact copy or you believe the works are substantially similar. If the latter, we have to see if there is access to the original work, and that it is more than a coincidence that the two works look similar. We are looking at circumstantial evidence: 1) the defendant had *access* to the plaintiff's work and 2) the degree of similarity between the two works.

> ***Access.*** The courts look to how popular the work was (one million copies sold; played on the radio for eight weeks at number one, sold only three copies at a local shop in the 1990s etc.) and geographically where the work was available to be seen (at Houston Quilt Festival). The court also looks to direct points of access to the work by the defendant (e.g. the plaintiff emailed a copy to the defendant in preparation for a podcast interview). Other considerations: Had permission been granted to use the copyrighted work? This could be a Creative Commons license, or one-on-one contract. If the work is under copyright and no permission has been granted, one should also check to see if the use qualifies under fair use or another exception. We'll talk more about this shortly.
>
> ***Degree of Similarity:*** This one is more complicated. *Why are they similar*? Was it subconscious copying? Direct copying? Both relied on public domain elements? My favorite case is based on Beanie Babies, where one company TY (manufacturer of said Beanie Babies) sued another toy company for copying their Pig named Squealer, and their cow named Daisy. The defendant said that cows and pigs were in the public domain. The court said, not these cows and pigs...because the Beanie Babies hardly looked like public domain cows and pigs! Ty, Inc. v. GMA Accessories, Inc. 132 F.3 11967 (7th Cir. 1997).[24]

---

[24] For a great source (of this picture and also more on copyright, see Brian Frye's Open Source Copyright casebook, http://copyrightlawcasebook.blogspot.com/2014/01/class-1-introduction-to-copyright.html. Brian has been a guest on our show a number of times.

Squealer is on the right, and the infringing "pig" is on the left.

Step 2: Inappropriate Copying. If there has not been indeed copying in fact, then the courts move to inappropriate copying, which can be a long, drawn-out comparison between the plaintiff's and the defendant's works. Interestingly, one of the key cases to be used for teaching law students is *Boisson v. Banian, Ltd,* 273 F. 3d 262 (2d Cir. 2001), a quilting case! But first, we begin with the classic case of *Nichols v. Universal Picture Co.*, 45 F.2d 119 (2d Cir. 1930), cert. denied, 282 U.S. 902 (1931). We touched upon the case earlier in the book, when we were discussing idea/expression dichotomy. Now let's look at it for infringement. In this case from 1931, Judge Learned Hand set out what we now refer to as the abstractions test.

Levels of Abstraction: On one end is a general idea of something--*Romeo and Juliet*--two families feud, and the boy and girl find love. As the idea gets more delineated, some stock characters might show up-the angry father, for instance. Then the idea with its characters gets put down on paper. It is that expression, the details, that are protectable. *Romeo and Juliet* (in the public domain anyway) is the same storyline as *West Side Story*, *Gnomeo and Juliet*, and even *Warm Bodies*. But the expression of the general theme and the stock characters are further delineated in each to create copyrightable works. When someone infringes, we are looking to see if the expression, not the general ideas or stock elements are infringed. If you are looking to the stock elements, one would have to see how much of the expression was copied.

Who decides? Generally, experts are brought in to determine the first part--was there copying? However, the second part--was there inappropriate copying?--is something left up to a judge or jury, a general view of how similar they are.

Judge Hand suggested that there were levels of abstraction: "Upon any work...a great number of patterns of increasing generality will fit equally well, as more and more of the incident is left out. The last may perhaps be no more than the most general statement of what the [work] is about, at times might consist only of its title; but there is a point in this series of abstractions where they are no longer protected, since otherwise, the [author] could prevent his 'ideas' to which, apart from their expression, his property is never extended. Nobody has ever been able to fix that boundary, and nobody ever can..." We've seen this before in our chapter on Ideas. It comes back when we are talking about infringement.

Ok. Let's look at the quilting case!

Judi Boisson of American Country Quilts and Linens designed two Alphabet Quilts on a five by six block grid; so too did Banian LTD. *Boisson v. Banian, LTD, 273 F.3d 262 (2d Cir. 2001).* Judi had been in the quilt industry for 20 years. She started in antique Amish quilts, and then in the late 1980s, began designing her own quilts, which were advertised in catalogs she published in 1993 and 1996. The quilts at issue were designed in 1991, and were called "School Days." There were two versions. The letters were hand drawn by Boisson, and she selected and arranged the various colors and placement of the letters. She included a copyright notice on the quilt, and she registered the quilts with the U.S. Copyright Office.

School Days I by Judi Boisson

She registered the quilts with the U.S. Copyright Office the same year she created the pattern. Remember, registration is important for a number of reasons. It creates a presumption that Boisson is the copyright holder. It also allows her to go to court, and if she is successful, potentially gain attorney's fees. Here is the digital record at the U.S. Copyright Office. Notice, she registered the quilt in VA, visual arts materials. Judi regularly registered her work. She has over 90 copyright registrations at the U.S. Copyright Office.

School days I / Judy Boisson.

Type of Work: Visual Material
Registration Number / Date: VA0000505332 / 1991-12-09
Title: School days I / Judy Boisson.
Description: needlework design : quilt.
Copyright Claimant: Judi Boisson
Date of Creation: 1991
Date of Publication: 1991-02-04
Copyright Note: C.O. correspondence.
Names: Boisson, Judi

In 1991, Vijay Rao was an electrical engineer who decided to start selling quilts by importing quilts from India and selling them through boutique stores and catalog companies. In 1991, he ordered the pre-made quilt, shown to him by a third party, and then after requesting modifications, reordered the quilt in 1994. He reordered once in 1995. Then, he voluntarily withdrew the quilt from market in 1998, when Boisson initialized the lawsuit.

Here are two of the allegedly infringing quilts.

So, what is interesting is one is a quilter, mass producing quilts. The other is a company getting quilts from a third party overseas. In 1997, Boisson sued for copyright infringement, false designation of origin and unfair competition. The first trial lasted three days. Boisson testified, as did her daughter. Expert witnesses testified for both sides including one of Banian's who testified about the history of alphabet quilts. At the end of the trial, the district court dismissed all of Boisson's claims. The District Court found

- The alphabet and the lettering are both in the public domain.
- Putting the alphabet into six rows of five blocks each is not protectable. Here, Banian presented evidence that alphabet quilts had existed for over a hundred years, including an example from 1900 that used the same format as Boisson's quilt.

- The color she chose was not protectable.
- The similarities between the two sets of quilts were only in the non-protectable items. So, no infringement was found.

Boisson appealed the decision. The Second Circuit reversed the trial court, and remanded it back to the trial court for further considerations. The Appeals court found that while the trial court used the right test, it failed to consider "the overall look and feel brought about by the creator's arrangement of unprotectable elements." While the alphabet and the use of colors was not protectable, Boisson's selection, arrangement, and coordination of non-copyrightable elements were protectable. "Copying the creative works of others is an old story, one often accomplished by the copyist changing or disfiguring the copied work to pass it off as his own. Stealing the particular expression of another's ideas is rightly condemned in the law because pirating the expression of the author's creative ideas risks diminishing the author's exclusive rights to her work, or as a poet said, taking all that she may be or all that she has been."

1. Ownership of a Valid Copyright

Because Boisson registered both "School Days" quilts within five years of first publication, the Copyright Act provides the presumption that she holds valid copyrights. 17 U.S.C. Section 410(c).

2. Actual Copying of Plaintiff's Work

The defendant did not dispute that there was actual copying. The court explains, "Not all copying results in copyright infringement, even if the plaintiff has a valid copyright. Plaintiff must also demonstrate 'substantial similarity' between defendants' quilts and the protectable elements of their own quilts."

3. Originality

The court looks at individual elements of the quilt to see how original each element is. If a work is not original, it is not protectable. The trial court had found that some of the elements in Boisson's quilts were unprotectable: the alphabet, the layout, and the color. The Appeals court reviewed. Originality, of course, does not mean novel, but merely that the creative work is from the "fruits of the author's intellectual labor." *Burrow-Giles Lithographic Co. v. Sarony, 111 U.S. 53, 60, (1884) as cited in Boisson*. But, not all creative materials are protectable.

Alphabet: The Appeals Court agreed that the alphabet is in the public domain.

> **Layout of Alphabet.** The district court found it in the public domain, but the Appeals Court did not.
>
> > "Not only did plaintiffs obtain valid certificates of copyright registration, but also the alphabetical arrangement of the letters in the five-by-six block format required some minimum degree of creativity, which is all that is required for copyrightability. Moreover, unlike the use of letters, no federal regulation establishes that the use of this layout is unprotectable. These factors create a

> presumption that the layout is original and therefore a protectable element. Therefore, if defendants want to contest this presumption, they bear the burden of proving that this particular layout is not original."

What is interesting is that the defendant did not provide enough proof to show that the layout was in the public domain. Absent evidence of copying, an author is entitled to copyright protection for an independently produced original work despite its identical nature to a prior work, because it is independent creation, and not novelty that is required. Judge Jerome Frank said that "an 'author' is entitled to a copyright if he independently contrived a work completely identical with what went before."

Lesson: if a work is registered, and you (the potential infringer) believe it is a public domain pattern, you have to put together a good case of why it is, or otherwise the court will presume that it meets the originality standard, and if registered with the Copyright Office, that the registration is valid. "Absent evidence of copying, an author is entitled to copyright protection for an independently produced original work despite its identical nature to a prior work, because it is independent creation, and not novelty that is required." B*oisson* at 271.

Color. Color, by itself, is not protectable, but as part of the selection, arrangement and coordination, it might be.

Once the Appeals court had gone through the elements, they turned to their improper copying analysis, or substantial similarity. The court turned to a *fabric* case, *Folio Impressions v Byer*, 937 F.2d 759 (2nd Cir. 1991). *Folio Impressions* concerns a fabric design with a rose that had been registered with the U.S. Copyright Office, where the rose repeated in horizontal rows against an ornate background. The Defendant contended that the design was not original or substantially similar to the plaintiff's. With the registration, the plaintiff was entitled to a presumption of validity that the defendant would have to overcome. The Appeals court found that the background had been copied from a public domain source, and so was not entitled to protection. The court then turned to the arrangement of roses, which were placed in straight lines. The court found enough creativity in the choice, although thin protection. The court found the same to be true for Boisson's quilts and so proceeded to the infringement analysis. Enough creativity for copyright, but thin protection.

The general test is the "ordinary observer" test where "unless he set out to detect the disparities, would be disposed to overlook them, and regard their aesthetic appear as the same." *Boisson* citing *Folio Impressions.* But in *Folio Impressions*, explains the court, the plaintiff designer created fabric by using a public domain document without changing anything. So, the Folio court found the need to have a "more discerning" observer in certain circumstances.

How does the "more discerning" test work? You look at the "total concept and feel" of the two works, but at the same time recognizing the public domain elements. "In the present case, while use of the alphabet may not provide a basis for infringement, we must compare defendants' quilts and plaintiffs' quilts on the basis of the arrangement and shapes of the letters, the colors chosen to represent the letters and other parts of the quilts, the quilting patterns, the particular icons chosen and their placement." And most of all, one should use common sense, says the court, in the comparison. The court then turns to looking at the two sets of quilts.

Boisson's School Days 1

Banian's ABC Green Version 1

What do you think? If you were on a jury, would you find them substantially similar? How would you go about doing the analysis?

Here is how the Appeals Court approached the question. Both Boisson and Banian quilts have the same formation of the alphabet, with different icons filling in the last row. Boisson's "School Days 1" has a cat, house, single-stared American flag, and a basket. Banian's "ABC Green Version 1" has a cow jumping over the moon, a sailboat, a bear, and a star. "ABC Green Version 2" has a bit of alteration. "All three quilts use a combination of contrasting solid color fabrics or a combination of solid and polka-dotted fabrics to represent the blocks and letters." Boisson. The court then does a comparison letter by letter.

A: Both quilts: dark blue on light blue background
B: Both quilts: red on white
D: Both quilts: polka-dots on light blue background
F: Boisson's is white on pink; Banian is pink on White
G: Both quilts: green background
H and L: Both quilts: blue on white background
M: Both quilts: yellow on white
N: Both quilts: green on white
O: Both quilts: blue on polka-dot background
P: Both quilts: polka-dot on yellow background
Q: Both quilts: brown on light background
R: Both quilts: pink of grey/purple background
S: Both quilts: white on red background
T: Both quilts: blue on white background
U: Both quilts: gray on white background
V: Both quilts: white on gray background

W: Both quilts: pink on white background
X: Both quilts: purple on light background
Y: Both quilts: yellow on light background
Z: Both quilts: navy or black

Boisson also noted that Banian's letters "J", "M", "N", "P", "R", and "W" copied her unique way of making the shapes. Note how carefully the court compares the two quilts. What the court is trying to do is see if Banian actually copied from Boisson, and looks to each element to see.

The quilting was also the same, with both having diamond-shaped quilting within the blocks and a "wavy" pattern in the plain white border that surrounded the blocks. They were all edged with ⅜" green binding. Substantially similar? What do you think? What did the court decide?

When you do the step-by-step analysis, it becomes clear that there was copying of the selection, arrangement, and coordination. The court thought so too: "We think defendants' quilts sufficiently similar to plaintiffs' design as to demonstrate illegal copying. In particular, the overwhelming similarities in color choices lean toward a finding of infringement. Although the icons chosen for each quilt are different and defendants added a green rectangular border around their rows of blocks, these differences are not sufficient to cause even the "more discerning" observer to think the quilts are other than substantially similar in so far as the protectable elements of plaintiffs' quilts are concerned." Not pirating all of it doesn't relieve them of infringement.

The court then turned to the comparison of Boisson's "School Days 1" and Banian's "ABC Navy."

Boisson's School Days 1

Banian's ABC Navy

In this case, the court did not find infringement. The icons are splattered throughout, instead of the last row. The color decisions are different. The quilting pattern was now a "zig-zag" instead of a "wavy" design. The binding is also a different color. The court turned to "School Days II" v. "ABC Navy." The court again did not see them as similar. Then the court looked at

"School Days II" versus "ABC Green" version. Here Boisson used seven horizontal rows of four blocks, with an addition of the single-starred American flag and a house. The court felt that the "total concept and feel" were different. Where "School Days II" focuses on patriotic colors, "ABC Green" focused on green, and so did not create the same impression. The court remanded the case back to the district court to determine remedies.

Lesson: the court only found infringement in one instance. It doesn't take much for a work to not be infringing. Seriously. Are you surprised?

What You Get If You Win and the Harsh Lessons from Boisson

So, you file a complaint, you go to court, and you win the case. That takes a lot of money and time. What is the payoff? There can be a number of ways the court awards you: statutory or actual damages, injunctions, and attorney's fees and costs.

Actual versus Statutory Damages. For copyright cases, sometimes it's hard to measure the harm, the actual damage. Copyright includes an alternative: statutory damages. You have to choose between actual damages and statutory damages. 17 U.S.C. Section 504(a).

Statutory damages can range from $750 to $30,000 per original work. It is based on the fact that work was registered, rather than on the number of times the work was copied. This can go up to $150,000 if the infringement is found to be willful. It's up to the court to determine whether it was. Willfulness is when "the defendant had knowledge that [his] conduct represented infringement or perhaps recklessly disregarded the possibility." Yurman Designs Inc. v. PAJ Inc., 262 F.3d 101 (2d Cir. 2001) as cited in Boisson 2003 at 15. And on the other side is the innocent infringer, where the court can exercise its discretion for the proper remedy. Boisson at 15. So, there are three categories: infringement, willful infringement, and innocent infringer. The court looks to a number of factors to determine the category of infringement: "plaintiff's lost revenues, defendant's profits, the value of the copyright and the deterrent effect of the award." *Sevents*, 2002 WL 31387224 as cited in *Boisson* 2003 at 15.

Injunctions

Injunctions are granted to prevent future infringements, either temporarily while the court case develops or permanently, as a result of the outcome of the case. There are two types of injunctions: temporary and permanent. They both stop people from doing the activity that is infringing--selling something usually. "Permanent injunctive relief will not be awarded in cases where there is no history of infringement, the defendant is cooperative in ceasing to sell infringing products and there does not exist any probability of future infringement." *Boisson* at 15.

Attorney's Fees and Costs

Because the work was registered with the U.S. Copyright Office, the court has at its discretion to award costs and attorney's fees. 17 U.S.C Section 505. The determination on whether attorneys' fees will be awarded is based on the conduct of the non-prevailing party. The court will look to who is considered the prevailing party, whether the lawsuit was frivolous, the non-prevailing party's motivation, whether settlement attempts were in good faith, whether the losing party was objectively unreasonable, and whether deterrence and compensation for the behavior is necessary.

Back to Boisson

So, what happened in *Boisson*? After the Appeals court found that there was infringement for one of the quilts, the trial court was required to assess the request for damages, injunction and attorney's fees and costs. Banian was not selling the infringing quilts any longer. So, the court did not find a need for an injunction to have him stop selling the quilts.

Statutory damages. Boisson had elected statutory damages. The court did not find Banian willful or innocent. The Defendant did have access to Boisson's catalogs and copyrighted designs, but that is not enough to establish willfulness, nor enough to establish innocence. The court looked to Boisson's profits, and did not see a reduction in the value because of Banian's version. Also, Banian did not mass market the quilts. Instead, he sold only 153 of them for a profit of $3,306. He also withdrew them in the market when he was faced with a lawsuit. The court also looked to Banian's saved expenses in relying on Boisson's design. The court found, that although Boisson claimed it took her a month to design, large portions of the design were in the public domain, and no evidence that in borrowing Boisson's design that expenses were saved. The court looked to the materials used to create the design--in this case Boisson used a pencil and tracing paper, along with labor. The court decided to award an additional $1000 for labor and saved expenses by Banian. The court also looked to Banian's profits. The gross revenue on the 153 quilts was $7,150, with a profit of $3,306. The court seems to be taking in actual profits, even though they can award a greater amount. This goes to the character of the Defendant. There was no evidence that Boisson lost revenue. And because Banian had already ceased selling the quilts, deterrence wasn't needed either, but did add $500 as a deterrent measure. The total was $4,806 in statutory damages.

Attorney's Fees and Costs. The court found Banian reasonable: he was just trying to sell quilts and that the Second circuit only found one infringing quilt. Boisson's settlement demands of $175,000 made it impossible for Banian to bring the case to an end; Banian was not objectively unreasonable. The court found no need for deterrence, as the defendant repeatedly tried to settle the case. So, no attorney's fees to Boisson.

The parties returned to court one more time in 2004 where both parties attempted to get an award for costs. Boisson submitted a bill of $4,488.60 for costs, and Banian submitted a bill of $8,889 plus attorneys' fees in the amount of $84,907. (Note how expensive it is to litigate.) So, how are costs determined? The court looks to Rule 54 of the Federal Code of Civil Procedure, which allows for cost by the "prevailing party." Rule 54 relates to costs including filing fees, transcript fees paid to court reporters, and costs in connection with witness attendance at trial. Attorney's fees are not included in Rule 54. But Rule 68 does include attorney's fees. Boisson v. Banian, 221 F.R.D. 378 (2004).

Rule 68, "Offer of Judgment" rule, is meant to encourage settlement. If a defendant makes an offer to settle, and the result of the case is less than the offer to settle, the defendant may under Rule 68 apply for costs. The court believed it did not include attorney's fees because to gain attorney's fees, one must be the "prevailing" party. Rule 68 had not been considered for copyright cases by the Second Circuit. But the court notes that only prevailing parties are eligible for attorney's fees. A non-prevailing party cannot recover attorney's fees as part of a Rule 68 award. But the 11th circuit did award attorney's fees on a Rule 68 offer to a defendant.

Application to Boisson

The court reviewed the history. The case began in March 1997, and by July 1998, Banian had made a Rule 68 offer of judgment for $12,000. The damages awarded to Boisson in 2003 was for $4,886. "This award was less favorable than Defendant's Rule 68 offer of judgment." Boisson 2004. Both parties believed they were the prevailing party because one quilt was found infringing, while the others were not. The district court found Boisson the prevailing party, but did not award attorney's fees or find willful infringement. The court also looked at plaintiff's lost revenues, defendant's profits, the value of the copyright, and the deterrent effect of the award. The Defendant litigated in good faith, and when a settlement was proposed by Boisson, it was for $175,000, more than willful infringement statutory damages.

Boisson can recover costs under Rule 54, but only up until the point that the Rule 68 offer had been put on the table, which was July 10, 1998. As the Banian's Rule 68 motion to recover costs post-offer, the court denied the attorney's fees because these are covered by the Copyright Act, and were not rewarded as part of that. The costs, however after July 10, 1998 are awarded to Banian after July 10, 1998. Banian's costs were $8,889.77. Boisson, even though she partially won, had to pay $8,889.77 to Banian.

What we Learn from Boisson

1. Get a good expert. Banian's expert on whether the alphabet quilt structure was in the public domain did not convince the court. Make sure to have support.
2. The outward appearance. The court was looking to the colors and shapes--the total look and feel. If it is too close, infringement will be found, but it is easy to change some elements, at least with this court, to find no infringement.
3. Just because you win, doesn't mean you get a lot of money.
4. You can get penalized for not settling. It's a gamble.
5. The Court may not agree with you. Boisson won only on one quilt, not the others. The others were deemed not infringing. She could have gotten more if she had settled for $12,000
6. The costs. We know that Banian had over $84,000 in attorney's fees. One would imagine so too did Boisson. It's a high price for both.

In the end, I'm not sure why Boisson pursued the claim. Banian stopped. She kept going. She likely felt that she had the right to pursue the copyright claim, and that she would be compensated accordingly. We reached out to get comment, but she didn't return our email.

Other Cases with Quilting and Fabric

Tufenkian Import/Export Ventures v. Einstein Moomjy (339 F.3d 127, 2d Cir. 2003)

This case concerned "two textile designs, each of which combines with modifications, the "primary border" and the "half field" of two unrelated public domain carpets..." The court explained, "Viewed uncritically, the two designs at issue are substantially similar. For the defendant's rug to infringe upon the plaintiff's design, however, the defendant's opposition must be substantially similar to that which is original in the plaintiff's expression."

Plaintiff James Tufenkian took two public domain images and put them together, modifying them in his computer. He used different components from the public domain images, and added some bits of his own creation, including stick-figure animals and castle-like figures. Defendant Bashian hired one of Tufenkian's former employees to help him design a rug. This was two years after Tukenkian's work had been marketed. The design team was familiar with Tukenkian's rug, and Bashian admits some copying occurred. There were new elements, but they were using the same public domain elements. The court found that "Tufenkian infused [the Heriz design] with sufficient originality to support copyright protection, that Bashian actually copied the Heriz, but that the result was not substantially similar to protected expression in the Heriz."

Just as in *Boisson*, the court was called on to separate what might be in the public domain from creative expression protectable under copyright. The district court used the "total concept and feel," just as in *Boisson*, using the "more discerning observer" test from *Boisson*: substantial similarity must exist among the protectable elements, and not the public domain elements. The court factored out the public domain elements. The court did not find similarities on the protectable items.

The Appeals court reviewed. The Appeals court begins with the principle: "all creative works draw on the common wellspring that is the public domain." What is interesting in the Appellate case is the judge ponders what is scène à faire with regard to rug patterns and how much of what the plaintiff changed is conventional. "Even the Heriz's pairing of the Battillossi half-field with the value-derived border was, arguably, a fairly simple exercise. One might contend that the pairing is too minor to surmount even the low threshold for copyright protection, or else conclude that it is protected only against very close copies."

Let's take this out to the world of quilting. Putting together blocks from our public domain may not render much or any protection if we apply this case. But here we see the court looking to what the plaintiff did to the public domain images: "The plaintiff not only cropped and elongated the Battillossi half-field, he also selectively eliminated numerous design motifs, creating a more open, less busy aesthetic." This is super important when thinking about traditional blocks, and especially the modern quilt movement.

The court explains about the rugs: "Of course, mere simplification of an ornate public domain carpet into a mass market knock-off may not be protectable. But the plaintiff's half-field modification was not a uniform or homogeneous simplification akin to removing all serifs from a font, blurring the petals on all flowers, or eliminating every third leaf on a stem. Rather, the plaintiff seems to have engaged in a selective and particularized culling of a leaf here, a complex of leaves and flowers there, and so forth. And close visual inspection of the two rugs confirms that the Bromley precisely mimics the Heriz in nearly all of these choices." This is super important. Altering-- adding or deleting --materials from a public domain work may create a new copyrightable work, but it does not change the status of the underlying work.

"This non-mechanical adaptation of individually unprotectable elements from the public domain is precisely the type of "original selection" that the Supreme Court indicated was protectable expression in *Feist*." Therefore, the court found the defendant's work infringing. The defendant added materials. That did not matter. So, when we take images from the public domain, delete and add additional creativity, we gain copyright in that version of the public domain work. It doesn't mean that others can't use that public domain image, but they cannot do what we did with that image.

Brown v. McCormick, 87 F. Supp. 2d 467 (D. Md. 2000)

Universal Studios and Amblin' Entertainment produced the film, *How to Make an American Quilt* in 1993. As part of the preparation, Patricia McCormick, President of the Southern California Council of Quilt Guilds, was hired to help with obtaining quilts for the filming. McCormick was charged with obtaining an African-American story quilt for the film that was to be called "The Life Before," and would comprise a series of blocks depicting an African-American family's history from life in Africa, capture, transshipment, slavery, and emancipation. The first try by the studio art department didn't work. McCormick reached out to Barbara Brown.

Patricia McCormick, was hired as a technical consultant on the film, and part of her job was to find quilts to be used as props. The script called for an African-American story quilt, which needed to have blocks that depicted the chapters of a family's history: "including life in Africa, capture and transshipment, slavery, and emancipation." McCormick found Barbara Brown to design it.

Barbara Brown was an African-American quilter in her 40s at the time. She was also a lawyer. In a *New York Times* article, it was reported that she was adding a civil rights section to the story quilt for the film "because my story does not end with slavery." She was also part of a movement in the 1980s to make African American quilts and guilds more visible. McCormick gave Brown the direction to create a quilt like Harriet Powers' Bible Quilt, but not a duplicate of the late 1800s quilt because it was so famous.

Harriet Powers was an African American woman, who was born a slave in 1837, had nine children, and became landowners after the Civil War. She lived on a farm in Clarke County, Georgia, who made the Bible quilt in 1886, which she exhibited at the Athens Cotton Fair that same year. Later, she would sell the quilt for $5 to Jennie Smith, but not before explaining the meaning of each panel, which Jennie recorded.[25] Powers passed away in 1910. The quilt is now housed at the Museum of American History.[26]

Harriet Power, "Bible Quilt" (1886)

Brown had a contract to create 15 block patterns for $750 total. She was not hired to make the quilt, "The Life Before." "in the Movie, one of the quilters, Anna (played by Maya Angelou), was an African-American who owned "The Life Before" quilt as a family heirloom." (473) She retained the copyright to the pattern. Universal was an authorized licensee to create two prop quilts for the movie. Patrick McCormick and another quilter created the actual quilt.

[25] "Briefly, the subjects are Adam and Eve in the Garden of Eden, a continuance of Paradise with Eve and a son, Satan amidst the seven stars, Cain killing his brother Abel, Cain goes into the land of Nod to get a wife, Jacob's dream, the baptism of Christ, the crucifixion, Judas Iscariot and the thirty pieces of silver, the Last Supper, and the Holy Family." https://americanhistory.si.edu/collections/search/object/nmah_556462

[26] Mary Fons, Quilt Scandal No. 002917: The Harriet Powers Bible Quilt, http://www.quilts.com/quiltscout/the-quilt-scout-the-harriet-powers-bible-quilt.html

Then, a second quilt design was required, "Where Love Resides," with 16 blocks that "would depict the Movie's main pictorial themes." (468-9) "In the movie, each woman in the quilting circle contributed to "Where Love Resides" a block depicting her own life story." (473) Instead of contacting Brown again, McCormick designed the blocks, except for one: The Marriage/Wedding Block. That was copied and altered from the Marriage Block from Brown's "The Life Before" quilt. The court explained, "In designing Anna's block, the Marriage Block, McCormick borrowed the basic design of the Wedding Block in "The Life Before."

The "Life Before" quilt was not featured in the film. But one of the blocks was. McCormick used the Marriage Block from "The Life Before" to link thematically the two quilts. The block had a scene of a black bird flying over a man and woman holding hands. "The Marriage Block differs from the Wedding Block in two major respects: (i) in the Marriage Block, the crow points downward rather than upward; and (ii) the Marriage Block includes a figure of the sun not present in the Wedding Block. With these exceptions, however, the Marriage Block is plainly derivative of the Wedding Block." (474) McCormick did not get Brown's permission. "McCormick, who has no legal training, did not appreciate that she had created a copyright problem." (474). And, Universal relied on McCormick. (This always seemed weird to me). This block appeared in the "Where Love Resides" quilt that was featured in the film and merchandising.

The "Where Love Resides" book by Patchwork (one of the parties sued" included both quilts in the book. Strangely, the book at issue was labeled "Motherhood" in the book, but it is clear which block was copied. You will see that the quilts themselves are different, but that one block is very similar

"The Life Before" by Brown

Where Love Resides Quilt (infringing block)

Now, let's take a look at the two blocks:

Brown's "The Life Before"

Where Love Resides Version (infringing)

And here is another block that seems to have the additional sun component

Another block from "The Life Before"

So, that was what was used without permission. Her other quilt did not make it into the movie.

Brown had been paid $750. The studio had used her pattern in beyond the two prop copies they had agreed upon and Brown retained the copyright. With each block she sent (by fax), she included © 1994 Barbara Brown. Sixteen counts of copyright infringement remained after summary judgment. The court divided them into seven groups:

1. McCormick's use of the Wedding Block to create the Marriage Bock
2. McCormick's display of "The Life Before" and "Where Love Resides" at exhibitions
3. Promotional materials using "Where Love Resides"
4. The book *Where Love Resides* using the quilts from the movie
5. Derivative version painted by John Simpkins
6. Unauthorized display of two quilts on two cable television shows
7. Display of Marriage Block in the other quilt in the movie itself

The parties could not settle. The court found:

1. McCormick infringed Brown's copyrighted Wedding Block: All displays of the Marriage block are infringement.
    1. Movie
    2. T-shirts and tote bag
    3. Tie-in book
    4. Display on television

    5. Display at quilt shows
2. The size, shape, placement, and orientation of the human and bird figures of the two blocks were "substantially similar".
3. John Simpkins work did not infringe Brown's copyright because it more suggestive of the quilt and not detailed enough to infringe.
4. The Studio went too far in using the quilt, and did not have the right to display it on television, in quilt shows, or in the tie-in book.
5. The studio was allowed to display "The Life Before" quilt in the Movie, but no on television, at quilt shows or in the tie-in book.

The court did not find the actions of the Studio or McCormick as willful (where the big money is). And Brown did not present evidence of substantial damages or the need for injunctive relief. So, Brown won. But what did the court award her?

- Actual damages of $50 for the use of the Marriage Block in "Where Love Resides."
- Actual damages against Amblin for $2.35
- Statutory damages of $7,000 against McCormick
- Statutory damages against Universal, and the publisher of $7,000

Even though the film made $29,111,120, Universal claimed $28,846,927 in distribution expenses and $29,620,190 in production in expenses, along with Amblin receiving a fee of $2,000,000 for services. The Movie cost more than $50 million, and so had not produced a profit. The book by Patchwork also lost money, $209,976. The painting created by Simpkins was for merchandising.

About the Quilt Exhibition: "In early November 1995, McCormick attended the International Quilt Festival in Houston, Texas, and worked in M & FM's exhibit booth, at which M & FM displayed both the finished and unfinished copies of the "Where Love Resides" quilt. The two "Where Love Resides" quilts and "The Life Before" quilt were displayed in Houston, Texas with the permission of Universal Merchandising." In the book, t-shirts and tote bags with the "Where Love Resides" quilt were giveaways to the public who attended. (The Quilt Festival attracts more than 50,000 attendees.) They were not sold, and so no profit was produced, and moreover, the court explained, Universal and M & FM spent money producing the t-shirts and tote bags just as they spent money advertising the Movie. This seems so disingenuous.

Brown would win on authorized display of her quilt: "Count III alleges that McCormick infringed all of Brown's designs by displaying "The Life Before" and "Where Love Resides" at exhibitions. Brown gave permission solely for the use of the patterns for "The Life Before" in the Movie. This permission extended to the use of "The Life Before" for promotional and marketing purposes; it did not, however, extend to McCormick's private use of the quilt at exhibitions. The Court, therefore, finds McCormick liable under this count with respect to "The Life Before." As the Court previously stated, "Where Love Resides" incorporates Brown's copyrighted Wedding Block. Any display of "Where Love Resides" is an infringement. Thus, the Court finds McCormick finds liable for the display of "Where Love Resides" at the exhibitions." (482). This seems promising. Brown will have justice. Then, "The Court found McCormick liable for the infringement alleged in Count III. Because Brown did not suffer actual damages and

McCormick did not earn any profits from McCormick's display of "Where Love Resides" at exhibitions, the Court awards nominal damages of $1." The damages? Nominal $1.

What should we learn from this? It's a disturbing lesson. This case is from a pre-Internet era, where we now understand that free and giveaways have value. So, it might be decided differently in 2020. But what this case says to me is that Brown's work, while infringed, was not valued, and even devalued by the court.

A Fabric and Pattern Designer Sues

Thimbleberries v. C & F Enterprises, 142 F.Supp. 2d 1132 (2001). Thimbleberries was the brainchild of Lynette Jensen, who designed and sold quilt patterns and fabric designs beginning in 1988. A year into her business, Jensen created a Christmas wreath pattern, which she displayed at the Houston Quilt Market and in Denver. Her quilt design was also featured in *America's Best Quilt Projects* in 1993. Lynette Jensen is big in the quilt world. She creates fabric for RJR Fabrics (https://www.rjrfabrics.com/lynette-jensen/). She publishes with C & T Publishing (https://www.ctpub.com/lynette-jensen/). She ran the first Block of the Month for Craftsy, and Thimbleberries, her business, was a presence in the quilting world.

Lynette saw a near identical copy of her pattern being mass-produced without her permission or a license. This is a pattern maker's worst nightmare. She saw it in a Charles Keath catalog in October 2000. She contacted a lawyer, who sent a cease and desist letter to stop all sales through the catalog. Thimbleberries also sent a letter to C & F Manufactures requesting they shop production and sale of the allegedly infringing products. Both the manufacturers and the catalog refused to stop selling the table linens using the Christmas wreath pattern. So, Thimbleberries sued.

We turn to the district court's decision relating to copyright. First, Thimbleberries waited more than five years from first publication to file for a copyright registration. That doesn't keep Thimbleberries from obtaining a registration. It just means that the court will look into whether the work has the sufficient amount of originality and protectability now, rather than, if filed within the first five years after publication, presuming that. Note: file within five years so that you have the presumption of originality and copyrightability.

Defendant argued the following:

> *Idea/Expression:* The Defendant thinks that "the idea of expressing a wreath in a pattern of squares and triangles may enjoy no copyright protection whatsoever, but that even if it does, such protection extends only to the "particular compilation of public domain squares, 90 degree triangles and border-strips in the particular colors, dimensions, background quilting stitches, borders and contrasting bow and wreath designs originally selected coordinated and arranged by Plaintiff." That would be fairly narrow copyright, and in many ways, mimic's the court in *Boisson* that felt that deviation in color and adding a few icons within the alphabet quilt made them seem different.
>
> *Merger Doctrine*. A work is not protected by copyright when the idea underlying the copyright can only be expressed in one way. 17 U.S.C. Section 102(b). What the defendant is arguing is that public domain shapes arranged in the form of a wreath is tied to the expression of that idea-the specific one created by Lynette Jenson, and therefore, is not protectable by copyright.
>
> Scène à Faire. A work is not protected by copyright if the expression in the work comes from a commonplace idea rather than creative efforts of the designer.

What does the court think?

Lynette does not have a monopoly on the idea of shapes arranged into a wreath. "However, as Thimbleberries easily demonstrates, the pattern which it seeks to protect represents only one of many ways to express a quilted wreath design." Thimbleberries' counsel provided nine other wreath patterns that were an arrangement of squares, triangles, octagons, and rectangles that were different from Thimbleberries. The court found that with this evidence, Thimbleberries had enough creativity to meet the minimum bar for copyright. "Moreover, the variety of patterns reveals that Thimbleberries' particular arrangement of public domain shapes is not at all compelled by the underlying idea." Merger doctrine does not apply.

Thimbleberries needed to prove that there was a "reasonable possibility" that the defendants viewed the Countryside Wreath pattern. It was featured in two international quilt shows in 1989, and sold in quilt shops around the country. But the court did not think that was enough. The defendant's designer, Judy Short, claimed that she did not go to the shows, does not frequent quilt shops, and did not see the publication. "The court finds dubious Short's assertion that she is a professional quilt pattern designer, yet she does not visit quilt stores." The problem was that Thimbleberries did not provide more specifics on distribution. More specifically, was it distributed near shops that Short might have visited? There was not enough evidence at an early stage for a preliminary injunction. That might come later. access was not proven definitively. So, the court moved on to the similarities between the two. The court used the 8th circuit's two step test: extrinsic analysis to determine whether the general idea of the two works were substantially similar, and if so, then a more subjective intrinsic test to "ascertain if they are so dissimilar that ordinary, 'reasonable minds' cannot differ as to the absence of substantial similarity in expression."

What did the court find? "A reasonable observer would easily recognize the similarities between the two wreath-shaped patterns as not only substantial but striking." Thimbleberries at 1140. The court explains: "To the ordinary observer, the two designs are, for all practical purposes, identical: the shapes of the designs are identical, consisting of sixteen exterior points of 45 degrees and six exterior points of 90 degrees; the number and placement of squares and triangles is virtually the same, except for four triangular pieces flanking the contrasting bow which have been removed from the defendants' design; and finally, the number of pieces, their scale and the proportions used in both designs are identical. For example, both patterns utilize six square pieces and eight triangular pieces, arranged the same way, to comprise the bow, which is placed in the identical location on the wreath. Most telling is the nearly identical arrangement of squares and triangles to create both the exterior shape of the wreath and the center hole design. The striking similarities between these two works stands in sharp contrast to the notably different wreath patterns created by other quilt pattern designers." Id at 1140.

The court did not think changes in the defendant's work were enough to be distinguishable: "To the contrary, the court finds that the subtle distinctions in color and fabric choice, background quilting stitches and border trim are irrelevant to the similarity determination because these features do not constitute the subject matter of the copyright." Id at 1140. The court even notes that the list of differences only highlighted to the court how much they are the same.

Then, the biggest blow to the defendant: "Finally, the court concludes that the two works are so strikingly similar as to preclude the possibility that defendant's designer independently arrived at the same result." In particular, the court believed the subtle changes looked as if the pattern maker was making deliberate changes to escape copyright infringement. The case would move forward because Thimbleberries would be able to establish copying occurred, and would likely prevail on a copyright infringement case. With this, Thimbleberries could show a presumption of irreparable harm, and obtain a preliminary injunction to stop manufacturing and selling the pattern until the case is resolved. Moreover, the court found that the economic hardship would fall to Thimbleberries if the pattern was continued to be mass-produced without a license in place. The court issued a preliminary injunction for Thimbleberries.

There are other fabric and quilting cases, of course. Let's examine two more.

The Schiffer Publishing v. Chronicle Books case[27]

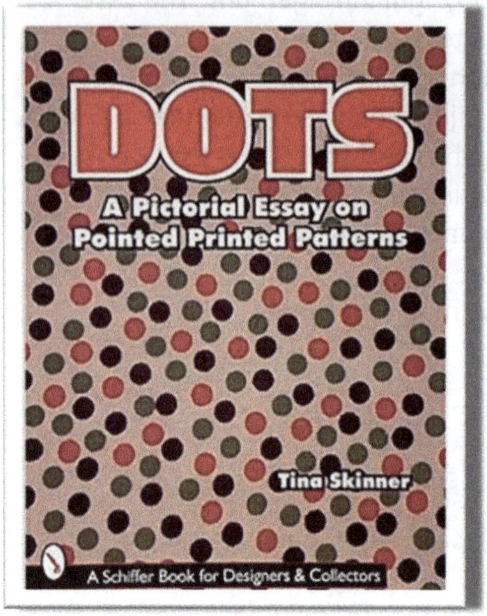

Here Schiffer's (the plaintiff) photographs were included in Chronicle Books without permission. The Court on January 11, 2005 awarded $150,000 in statutory damages and permanently enjoined Defendant from selling their book, *1000 Patterns*, within the United States. The Court later awarded Plaintiff over $50,000 in costs and over $205,000 in attorney's fees.

Let's take a look at this case and see what happened: Schiffer created photographs of fabrics and textiles, which the court concluded had valid copyrights. The books included are *Dots: A Pictorial Essay on Pointed Printed Patterns* and *Paisley: A Visual Survey of Pattern and Color Variations*, which contain photographs of fabrics and fabric swatches. The books were registered with the United States Copyright Office.

Between 2001 and 2002, Ivy packaged *1000 Patterns*, a history of pattern making, and included over 100 source images from Schiffer books, including three Schiffer images for the cover of the book. (That's never good.) The court found infringement, and awarded attorney's fees, costs, and willful infringement damages. Ivy had argued that the photographs were not original enough to obtain copyright; the court disagreed. There were 118 photographs at issue. Ivy deliberately copied from Schiffer books; there was even a memo acknowledging it. That's willful infringement. Publisher to publisher willful infringement is never, never good. The court found originality in the photographs, and willful infringement in Ivy.

The Paula Nadelstern Case

One of the most famous cases is that of Paula Nadelstern, a famous quilter.[28] She is most famous for her kaleidoscope quilts, especially because of a lawsuit. The defendants were Couristan, the Houston Convention Center Hotel Corporation and Hilton Hotels Corporation. Couristan is a manufacturer and vendor of carpets. I think it was one of the greatest thrills of the project to chat with Paula about this very famous quilt copyright case.

Paula began experimenting with kaleidoscopes in 1986l, and they just kept interesting her. She began focusing on Kaleidoscopes, including publishing the book, in 1996 *Kaleidoscopes & Quilts* with C & T Publishing, who registered the copyright, as they do.

---

[27] See *Schiffer Publ'g v. Chronicle Books*, 350 F. Supp. 2d 613 (E.D. Pa. 2004) (" Summary Judgment Opinion"); *Schiffer Publ'g v. Chronicle Books*, Civ. A. No. 03-4962, 2004 U.S. Dist. LEXIS 23052, 2004 WL 2583817 (E.D. Pa. Nov. 12, 2004) (" Infringement Opinion"); *Schiffer Publ'g v. Chronicle Books*, Civ. A. No. 03-4962, 2005 U.S. Dist. LEXIS 416, 2005 WL 67077 (E.D. Pa. Jan. 11, 2005) (" Damages Opinion"); and Schiffer Publ'g v. Chronicle Books, (E.D. Pa May 24, 2005) ("Attorney's Fees and Costs")

[28] *Nadelstern v. Couristan*, Inc. et al., No. 06 CV 0248 (JFK) (S.D.N.Y. June 26, 2006).

Kaleidoscopes & quilts / Paula Nadelstern.

Type of Work: Text
egistration Number / Date: TX0004428505 / 1996-11-20
Title: Kaleidoscopes & quilts / Paula Nadelstern.
Imprint: Lafayette, CA : C&T Pub., c1996.
Description: 144 p.
Copyright Claimant: Paula Lyman Nadelstern, 1951-
Date of Creation: 1996
Date of Publication: 1996-10-18
Basis of Claim: New Matter: additions.
Names: Nadelstern, Paula Lyman, 1951-

Record at U.S. Copyright Office

In 2005, Paula was attending Houston Quilt Market and Festival, a staple event for the quilt industry. A Hilton had been built that connected with two floors of skywalks to the Houston George Brown Convention Center, where the Quilt, Inc. shows are held annually.

As Paula tells it, she was at a booth at Market when people began coming up to her and congratulate her on the rugs in the new hotel in the skywalk to the Convention Center. She did not know what they were referring to. "They were suggesting that the carpet looked like my work." She went over. "My first response is, 'Oh, they like me! They picked mine. That's so familiar...' But my second reaction, and I think it is a very female reaction was, 'How did I let them do this to me? It's my fault.' "Now, it was my fault that a big corporation stole my designs without letting me know, and I come out of that thinking it's my fault." (Interview with Just Wanna Quilt). Her friends took photographs. But after the show, she went on with her other life obligations. The first attorney she talked to didn't think she had a case. At the time, she was (and continues to be) at Benetex. "The woman who was head of the studio" asked her about her lawsuit, and she said, "I'm just going to give it up. I can't be angry about it anymore. There's nothing I can do. This is what the lawyer told me. I'm letting go." The woman suggested a lawyer that she had seen him give a talk about copyright, George Gottlieb, who is well-respected, well-known intellectual property attorney in New York. Paula wrote an email to George to appease her colleague. He took the case.

George informed Paula that indeed they did have a case. It began with the U.S. Copyright Registration certificate. "I never registered the copyrights in my quilts at the time. I thought it was enough for me to embroider the letter "c" with my initials and the date." explained Paula. But C & T publishing did. That was important. She hadn't registered the quilts. "If they had taken a picture at a quilt show, I wouldn't have had anything. But the fact that they took the images from my first C & T book."

George set the defendants a cease and desist letter to no avail. The carpet company was in New Jersey. Paula confessed, "If they had just said, 'We're so sorry. Come on by. Come to us, and let's figure this out,' I would have settled for nothing. That's not what they did." The case went on for two years. "They went after the C & T book."

The case was filed in federal court in New York. To the infringement charge, here's what the defendants' response was. From the complaint filed with the court, the carpet company,

Couristan denied needing any "permission, license or consent" with regard to the "design, manufacture and installation of the carpet at issue...because said carpet did not infringe any purported copyrights of the Plaintiff."[29] They also denied the VARA claim.

As to defenses, they alleged an invalid copyright registration, that the Plaintiff was not the lawful owner of the copyrights and therefore lacked standing, that the Plaintiff had committed fraud upon the Copyright Office, that the works were not substantially similar, or alternatively Couristan's use falls under fair use, and that Defendant's actions were not willful. The defendants also counterclaimed. They claimed that Nadelstern used third parties' fabric designs in her quilts in order to create a kaleidoscope pattern, and that she is infringing on the use of those fabrics. About this, Paula responded in our interview, "If they had done due diligence, the fabric companies sought me out. The sent me more fabric that I could ever need or want. Because they want their fabrics in a book. That's how the industry has evolved."

Turning to her 1996 book, "*Kaleidoscopes & Quilts*," third party fabrics are used throughout the book, creating derivative works of the fabrics. Here is where the fraud upon the Copyright Office comes in: the defendants claim that Nadelstern should have disclosed the third-party fabrics that are part of her book as pre-existing, and that she did not have permission to photograph the fabrics themselves. Because of this, the defendants want her copyright registration declared invalid and unenforceable. The defense was focused only on discrediting the book.

After two years, the parties went to mediation. In New York, cases are required to go to mediation before going to court. Recalling back, Paula said, "They were so patronizing. And so was the mediator. ...He was that set me off to dig in my heels. When he came into the room, he said, 'I know nothing about quilts. If you just let them put your name on their website, you'll be famous." Paula Nadelstern was already a famous quilter. "The whole mediation, ignoring me... they all assumed the little quilter would go away," and that they could drag out the case. Most artists couldn't afford the attorney's fees, but Paula had an arrangement with George that was on a contingency basis, rather than hourly. "I was the only woman there. Everyone else was a man in a suit. My quilts were hanging but nobody looked at them and nobody cared." The day continued. The mediator had to leave.

"I got a message that the head of the carpet company wanted to talk to me alone." George thought it was ok, and the mediator said, "Yes, you can talk to anybody." Paula said, "Then I want to talk to this man, Marcus M., the head of the carpet company's design department." Marcus comes in from Dallas, dressed in shorts. In the boxes and boxes of papers they had received through discovery, there were notes that said "refer to book, refer to book with the page." George would write an article about the case for Studio Art Quilt Associates Journal. He wrote, "During the course of the investigation, as part of discovery, we were able to learn the exact number of blocks taken from Paula's quilts, that images of the carpeting appeared on the hotel's website, the size of the copied carpet, and sales figures relating to the carpeting."[30]

Paula wanted to know how they got her book. She asked Marcus. "How did you do this to another artist?" Marcus responded, "We were told that kaleidoscopes were a generic term, and

---

[29] Defendants' Amended Answer to the Complaint and Counterclaim, 2006 WL 2307184

[30] George Gottlieb, Esq. and March P. Mistal, Esq. *Settlement Reached in Nadelstern Copyright Case*, SAQA Journal, Winter 2008, 6-7.

we were working through the interior decorator." The interior decorator had them given them a storyboard that described what the Hilton wanted, including what the carpets would look like. "They had a picture of one of my quilts from my first C&T book. They just had it on the storyboard. When they asked what it was, they said kaleidoscopes." The President of the carpet company asked, "What would it take to settle?" Direct evidence of access and copying. They settled that day. And, Paula included in the settlement that her name would be included on the website, and a plaque at the Hilton.

She ended the story: "So the key to my story, this was the lesson is that copyright is not enough. I have to register my quilts. I had to register my copyright. Everybody needs to learn to register their copyright when they are making quilts, and making patterns. It's not that expensive, and you have to do it. I never use the word 'lucky'. The fact C & T Publishers registered the book, that's what made it a case. And they took everything straight from the case. And the interior decorators had a copy of my book in their Dallas library."

Now the Hilton changed the carpet. Throughout the years, when they had to change the carpet, they had to pay Paula a royalty. "I used to tell everyone to walk on the carpet and shuffle their feet."[31]

Her attorneys concluded their article in SAQA Journal with the following: "One of the lessons to be learned from the case is the following: If the creator thinks he or she has a good case, he or she should meet with several different attorneys who specialize in intellectual property, and especially copyright, to find an attorney that believes that there has been an infringement. If the case is a strong one, it is possible to make a financial arrangement with the attorney whereby the artist does not have to bear the entire cost of the case until there is a settlement."[32]

---

[31] Paula had one more thing to add: "And another interesting thing, George called this a t-shirt law. They wanted to measure the carpet to pay royalties only on the exact parts that infringed her designs. The rest that off goes to the side to doors and windows is an all-over pattern that she had not designed, so she shouldn't get a royalty for those inches." George said that no. They owed for the whole space, and not just the "t-shirt" design.
[32] Id at 6.

A Just Wanna Quilt Example

Now, with everything we have learned, let's look again at the Gypsy Wife quilt, and the one made by the Quilting Army.

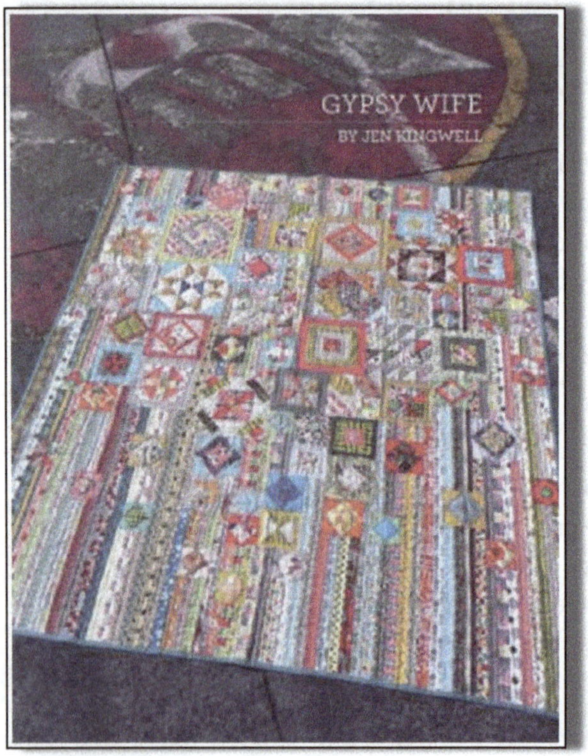

Gypsy Wife pattern cover

Quilting Army Quilt

First, I check to see if Gypsy Wife is registered with the U.S. Copyright Office. In this case, it is not. While the author is foreign (and so could go to court without registering), no statutory damages or attorney's fees would be available until registration. And so, the question to ask is what kind of actual damages (lost profits, for example) could the author prove that occurred because of my work, even if I sold it? Additionally, no copyright notice has been included on the pattern. Kingwell still holds a copyright, but I could claim I was an "innocent infringer" without notice, which potentially reduces statutory damages (which are not currently available) dramatically.

Next step: confirm that the plaintiff **owns the copyright** and that the **copyright is valid.** The plaintiff has the burden to prove that they own the copyright (e.g. employment agreements, business records, etc.). There also could be transfers of ownership, licensing deals, and other aspects that affect who is considered the copyright holder.

Is the copyright valid? The work at issue (the Gypsy Wife Sew-Along) must meet the requirements of copyright: a work of authorship that is original, minimally creative, and fixed. 17 U.S.C. Section 102(a). The Plaintiff will have the burden of proving this, and if a certificate of registration is issued within five years of first publication, it is *prima facie* evidence that the copyright is valid. This is another reason to register your work promptly with the U.S. Copyright Office. In Meaghan Hemmings Kent and Joshua J. Kaufman's *An Associate's Guide to the Practice of Copyright Law*, they caution, "Take some time to seriously think about whether your client's work is copyrightable. Consider the defendant's potential arguments, including merger doctrine and non-copyrightable elements, and be sure that you have reasonable counterarguments. And remind your client that the underlying idea is not protected by copyright." (111). These are all good points to remember.

Infringement of an Exclusive Right

As a reminder, the exclusive rights include reproduction, creating a derivative work, distribution, and public display (for art works). Did we make a copy? To prove that we did you must prove copying and substantiality of copying protected expression (inappropriate appropriation).

Was there copying? This can be direct evidence (defendant admits to copying) or indirect evidence. We do not admit to copying. We're going to look at indirect evidence: access + substantial similarity to the expression (and not idea) of the copyrighted work, or alternatively, strikingly similarity so that independent creation would be unbelievable. In our case, we'll look at indirect copying. Yes, there is proof of access. We had a copy of the book, ran a Gypsy Wife Sew Along, and it is a very popular pattern. Members of the QA saw it at Paducah and came home wanting to do it. That was easy.

Infringement filter for copying. Was there copying? There can be similarities. This would be up to a jury to decide. If access + substantial similarity is found, then you move to part 2, inappropriate appropriation.

> Was there inappropriate appropriation? Did we copy sufficiently protected expression of the plaintiff's? We have to look to the Nichol's case again.
>
> Here is our base:
>
> Gypsy Wife: Common blocks of varying size with stripes of two sizes. Square in a square is used as fillers, along with complicated individual blocks. Stripes are all vertical, and look as if they move through the blocks.
>
> QA Quilt: Common blocks all finishing at six inches (different ones from GW) with all one inch stripes, and with some horizontal stripes connecting blocks, along with some connected by one inch vertical stripe. The clumpy stripes are horizontal, rather than vertical.

Nichol's Level of Abstraction:

- Idea of vertical/horizontal stripes: Both have it; QA has consistent one inch; GW has two sizes, one inch and a half inch. QA has horizontal stripes; GW has vertical. Both have the colors continuing through the blocks.
- Common blocks: not protectable or excludable (and the same common blocks not used)
- Strip layout: not excludable

The question is was our selection, arrangement, and coordination of blocks and stripes so substantially similar to the GW to constitute inappropriate copying? Because there are so many elements in the public domain, we turn to the more discerning ordinary observer test for the question of inappropriate copying. You look at the "total concept and feel" of the two works, and at the same time recognizing the public domain elements.

Your answer, jury?

As the defendant, I would argue that we were inspired by GW, of course, but that what we took was nonprotectable elements: using common blocks and the idea of stripes to set the blocks. We used both horizontal (the majority) and a few vertical. That was different from the GW. I would also argue that I built upon the unprotectable elements created by a giant, but that we would have to see if Kingwell was the first (and likely not) to combine public domain blocks with vertical stripes. Finally, I would suggest that the distinctiveness of the GW is the blocks themselves and placement. Ours has none of the same elements. The more discerning ordinary observer test requires you to look at "those elements and only those elements that provide copyrightability to the allegedly infringed compilation." Is there an "enormous amount of sameness"? If there is different placement, there will not be infringement.

Applying Brown: is the size, shape, placement, and orientation of the QA quilt substantially similar to GW?

Applying Boisson "more discerning ordinary observer test": which elements are in the public domain and which are protectable? In this case the selection, arrangement, and coordination including the layout and specific choices were compared to the alleged infringing quilts.

Thimbleberries: extrinsic test - how similar is the general idea behind the work(s); and then intrinsic test: ascertain if they are so dissimilar that ordinary "reasonable minds cannot differ as to the substantial similarity in expression." The court compared the number and placement of squares and triangles, and the scale and proportions used in both designs. In this case, the court found them strikingly similar.

Take away: Creating a New Work

- Think about how you are inspired by others.
- Make sure it is the idea and not the expression.
- Be aware of where inspiration comes from, and check its copyright status before using it.
- Think about protectable expression (selection, arrangement, and coordination) versus unprotectable elements.
- Make sure your own selection, arrangement, and coordination is substantially different.
- **Document your process and progress (see appendix with Notebook worksheet pages).**

And...

- Register your work. If the quilts matter, register them (you can register up to 10 unpublished works, and each qualify for their individual copyright). If the patterns matter, register them. Your book publisher will likely register your work, but check.
- Lawyer can be expensive. You will likely only sue if a sizable corporation is involved.
- Don't be vain. Don't bring lawsuits merely because of your ego, unless you want to pay in the end, even if you win.
- Winning a lawsuit does not mean you are golden. The settlements are not always big; and the attorney's fees can be high.

13: Moral Rights

What are Moral Rights

So, you take pictures at a quilt show, and you post them online. You didn't include the information card, and suddenly people are screaming at you. Why? Right of attribution.

Section 106A of the 1976 Copyright Act addresses the rights of attribution and integrity for certain authors under the Copyright Act. These are called moral rights. Moral rights are distinct from the economic rights we've been discussing (Section 106 rights of copyright, distribute, derivative, public display and public perform).

This part of the Copyright Act is called the Visual Arts Rights Act, or VARA, as it is often referred to. It provides special protection to certain artists for right of attribution and integrity.

Tricia Royal's letterpress print available at http://bitsandbobbins.com/

Works of Visual Art

Only works of visual art get moral right protection in the United States. That is *not true around the world,* where most countries have a vibrant and extensive moral rights system. The definition of a work of visual art in the United States becomes important. That is found in 17 U.S.C. Section 101:

> A "work of visual art" is—
>
> (1) a painting, drawing, print, or sculpture, existing in a single copy, in a **limited edition of 200 copies or fewer that are signed and consecutively numbered by the author**, or, in the case of a sculpture, in multiple cast, carved, or fabricated sculptures of 200 or fewer that are consecutively numbered by the author and bear the signature or other identifying mark of the author; or
>
> (2) a **still photographic image produced for exhibition purposes only**, existing in a single copy that is signed by the author, or in a limited edition of 200 copies or fewer that are signed and consecutively numbered by the author.
>
> A work of visual art **does not include—**
>
> (A) (i) any poster, map, globe, chart, technical drawing, diagram, model, applied art, motion picture or other audiovisual work, book, magazine, newspaper, periodical, data base, electronic information service, electronic publication, or similar publication;
>
> (ii) any merchandising item or advertising, promotional, descriptive, covering, or packaging material or container;
>
> (iii) any portion or part of any item described in clause (i) or (ii);
>
> (B) **any work made for hire**; or
>
> (C) any work **not subject to copyright protection** under this title.

Let's unpack. Works of visual arts are not mass-produced commercial works; they have to works produced with less than 200 copies and signed. They are not practical. They are not promotional materials or advertising. They are not work made for hire. And they have to be under copyright. And not every photograph counts. VARA is a bit picky. A work of visual art is something unique, or at least 200 copies or less. The focus seems to be on fine art and gallery art, but in recent years, graffiti cases have successfully used VARA in court.

The Rights

If you meet the qualifications, here are the following rights you obtain under VARA.

- Right to claim authorship of the work. (The right to be named)
- Right to prevent the use of his/her name as the author of a work of visual art, which he or she did not create.

- Right to prevent use of the author's name as the author of the work of visual art in the event of a distortion, mutilation, or other modification of the work, which would be prejudicial to his or her honor or reputation.

There are also provisions with respect to artwork incorporated into buildings, which is beyond the scope of this book.

Exercise of the Rights

Only the author (whether or not the author is the copyright holder) has VARA rights. Modifications of the work that are a result of time and conservation are not considered a violation of VARA. The rights may not be transferred, but the rights may be waived by express agreement in writing by the author. The writing must identify the work, and the uses of that work to which the waiver applies. Ownership of the copyright, the work itself, and the VARA rights are each distinctly separate.

Duration

The VARA term is different from the economic term of the work.

- Works created **after 1990** (when VARA was enacted): life of the author.
- Works created **before 1990** but title was not transferred from the author (meaning the original author still holds the copyright): life plus 70

Many have commented on the weirdness of the duration of VARA, and that works before 1990 that were sold or otherwise transferred do not gain VARA protection.

Remedies: You can get the same remedies as under the economic rights portion of the Copyright Act: injunctions, impounding, actual damages, statutory damages, costs, and attorney's fees. Statutory damages for moral rights begin at $500 and go up to $20,000, and if willful, $100,000. If the violation was deemed an innocent infringement, the damages can be reduced to $200.

No Registration Required: VARA does not require that a work be registered to be protected.

Back to Paula Nadelstern

Paula Nadelstern sued for copyright infringement because C & T registered the book, and the defendants had *used the book as a model for the carpets* at the Hilton. Paula's legal team also included a VARA claim on the quilts themselves. From the original complaint: "Defendants Couristan, Hotel Corporation, and Hilton have willfully violated plaintiff's rights under Visual Artists Rights Act, 17 U.S.C. Section 106A by manufacturing, causing to be manufactured, importing, vending, distributing, selling, displaying, and/o promoting carpets which are direct copies of plaintiff's unique works of visual art (kaleidoscopic quilts)..." More specifically, the complaint asserted that the defendant violated Paula's 106A(a)(1)(A) right to claim authorship (attribution right) and 106A(a)(3)(A) right to prevent intentional distortion, mutilation or other modification...which is prejudicial to her reputation (right of integrity). Remember when Paula said she got her name on a plaque and on the website? That's settling the right of attribution claim. And replacing the rugs when they were worn and paying an additional royalty fee? Likely part of the right of integrity portion of the settlement. What is most interesting, and something to think about is that VARA did not require Paula to register the quilts. She had not registered the quilts, only the book. But she was still able because of the way the statute is structured, to sue on VARA claims. This potentially adds statutory damages, up to $100,000 if willful. We do not know the terms of the settlement.

Takeaway

- Sign copies and keep copies to under 200
- Make sure your work fits within the acceptable categories
- Make sure your work is not considered a work for hire
- You do not need to register the work to file a VARA claim, even to get willful damages
- The two key rights are attribution (right to be named) and integrity (right to prevent intentional distortion, mutilation, or other modification which would prejudice the reputation of the author).

Part 4:
An Approach to Fair Use for Artists

14: An Introduction to Permissible Uses

When Can You Make Use of a Copyrighted Work

From the beginning of this book, we've noted that copyright is not an absolute property right, meaning that others can use a copyrighted work *while it is under copyright*. These are sometimes called permissible uses: if a third party engages in these uses, they are not considered infringement. The most famous of these is fair use. But there are others. This chapter briefly touches upon some of them. All of these are limitations on the exclusive rights of copyright holders. This section focuses on U.S. copyright law, but many of the concepts and terms are used around the world.

Permission: You can ask the copyright holder for permission to use the work. This includes a license, either exclusive or non-exclusive to engage in one of the exclusive rights. You can also obtain an assignment, which must be in writing, transferring the ownership of the work, either in part or in whole. This is literally a permissible use. For example, for this book, I asked permission to use a number of the photographs throughout the book, as a courtesy, and also because I didn't think my use always fell under fair use. I also wanted to alert the author that they were in the book, and to make sure I got the attribution right. Permission allowed me to feel comfortable with my choices.

First Sale Doctrine: Section 109(a) in the Copyright Act, "limitations on exclusive rights: effect of transfer of particular copy or phonorecord," spells out the First Sale doctrine. You can sell or otherwise dispose of the copy of a work. We've discussed this before.

Why digital copies are not included under First Sale: Digital copies are not included under the First Sale doctrine because First Sale has to do with the distribution right. Once a physical good is sold, the copyright owner has no authority to control further distribution. That makes sense, yes? But digital copies are just that – a copy. When you purchase a digital good, you are being given permission to download and make a copy of the work (the actual papers you print). You are not being given a physical good. You cannot transfer your right to make a copy to someone else under the First Sale doctrine.

We're looked at First Sale before. We used First Sale for a number of the projects in the book, including the Splendid Sampler project, where we ripped up the book and sent pages to people to make blocks. Interestingly, nearly everyone sent *back* the pages with the block!

Displaying a physical copy: Section 109(c) allows you to display the copy you own publicly to viewers present at the place where the copy is located. This means you can display a copy to sell it, for example. So, if I buy a copy of a piece of art, I can display said work for sale. That does not necessarily mean I can make a digital copy and post the work online. That would be making a copy, displaying and distributing the work.

Classroom Uses: Section 110 provides limitations on exclusive rights in the form of exemption of certain performances and displays. Section 110(1) applies in face-to-face teaching and allows you to perform or display materials without permission from the copyright holder. Think of performing a play in a high school classroom or showing a film. (This does not include coverage if the high school performs the work and sells tickets). It does not give you the right to make copies of anything. This does not apply to hand-outs or other reproduced materials, only the physical presentation of the materials. Section 110 also applies to performances or displays of a religious nature in the course of services at a place of worship or other religious assemblies. Again, no copies made, strictly performance and display. County fairs, veterans' organizations, and nonprofit fraternal organizations where the public is not invited fit into Section 110 exceptions as well. There are also special provisions under Section 110 for the blind, restaurants, and places selling televisions and other devices.

Taking Pictures from the Street of Architectural Works: If a building is ordinarily visible from a public place, the public has the right to make, distribute, and publicly display pictures, paintings, photographs and other pictorial representations of the building. 17 U.S.C. Section 120.

Library Uses: Section 108 concerns special limitations on exclusive rights for reproduction by libraries and archives. Some of these are for preservation purposes. Interlibrary loan and patron copies are also part of this, as are photocopy machines in a library. This section protects the library from liability from patron misuse from these and other activities. Section 108 does not reach the individual library patron. Libraries are protected from their patrons' copying, Patrons may be protected by fair use and personal use, but they may also be engaged in infringing activities.

Fair Use: Fair use is a term that many people know. We're going to go through what it is, and how one applies fair use in a number of situations. Let's first understand the structure of the law, Section 107 of the 1976 Copyright Act. Fair use allows for uses by third parties without permission while the work is still under copyright. Typical uses are criticism, comment, news reporting, scholarship, research, and teaching. Fair use has also been used in technological instances for indexing (think Google searches), time-shifting (think DVRs), and parodies (think Saturday Night Live).

- Fair use is the mechanism that allows us to comment upon and criticize works -- like in a news story or online reviews. Fair use allows us to write biographies, to write papers, to copy newspaper article for classroom use. But fair use goes further than that. It allows thumbnail images on Google and other search engines. It allows indexing, also by search engines. It also sometimes allows artists to use others' work, transforming them into something else. And through the years, fair use has been expanding. Fair use is important, but it is also difficult to understand.

- Fair use also allows us to make physical and digital copies – for research, scholarship, personal use, and even for classroom use in some cases. You have to review fair use. If the copies are for personal use, and it is not a market substitute, fair use likely applies.

- Fair use *is not* about using 10% or some other formula to create or differentiate the piece. Instead, it is a balancing test to determine whether the use by a third party is fair to the copyright holder. There are four factors you have to consider. We will look more carefully at fair use in the next chapter.

We used fair use in this book as well, especially when I was commenting or criticizing using an image, and when I took a screenshot of something to compare it to something else.

Tolerable Uses. This is what one motion picture content owner once referred to regarding fan works. These do not necessarily fall under fair use, but as a society, we tolerate them. The content owners can decide at any time *not to tolerate them*, at least until there is a court case that further delineates fan-based works. Fan art is often put into this category.

Trademark and Right of Publicity Fair Uses and the First Amendment. Finally, we will be looking at the role of trademark and the right of publicity in artwork, and how that interacts with the choices you make as an artist.

Copyright Hyper Compliance: where you don't do something, you may self-censor, because you think it is not allowed. I see this *all of the time*. We've started to address this in the previous chapters. Fair Use is one more area where there is often confusion and fear in applying the doctrine. We're trying to change that with the following chapters.

15: Copyright Fair Use Basis

"Fair use [is a] non-infringing, unauthorized use of Copyrighted materials—under some circumstances."[33]

Fair use has become a very important force in our copyrighted world. For example, Google thumbnail image searches occur because of fair use. Transformative use for artists has had tremendously positive court cases in the last decade. (We'll talk a good deal more about transformative uses, particularly for artists shortly, and in its own chapter!) More and more uses fall under fair use. Additionally, copyright holders must be aware that they are required to do a fair use analysis of the infringing use before they assert a notice-and-takedown on social media platforms.

The dancing baby who caused all the fuss.

Traditionally, fair use came after a court found infringement, as a defense to the behavior. But in the new age of the Internet, *Lenz v. Universal Music Corp.*, 801 F.3d 1126 (2015), often referred to as the Prince Baby case, changed all that. Now copyright holders are required, in some instances like filing a notice-and-takedown with an Internet service provider (think YouTube, Facebook, etc.) to do an analysis to confirm that there would be no exceptions or potential defenses to the infringement. That happened because of this cute baby in the picture above.

Stephanie Lenz took a 29-second video of her toddler in a walker, who bouncing and walking to Prince's "Let's Go Crazy." It's heard faintly in the background. Universal, who owned the rights to the song, asked YouTube to take down the video through Section 512 notice-and-takedown procedures. Stephanie fought back, turning to the Electronic Frontier Foundation, a non-profit that helps people with copyright issues. Some stuff happened. In the end, the Appeals court ruled that copyright holders have to take into consideration whether there are any fair uses before filing a notice and takedown of something online. Meaning, that it was OK for Stephanie to post the video of the baby with the incidental Prince music in the background. The court found the use to be *de minimis*. This raises the bar for copyright holder filing notice-and-takedown complaints on platforms like Pinterest, Instagram, Facebook, and of course YouTube against other parties' using their copyrighted works, and brings more balance to the system.

[33] Fair Use in the Visual Arts, Center for Media and Social Impact, https://cmsimpact.org/wp-content/uploads/2016/01/caa_slideshow_updated_online.pdf

A Culture of Fair Use

The Lenz case does not stand alone. There has been a movement to strengthen fair use for more than a decade. We began the book discussing the efforts of the Center for Media and Social Impact at American University to standardize fair use, so that it was more useful in the form of Codes of Best Practices. That project has succeeded tremendously. While they focus on various types of groups, their conclusions are often very similar. (I worked on the poetry project as a reviewer.) Here is what I glean from their approach to fair use. Let's look briefly at the Code of Best Practices for Visual Arts with the College Art Association (CAA).

In a 2014 CAA study, 70% of the respondents said they use copyrighted works of others in their own works.[34] This could be in the form of writing about art, teaching, and managing museums, and making art. But the study also found that "1/3 of the visual arts community had avoided or abandoned work because of copyright concerns." The kinds of questions they reported included:

> "I found a suitable image online to illustrate my article. Do I still need a license?"[35]
> "Can I use some photos I took of an artist's work on my online course site?"[36]
> "I'm making art from found images. Do I need to get permission to use them?"[37]
> "Can I use pictures from our exhibition in museum publications?"
> "Can we put our archival collection online?" Can we take pictures of quilts at shows and post them online? What about Pinterest posting?[38]

In the next few chapters, I hope you start to feel more comfortable with fair use, and that you can start to answer the questions above, when they are related to creating art.

---

[34] https://cmsimpact.org/wp-content/uploads/2016/01/caa_slideshow_updated_online.pdf

[35] That depends on the use. We'll be learning about this shortly. Commercial use? Likely yes. Personal use? Likely no. How transformative is your use? (We'll be learning what this means). Just a lot of questions.

[36] Again, depends. Are you criticizing and commenting on the work? More likely, yes. Are you just using it as decoration? Likely no.

[37] Again depends. Are you taking little bits of the images? Are the images still under copyright? Are you using them to comment/criticize? Are you making a parody?

[38] So technically could be considered infringement, but we see these uses as non-infringing uses. Ideally, you include the right of attribution, but even that doesn't always happen. Think of how Pinterest has made its business model on people pinning other people's photographs!

Section 107: Fair Use Walkthrough

Fair use means uses by a third party that happen when the work is under copyright without the permission of the copyright holder. So, let's go through the statute and then we will turn to recent cases: one where the court found fair use (a photographer's photograph was used without permission), and one where the court did not find fair use and the U.S. Postal Service was required to pay $3.5 million for the use of an image of the Statue of Liberty. Let's make sense of these two cases using fair use.

Fair use is found as Section 107 of the 1976 Copyright Act. It applies only to works potentially infringed in the U.S.

> *Preamble*
>
> Notwithstanding the provisions of sections 106 and 106A, the fair use of a copyrighted work, including such use by reproduction in copies or phonorecords or... by any other means specified by that section, for purposes such as criticism, comment, news reporting, teaching (including multiple copies for classroom use), scholarship, or research, is not an infringement of copyright.

Section 106 refers to the rights you get as a copyright holder and Section 106A refers to moral rights for some kinds of artwork. So, the first sentence reads, **"Notwithstanding the rights given to copyright holders, the fair use of a copyrighted work is not an infringement of copyright."**

The fair use of a copyrighted work is not an infringement of copyright. That's the essence of Section 107. You have not committed infringement if fair use is found.

The preamble gives examples of what might be included as a fair use. Making copies for *the purpose* of:

- criticism,
- comment,
- news reporting,
- teaching (including multiple copies for classroom use), scholarship, or
- research.

Note: this is a "such as" list, and therefore the purpose doesn't have to fall under one of the categories. In fact, we've seen Google use fair use as a defense for *indexing* and creating thumbnail the world's photographs and even millions of whole books still under copyright, both in order to search. The category of *parody* (think Saturday Night Live) also falls under the purpose of fair use, connected to criticism and comment, but nonetheless its own type of fair use. Neither the word "indexing" or "parody" are listed in the statute. "Such as" allows that, and other uses. Also notice that copies for classroom use falls under this. We'll get to that shortly, once we are through how to understand and apply the four factors.

Four Factors of Fair Use

Fair use balances the copyright holder's rights with the unauthorized user's needs (some even say rights!). We call that the four-factor test.

> **[Preamble]** Notwithstanding the provisions of sections 106 and 106A, the fair use of a copyrighted work, including such use by reproduction in copies or phonorecords or by any other means specified by that section, for purposes such as criticism, comment, news reporting, teaching (including multiple copies for classroom use), scholarship, or research, is not an infringement of copyright. In determining whether the use made of a work in any particular case is a fair use the factors to be considered shall include—
>
> **[Four Factor Test]**
>
> (1) the purpose and character of the use, including whether such use is of a commercial nature or is for nonprofit educational purposes;
> (2) the nature of the copyrighted work;
> (3) the amount and substantiality of the portion used in relation to the copyrighted work as a whole; and
> (4) the effect of the use upon the potential market for or value of the copyrighted work.
>
> The fact that a work is unpublished shall not itself bar a finding of fair use if such finding is made upon consideration of all the above factors.

Over the years, the four-factor test has had a lot of cases that help us to understand what it means, and this is a whole area of subject for copyright scholars and attorneys. We're going to try to keep it simple in this chapter. In later chapters, we will look at cases specifically related to artists and their use of fair use in their creative work.

First Factor: The purpose and character of the [third-party] use

This is considered very important and can get complicated. There are a number of questions to ask. We are looking to the potentially infringing use. What is this third party (that could be you) doing with someone else's work?

Non-profit educational use? Are you a non-profit using someone else's work? Courts are more likely to find in favor of the use when it is for non-profit or educational purposes, but again, not always.

Is it a commercial use? Weighs against third party use. (But not dispositive, or conclusory. Some commercial uses are ok, like parodies). This is complicated. Rather is the work in question (the one being infringed) being sold by the infringing user? If a website uses a photograph, but is not selling the photograph (even if it is selling other things), then the use is likely to be ruled non-commercial. Things that are considered commercial include images used on an advertisement; on a product that someone is selling; or on the cover of a book (to sell that book). Just because a use is found to be commercial does not defeat a fair use being found. We'll see an example of that when we get to parody.

Is it a parody? Weighs in favor of third party use. The courts give a lot of leeway to works that are parodies that make fun of, that comment on, and or criticize the original work. This is super important to our democracy and our society. If a work is a parody, the four-factor test takes a different turn in some ways. We will see that shortly.

What is a parody? That was defined in Campbell v. Acuff-Rose Music Inc. by the U.S. Supreme Court (510 US 569 (1994)). There, 2 Live Crew used the Roy Orbison's "Oh, Pretty Woman" to make their own version, which it degenerates into "big hairy woman" and "two-timing woman" and references to looking like "Cousin It" (a character from the fictional Addams family), among other things. It has the same distinctive bits of music that we all know from Roy Orbison's. The court found the band was commenting on the original and making a statement. The listener holds the original (Roy Orbison) and the new one (2 Live Crew) in their head at the same time. We'll look more carefully at this case shortly. You can find a copy of both songs on YouTube and several digital music services. It's worth listening to them to understand the controversy that generated the case and the court's decision.

Is the Use Transformative? This is a big one. Have you somehow transformed the original into something else? It is a use different from the original, and somehow you are commenting, criticizing, or transforming the old work in the new work. This is a very important category for artists. Art often falls under transformative. When you use a pre-existing artwork in a new context, the work may fall under fair use. We'll talk more about this in the next chapter.

Second Factor: The nature of the copyrighted work.

You look to the original work -- the work being used. Is it fictional or factual?

A work of fiction has greater protection from fair uses, we still see a lot of fan art and fiction arising from fictional work. In contrast, history, directions, and other non-fictional copyrighted works do not get as much protection under the fair use analysis. Artwork gets more protection. A photograph of the Washington Monument gets less. (Factor two was easier. It usually is. Sometimes there's a question of whether something falls into fact or fiction). Can you see why? Facts are not protected by copyright, only the selection, arrangement, and coordination. Fiction is creative. Fictional works get more protection. Factual works get less.

Third Factor: The amount and substantiality of the portion used in relation to the copyrighted work as a whole.

How much did the third party take? This can be complicated, too. The amount is analyzed both for its qualitative and quantitative quantities.

If you take the "the heart of the work" and there's no reason to buy the original, that's not fair to the copyright holder. There is no magic number. But think of it this way, if what you are doing is a market replacement, that is not a fair use. Parody aside, the more you use, the less likely the court will find fair use. And if you take the reason people would buy the original work, then, the court is less likely to find fair use. This is both a qualitative and quantitative analysis. There are no hard and fast rules: no 10%, one chapter, or the left arm or the top of the picture. You have to focus on the questions and purposes of this factor. How much did the person using the copyrighted work take? Does the new work take the key or "heart" of the original? Does the new work co-opt the most distinctive or memorable aspect of the original? We want to see how much. As a note, just because you change the media (from 2d to 3d as in Rogers v. Koons, 960 F.2d 301 (2d Cir. 1992) it is not enough to protect you from fair use violations. If you replicate a creative work (the photograph) in wood or oil paint or mixed media, your work fails this third factor.

And of course, there is an exception. If you are creating a parody (commenting on a thing in a way that conjures up the original thing, again think Saturday Night Live), you must/can take the "heart of the work" – because you need to conjure up the original. The whole point is to identify an original work, and by making fun of it, comment on and criticize it. If a parody failed to mimic the dress, accent, and physical appearance of a celebrity, the audience would not understand that they were seeing a commentary on something.

Fourth Factor: The effects of the use upon the potential market for or value of the copyrighted work.

This is often seen as the most important factor. Is what the third party doing a market replacement or taking away licensing opportunities? This used to be seen as the most important factor. If you are taking away/substituting for economic opportunity with your use, the court would not find fair use.

Note: commenting, criticizing, and parody are NOT subject to this requirement. The thinking is that the copyright holder would never give permission to have a bad review or be made fun of. So, the fourth factor does not apply.

The Last Bit of the Statute: There's one more element: "The fact that a work is unpublished shall not itself bar a finding of fair use if such finding is made upon consideration of all the above factors." That's the last bit of the statute. This means that fair use can be applied to any work, not just ones out in the public, although courts often care whether the work had been circulated by the content owner (e.g., posted online) or keep unpublished (e.g., grandmother's diary in the attic).[39]

That's the statute. Now, let's look at some examples.

Examples of fair use:

- I write a biography and use quotes from a number of letters and novels of my subject. I use only what I need to in order to comment on the quotes and cite the original works. (Fair use, scholarship)

[39] If you have been given them as part of a will, you usually inherit the copyright too, and then you are the copyright holder provided the giver has the right to grant you such rights.

- I take a quote from a poem, and create a quilt using the quote and my interpretation of that poem. (Fair use, comment/criticism, and transformative use).
- I make a copy from five different books of how each approached the technique of perfect flying geese (a quilting block that is rectangular and made of three triangles). I bring them to class to teach each of the five different strategies. Because it is a small amount and the lesson is about comparing techniques that qualifies as fair use. I However, if I copy a whole book or a good part of it, and do not require the students to purchase the book, that is violating factor four and is unfair to the copyright holder. As part of this, I would include the full citation for each book on the copy for both reference and marketing in case others want to pursue that particular technique.
- I am a collage artist. I take bits from a variety of sources, and carefully craft a message that reflects on the original sources. We will talk more about artist uses of fair use in the next chapter.

Fair use is an important tool for artists. If you are using/incorporating someone else's work in your work, stop and think about why. Go through each of the four factors. Does it make sense to call it a fair use? If not, are the parts that you are using in the public domain? If not, are you going to seek permission? If not, you may be infringing. Let's take a look at a case, where the court did *not find fair use.*

Brammer v. Violent Hues

In *Brammer v. Violent Hues Production, LLC - District Ct. Eastern District,* No. 18-1763 (4th Cir. 2019), plaintiff professional photographer Russell Brammer took a time-lapsed photograph of the Adams Morgan neighborhood in Washington DC. He shared it on his website, and also put in online image sharing websites, including Flickr. He included © All rights reserved behind the photograph on Flickr. (For his work, got to www.flickr.com/photos/rbrammer) Bra mmer regularly sells physical prints of his photographs for $200-300, and on two occasions licensed an image for $1250 and $750.

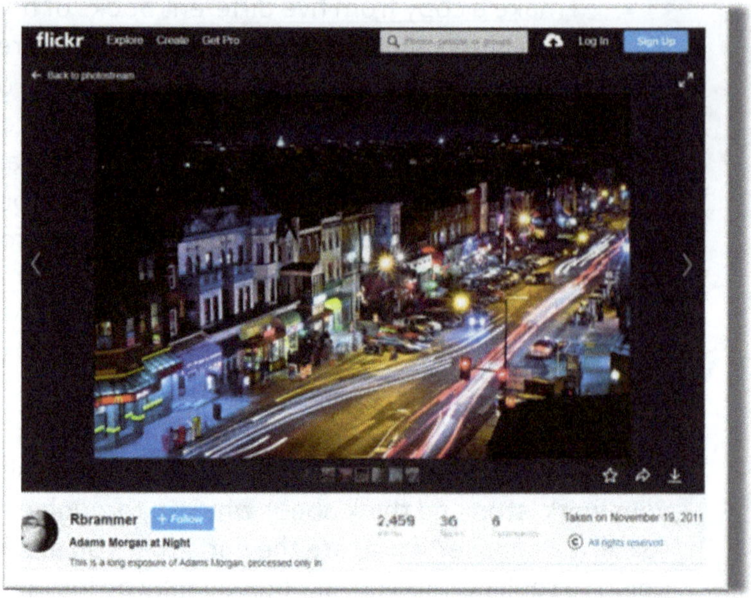

Brammer's original photograph on Flickr. Notice © on the right hand side

Violent Hues version (notice the middle image)

Defendant Fernando Mico, the owner of Violent Hues film company was running the Northern Virginia Film Festival, a revenue generating event, according to the court. Mico found the photograph through a Google Image search, which led him to Flickr, and Brammer's image. Mico believed that if it was on Flickr, it was out of copyright. (Now, that's not reading very carefully. Each Flickr image indicates the rights statement from the author, "all rights reserved" or some form of a Creative Commons license. You choose it as part of setting up your profile.) Mico posted on the www.novafilmfest.com website.

Brammer found it, and had his attorney to send a letter asking for compensation for the use. Mico removed the image, but refused to pay compensation. Brammer still sued.

The district court granted Violent Hues motion for summary judgment, finding fair use in favor of Violent Hues. The district court found that the use was different, that Brammer was (first factor) "expression," while Violent Hues' was "informational." The court thought it was (second factor) factual content. Violent Hues had cropped the photo, so didn't use all of it (third factor), and regarding the market, said that Brammer could get fees for others and Brammer doesn't put enough effort into marketing. (fourth factor). The court also said Violent Hues just didn't know, and so that should be taken into consideration. Brammer appealed. (I personally think this was a terrible decision and would, if it had been an exam answer, gotten no higher than a "c" grade.)

The 4th Circuit appeals court returned to fair use. Let's look step by step.

First Factor: nature and character of use

The Appeals court found Violent Hues use of Brammer's image to be commercial, because it was used to promote a for-profit film festival. The court asked, "was the use exploitative, in that others usually pay to engage in similar conduct?" (11) NFL teams, for example, license their copyrighted logos for use in commercial products, citing *Bouchat IV*, 619 F.3d at 311. The Appeals court found this case similar, and that it is customary to license stock images. Brammer sold licenses for just such a use, and Violent Hues did not pay the fee. The first factor weighs again Violent Hues.

As to Violent Hues' "I thought it was free" argument, copyright assumes good faith. Moreover, Violent Hues did not offer evidence that it indeed acted in good faith: "At best, Violent Hues appears to have acted negligently" especially when "© All rights reserved" was included next to the photograph.

(The Appeals court also found that the use was not transformative, a term we will learn more about in the next chapter).

Second Factor: the nature of the copyrighted work

We look to the Brammer's original photograph. Here the court is assessing the "thickness" or "thinness" of the copyright protection. How strong is the protection? The court looked to the range of creative choices in creating the photograph. Photographs are generally considered creative works (as opposed to factual works), and "have long received thick copyright protection" even when depicting factual events. 15 citing *Monge*, 688 F.3d at 1177. The court explained, "In taking the photograph at issue here, Brammer made many creative choices, which entitles Brammer's work to thick protection. The second factor weighs against Violent Hues.

Third Factor: amount and substantiality taken

For fair use, the goal of is to take "'no more...taken than necessary.' to accomplish the secondary user's purpose" 17 citing *HathiTrust*, 755 F.3d at 98 quoting *Campbell* 510 U.S. at 589. Violent Hues used ½ of the photograph, cropping out negative space, but keeping "the most expressive features, which constituted the 'heart of the work.'" 17 citing *Sunderman*, 142 F.3d at 205. Since the work was not transformative or a parody, there is no defense in taking the "heart of the work." The third factor weighs against Violent Hues.

Fourth Factor: effect on the market

How does the defendant's use harm the market for the original work? The court explains, "A 'common sense' presumption of cognizable market harm exists when a commercial use is not transformative but instead 'amounts to mere duplication of the entirety of an original.'" 18 citing *Campbell,* 510 U.S. at 591. Brammer licensed this exact photograph for the same purpose of representing a particular neighborhood in Washington, D.C. The fourth factor weighs against Violent Hues.

All four factors weigh against Violent Hues' fair use defense. The court ends with two important points.

> About the nature of our Internet world: "We reach our conclusion with the recognition that the Internet has made copying as easy as a few clicks of a button and that much of this copying serves copyright's objectives. Many social media platforms like Twitter, Facebook, and Instagram are specifically designed for the participatory 'sharing' --or copying -- of content. We express no opinion as to whether such sharing constitutes fair use. We note, however, that Violent Hues' use is not of this kind." (20)

> And about Violent Hues' use: "Violent Hues did not comment on the Photo, promote the Photo, "remix" the Photo or otherwise engage with the Photo in a way that might stimulate new insights. What Violent Hues did was publish a tourism guide for a commercial event and include the Photo to make the end product more visually interesting. Such a use would not constitute fair use when done in print, and it does not constitute fair use on the Internet." (20).

16: Copyright Fair Use & Art

When Can You Make Use of a Copyrighted Work

In 2009, Shepard Fairey was sued for using a picture of Barack Obama that was taken by Associated Press (AP) photographer Mannie Garcia. Fairey's art from that photograph has become iconic. At the time, fair use did not cover what he had done. It didn't fit into the categories we all now know. Everyone thought that the AP would win. The parties settled. Fairey should have gotten permission to use the photograph, everyone said. Over a decade later, fair use looks a lot different, and in part that is because of a concept called *transformative use*. Many believe that if the case was brought today, Fairey would win, and in some cases, the AP would not have even pursued the case. That is the story of this chapter. For artists, the concept of fair use, and in particular, transformative use under fair use can be powerful, and a tool not to be dismissed.

Transformative Uses

The transformative journey begins with the U.S. Supreme court case *Campbell v. Acuff Rose*, 510 U.S. 569 (1994), where 2 Live Crew, a rap group, took Roy Orbison's song "Oh, Pretty Woman," and made it their own. We discussed that a bit previously. "Pretty Woman" sounds strangely similar to the Orbison "Pretty Woman," but instead of putting a woman upon a pedestal to admire as Roy Orbison had done, the song is anything but flattering. And it has a different feel. Here are some of the lyrics from Verse 4.

> Two-timin' woman] Girl, you know you ain't right
> [Two-timin' woman] You was out with my boy last night
> [Two-timin' woman] That takes a load off my mind

> [Two-timin' woman] Now I know the baby ain't mine
> [O-o-o-o-oh, two-timin' woman]
> All: O-o-o-o-oh, two-timin' woman!

In 1994, Justice Souter, writing for the U.S. Supreme Court found that the 2 Live Crew song was a parody of the first "Oh, Pretty Woman". And this decision in some way set us on a new course with fair use. Let's take a look at the case briefly.

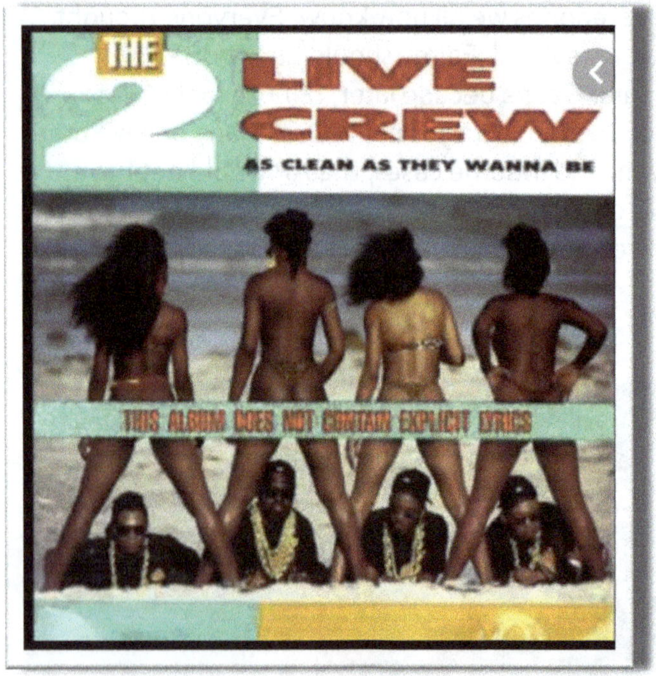

When 2 Live Crew decided to write their own version of "Oh, Pretty Woman", they contacted Acuff-Roses Music to obtain a license to create a parody. Acuff-Roses denied them a license. The rap group decided to move forward with the song anyway, and within a year, the recording had sold over 250,000 copies. Acuff-Rose was not pleased. The case worked its way through the court system. The district court found 2 Live Crew's version to be a parody of the original, which is covered under fair use. The Court of Appeals reversed, finding it unfair and taking too much of the work, and harming the potential market for the original song because of the commercial use of the 2 Live Crew version. Then the U.S. Supreme Court weighed in: they found that 2 Live Crew's version was a commercial parody that fell within fair use, and that what 2 Live Crew did was a "transformative use."

The court, in summary, explained that every work borrows from those before, but we see a tension of how much one can borrow before it becomes infringement. Fair use was developed by Justice Joseph Story (1779-1845) to find that balance between borrowing and the copyright holder's exclusive rights. The Supreme Court then turns to Section 107 of the Copyright Act, fair use. There are no bright line rules with fair use, no 10% rule, and no chart to review. The preamble even suggests that fair use can be many things, with the language "including" and "such as". (We know this already, right?) Justice Souter includes the Preamble:

> "Notwithstanding the provisions of sections 106 and 106A, the fair use of a copyrighted work, **including** such use by reproduction in copies or phonorecords or by any other means specified by that section, for purposes **such as** criticism, comment, news reporting, teaching (including multiple copies for classroom use), scholarship, or research, is not an infringement of copyright. In determining whether the use made of a work in any particular case is a fair use the factors to be considered shall include—" 17 U.S.C. Section 107.

The reason the court had to begin here was parody had not been included in the statute by word or name, they had to determine if it feels within the purpose or meaning of the statute. So, Justice Souter returned to Justice Story: "The central purpose of this [fair use] investigation is to see, in the words of Justice Story's words, whether the new work merely "supersede[s] the objects" of the original creation,...or instead adds something new, with a further purpose or different character, altering the first with new expression, meaning, or message; it asks, in other words, whether and to what extent the new work is **"transformative."** Transformative works, according to the court, "lie at the heart of the fair use doctrine's guarantee of breathing space within the confines of copyright."

The Court placed parody within comment or criticism, categories which *are* mentioned in the Preamble. The Court explains the definition of a parody: a "literary or artistic work that imitates the characteristic style of an author or work for comic effect or ridicule." The parodist quotes the original material to comment on the author's work. There is critical commentary in the use of other work. If this is missing, it is not parody; it is merely borrowing someone else's work to avoid the "drudgery in working up something fresh...Parody needs to mimic an original to make its point..." Here, the Court found 2 Live Crew's work to be a parody. The Court found that parody had "transformative value." You don't have to ask permission to comment or criticize a copyrighted work. That would just not make any sense at all.

The Court also tackled the question of commercial use, as it is mentioned in the first factor of the statute: "the purpose and character of the use, **including** whether such use is of a **commercial nature** or is for nonprofit educational purposes." The Court reasoned, because the statute uses the word "including", commercial uses is a factor only, and not determinative. Many activities, including news reporting, teaching, and scholarship, can be done for profit. And so, fair use does apply in commercial uses. We just have to evaluate the whole, and not only that one factor; the same is true for non-profit purposes too. Wholesale copying of a workbook in a non-profit educational use would likely not be seen as fair use, for example. Where the line seems to be drawn, then and now, is barring fair use to be used for commercially advertising a product, even if it is a parody.

What about the amount taken (factor 3), in this case, a good deal of the sound of the musical score, melody, and tempo of "Oh, Pretty Woman." For parodies, often you must take the "heart of work" to connect to the original work. In non-parody cases, taking the "heart of the work" often plays against the one using fair use as a defense. Not in parodies.

Then the court turned to the fourth factor, on economic impact on the original work. Traditionally, this had been one of the most important factors. With regard to a parody, this is less of a factor, because it does not offer itself as a substitution for the original: "the role of the courts is to distinguish between '[b]iting criticism [that merely] suppresses demand [and] copyright infringement [which] usurps it.' Citing. *Fisher* v. *Dees*, 794 F. 2d, at 438. In fact, the Court goes further to say that there is no derivative market (for licensing) for critical works. The copyright holder cannot control that market. This started a serious reliance of "transformative uses" and "parodies." There were a few more developments that were important too.

The Jeff Koons Cases

Artist Jeff Koons was sued four times in the U.S., losing the first three cases, and winning the fourth. What changed? Let's see what he learned.

In *Rogers v. Koons*, 960 F.2d 301 (2d Cir. 1992) concerned the event where Koons took Art Roger's professional postcard photograph depicting a couple with puppies and turned it into a colored 3D sculpture. Koons literally ripped the copyright notice off of the postcard, and sent it to Italy with instructions to reproduce it, but with the puppies turned blue, the noses exaggerated on the couple, and flowers added to their hair. It was part of his "Banality" series and he was sued for four other uses of someone else's work in the same show, including in France. Note: this case was decided two years before the Campbell case, but the outcome would likely have been the same at the time. The court did not find his work to be a parody: "The problem in the instant case is that even given that "String of Puppies" is a satirical critique of our materialistic society, it is difficult to discern any parody of the photograph "Puppies" itself." Moreover, by ripping off the copyright notice, they found he was working in bad faith, "primarily for profit-making motives, and did not constitute a parody of the original work." Koons produced four copies of the sculpture, which together sold for $367,000. His other two court cases making similar claims and Rogers' around the same time suffered the same fate. He could not use another artist's work to comment generally on the materialist nature of society.

Original Rogers photograph (left) next to Koon's 3D colorized statue (right)

Then in 2006, the Second Circuit again heard a Jeff Koons appeal in Blanch v. Jeff Koons (467 F. 3d 244, 2006), and this time he won. Fourteen years later, both Koons and fair use had become savvier. Here Koons had taken a commission to create a collage painting, titled "Easyfun-Ethereal", and as part of that had included images from advertisements and his own photographs, which were scanned into a computer and then the resulting image was printed as a template for his assistants to paint billboard-sized – 10' x 14' canvasses. They made 7 of these, and one, "Niagara" is the subject of the lawsuit.

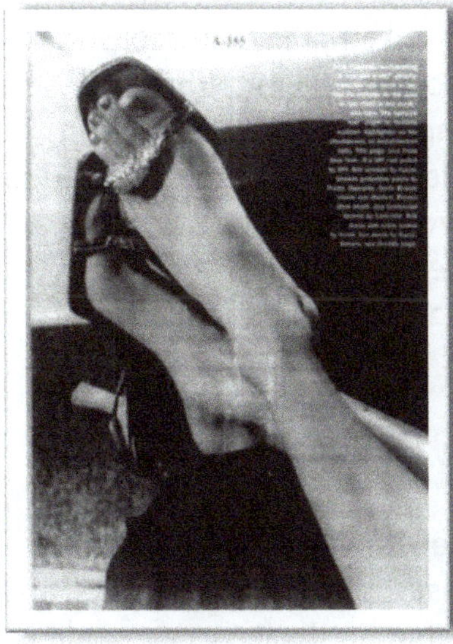

Original photograph by Andrea Blanch "Silk Sandals" as published in the August 2000 issue of Allure Magazine (left) next to Koon's collage and colorized version entitiled "Niagara" (right)

Koons had taken the legs from an advertisement, and like "Puppies," altered the image, including colorization, and changing the direction. The legs from "Silk Sandals" were positioned with other legs, and not all of the picture had been taken, just the feet/legs had been lifted off the background and out of context. Koons explained that he juxtaposed women's legs again a background of food and landscape: "he intended to "comment on the ways in which some of our most basic appetites -- for food, play, and sex -- are mediated by popular images." He further explained, "By re-contextualizing these fragments as I do, I try to compel the viewer to break out of the conventional way of experiencing a particular appetite as mediated by mass media." How would the court view this use of someone else's professional photograph? The court found, in the post-Campbell world, that Koon's use of the "Silk Sandals" legs was "transformative." The court explains, "Koons asserts -- and Blanch does not deny -- that his purposes in using Blanch's image are sharply different from Blanch's goals in creating it." The court articulates a test:

> The test for whether "Niagara's" use of "Silk Sandals" is "transformative," then, is whether it "merely supersedes the objects of the original creation, or instead adds something new, with a further purpose or different character, altering the first with new expression, meaning, or message." The test almost perfectly describes Koons's adaptation of "Silk Sandals": the use of a fashion photograph created for publication in a glossy American "lifestyles" magazine -- with changes of its colors, the background against which it is portrayed, the medium, the size of the objects pictured, the objects' details and, crucially, their entirely different purpose and meaning -- as part of a massive painting commissioned for exhibition in a German art-gallery space. We therefore conclude that the use in question was transformative.

Koons had learned how to make his work transformative. What a difference 14+ years made. He also started to think about transformative fair use as an artist – if he was going to use others' work without permission, he had to start thinking about *why* he was using them as part of the process.

Let's look at the Third Principle of the Code of Best Practices of Visual Art for the Center for Media and Social Impact at American University.[40] "Artists may invoke fair use to incorporate copyrighted material into new artworks in any medium, subject to certain limitations...."[41] The limitations include that the artist should include materials **creating "new artistic meaning,"** and **should be justified by the artistic objective**, with **artists able to explain the rationale for the use** and **why they are integral to the meaning of the new work**. And when using the work of someone else, make sure to cite the source when possible. This IS the Koon's case, the fourth one he finally won, right? Let's take a look at a few other cases, and see how transformative use continued to grow in power.

Transformative Artwork and Fair Use

The concept of transformative fair use is now firmly established, and in particular, with art. According to the Copyright Office's Fair Use Index, we have 25 cases concerning artworks, and a few more are currently working their way through the courts. What do these 25 cases tell us about transformative use in artwork, and thinking about the use as an artist? Let's take a look at a few of them.

Andy Warhol Foundation for Visual Arts v. Goldsmith is the most recent transformative fair use case, decided in SDNY on July 1, 2019.

[40] Code of Best Practices in Visual Arts, Center for Media and Social Impact, American University, https://cmsimpact.org/code/fair-use-for-the-visual-arts/.

[41] College Art Association, 2015; https://www.collegeart.org/pdf/fair-use/best-practices-fair-use-visual-arts.pdf; last accessed 1/12/2020)

Andy Warhol Foundation for Visual Arts v. Goldsmith 382 F. Supp. 3d 312 (S.D.N.Y.2019)

Original photograph by Lynn Goldsmith (left) next to Warhol version in Vanity Fair (right)

Like in the Koons cases, the photograph at issue was taken by a professional photographer, this time by Lynn Goldsmith. The photograph in this case was a photograph of Prince, taken in 1981. The photograph was licensed by Vanity Fair r4om Goldsmith in 1984 for use as an artist's reference in connection with an article about Prince. Vanity Fair hired Andy Warhol, who transformed the actual photo into a sea of colors. After Prince's death in 2016, Vanity Fair republished the Warhol art work based on the photograph, and that's when the photographer, Goldsmith got upset, believing the Warhol work was copyright infringement. The district court went through the four factors of fair use.

First Factor: nature and character of (third party) use

While commercial in nature, the Warhol version added value to the public interest, and transformed Goldsmith's black-and-white photograph from someone portrayed as a "vulnerable human being" into a "larger than life figure. Warhol made it into his own style. (Think back to Shepard Fairy at the beginning of this chapter. Didn't he do that too?)

Second Factor: nature of the copyrighted work

While the original work was unpublished and creative (favoring Goldsmith), the work was licensed previously as a source for the final work.

Third Factor: the quantitative amount and qualitative value of the original work

The amount and substantiality of the work. The court found that Warhol removed the protectable items – namely the lighting, angle selection, and expression. This is interesting. Thinking back to a very old case involving Oscar Wilde (Burrow-Giles Lithographic Co. v. Sarony, 111 U.S. 53, 1884), photography was given copyright protection *because* of the photographer's selection, arrangement and coordination for the photograph. Here the court is saying that the transformative nature of Warhol's work stripped those from the photograph. Does that mean that fair use is not necessary because in his use, he did not infringe a copyrighted work? It's a strange and interesting argument.

Fourth Factor: effect on the market

The effect on the market, the court found that Warhol's work is not a market substitute for Goldsmith's. Again, weird. Couldn't there be a market for licensing images to artists for this purpose? And of course, what about the original license for the photograph? What is the take away lesson here? Use a photograph; strip it of its copyrightable choices; and make it your own. No need for a license. This is an incredible statement for artists using others' photographs. Less good for photographers. This is very different from the Shepard Fairey case. How did we get here? We've seen cases before this where the creep of transformative use is apparent.

Cariou v. Prince 714 F.3d 694 (2d Cir. 2013) (2013)

This is an important case for artists, and I think in part, where the creep of transformativeness for artists really gets traction. In 2000, Patrick Cariou published a book, *Yes Rasta*, a book of portraits and photographs taken in Jamaica. Richard Prince, a famous artist, took the photographs and created paintings and collages, which were exhibited at a gallery. He did not get permission to use the images.

Prince had purchased a copy of the book, and had torn 35 of Cariou's photos out, and pinned them to a piece of plywood. He started altering the photographs with paint. He purchased three more copies of *Yes Rasta.* He created a series of works. (So far, he has not done any copying. He purchased a book, and with his First Sale doctrine rights, has done with it what he imagined. Some courts see this as totally legal; others see this as a violation of the original artist's derivative work – we have a circuit split at the moment. But the court does not go there. Instead, it focuses on fair use.

Photograph by Patrick Cariou from Yes Rasta (left), next to Prince's collage of them (right)

Original Cariou's photograph (left) next to Prince's "painted" version (right)

The last one is really famous, where Prince added blue paint to the original photograph. Each artwork had varying degrees of the *Yes Rasta* images. Some were visible; others were obscured. The court also noted that the book itself was 9.5" x 12", whereas Prince's paintings were 72" x52", 100" x104", and 40" x30", significantly larger.

Prince's *Canal Zone* show included a catalog, which included copying and distributing Cariou's underlying photographs, which was different from Prince ripping out pages. Prince, again, did not obtain permission from Cariou. Cariou learned that his photographs were in Prince's show; Cariou was also looking to put his own images into a show, and so Prince's use of Cariou's images became a market replacement in Cariou's view, because his work was seen as already having been exhibited by Prince, but with no recognition of his work. It was Prince's show, not Cariou's.

The Second Circuit began its analysis. The district court had required that under the first factor, "to qualify for a fair use defense, a secondary use must 'comment on, relate to the historical context of, or critically refer back to the original works.'" Cariou, 784 F. Supp. 2d at 348." The Second Circuit appeals court responded: "The law imposes no requirement that a work comment on the original or its author in order to be considered transformative, and a secondary work may constitute a fair use even if it serves some purpose other than those (criticism, comment, news reporting, teaching, scholarship, and research) identified in the preamble to the statute." (citing Campbell at 577; Harper & Row, 471 U.S. at 561.) Instead, the court believed the Supreme Court required a "new expression, meaning or message", citing *Campbell* and *Blanch v. Koons*. The commenting/criticism/parody had been removed. This is HUGE. The court found that all but five of Prince's art works using Cariou's photographs were transformative, creating a new expression, meaning or message, with a different approach or aesthetic. "Here, looking at the artworks and the photographs side-by-side, we conclude that Prince's images, except for those we discuss separately below, have a different character, give Cariou's photographs a new expression, and employ new aesthetics with creative and communicative results distinct from Cariou's."

On the five works the court did not agree were fair use, they stated "As indicated above, there are five artworks that, upon our review, present closer questions. Specifically, Graduation, Meditation, Canal Zone (2008), Canal Zone (2007), and Charlie Company do not sufficiently differ from the photographs of Cariou's that they incorporate for us confidently to make a determination about their [...] transformative nature as a matter of law. Although the minimal alterations that Prince made in those instances moved the work in a different direction from Cariou's classical portraiture and landscape photos, we cannot say with certainty at this point whether those artworks present a "new expression, meaning, or message."

After Cariou, artist communities felt both panicked that their works could be appropriated, and also felt new artistic freedom to use others' works, as long as they created "new expression, meaning or message."

Seltzer v. Green Day, Inc., et al., No. 11-56573 (9th Cir. 2013)

In 2013, the Ninth Circuit also found fair use in a case involving the band, Green Day. David Seltzer created street art in Los Angeles of a screaming, contorted face called "Scream Icon". Seltzer made pictures of this work in various sizes with adhesive backs and both gave away and sold them. The Court explains, "Since then, Seltzer has moved on to other projects, but at times he has used *Scream Icon* to identify himself and his work's presence by pricing it on advertisements for his gallery appearances, and at some point he licensed it for use in a music video." Now, one would think this seems like the case we saw with Brammer and the film fest case.

Photographer Roger Staub took a picture of the corner of Sunset Boulevard and Gardner Avenue, which was covered in graffiti and posters, and included a "weathered and torn copy of *Scream Icon.*" Staub added it to his personal library. In 2009, Staub was hired to create a video backdrop for Green Day's set list for their upcoming concert. For the eighth song of the album, "East Jesus Nowhere," Staub created a four-minute-long video where there is a brick alley covered in graffiti, and where "at an accelerated pace... [graffiti artists come and go, adding new art, posters, and tags to the brick alleyway. The graffiti includes at least three images of Jesus Christ, which are defaced over the course of the video. Throughout the video, the center of the frame is dominated by an unchanging, but modified, *Scream Icon.* Staub used the photograph he had taken at Sunset and Gardner, cut out the image of scream Icon, and modified it by adding a large red "spray-painted" cross over the middle of the screaming face. He changed the contrast and color and added black streaks running down the right side of the face." IIs this starting to feel more like the Andy Warhol case? The district court found fair use, and awarded $201,012.50 in attorney's fees to Green Day. Seltzer appealed. (Remember, the artist brought the action; he lost to Green Day, and is now responsible for over $200,000 *to Green Day.*

Original "Scream Icon" by David Seltzer (left), next to Green Day's "religious" version (right) used during their song "East Jesus Nowhere"

Let's look at how the appeals court approached the case.

First Factor: purpose and character of the use

The court turns to defining transformative, recognizing that this is complicated. The court returns to the roots of "transformative" in their analysis. Judge Leval in *Towards a Fair Use Standard*, 103 Harv. L. Rev. 1105 (1990) expressed what "transformative" means, which was adopted by the U.S. Supreme Court in Campbell:

> The use must be productive and must employ the quoted matter in a different manner or for a different purpose from the original. A quotation of copyrighted material that merely repackages or republishes the original is unlikely to pass the test; in Justice Story's words, it would merely "supersede the objects" of the original. If, on the other hand, the secondary use adds value to the original—if the quoted matter is used as raw material, transformed in the creation of new information, new aesthetics, new insights and understandings—this is the very type of activity that the fair use doctrine intends to protect for the enrichment of society. (As cited in Seltzer v. Green Day, Inc.,725 F.3d 1170 (9th Cir. 2013))

Using Judge Leval's language, the court finds Green Day's use of *Scream Icon* transformative.

- The *Scream Icon* is used as "raw material"
- The music is street-art focused
- "The message and meaning of the original *Scream Icon* is debatable. To us, it appears to be a directionless anguished screaming face." Seltzer confirmed that it was about youth and skateboard culture in Los Angeles.
- Green Day transformed the message into something having to do with religion with "new information, new aesthetics, new insights and understandings".

The court explains, "an allegedly infringing work is typically viewed as transformative as long as new expressive content or message is apparent." Green Day's work is considered transformative. About the commercial nature of the use, the court found it "only incidentally commercial; the band never used it to market the concert, CDs, or merchandise." The first factor weighs in Green Day's favor. Do you agree with the court so far?

Second Factor: nature of the copyrighted work

The court finds that *Scream Icon* is a creative work deserving strong protection. Then, strangely, the court turns to whether the work was published, finding that *Scream Icon* was "widely disseminated, both on the Internet and the streets of Los Angeles before Green Day used it in their concert." Strangely still, the court finds that wide dissemination weighs in favor of fair use. No further analysis is given. "Considering this factor as a whole, it weighs only slightly in Seltzer's favor." Does this surprise you? Making you a bit nervous?

Third Factor: amount and Substantiality of portion used

The court recognizes that Green Day copied most of *Scream Icon*, both quantitatively and qualitatively, but says the image is not "meaningfully divisible." The court found that the entire work was necessary to achieve Green Day's "new expression, meaning or message." The court decides the third factor "does not weigh against Green Day."

Fourth Factor: effect on the market

Even though Seltzer had licensed the image to a music video, he had not shown how much revenue he had earned, and how the music video was used by the band. The Court said that Seltzer did not show harm to an existing market or a market Seltzer was likely to develop, and so weighed Factor four in favor of Green Day. To me, this is really the most surprising.

So, the court found fair use in Green Day's use of Seltzer's *Screen Icon.* The court then turned to the $200,000 award to Green Day in attorney's fees.

How are attorney's fees decided?

Attorney's fees are not automatic. There are five non-exclusive factors courts look to: "1) degree of success obtained; 2) frivolousness; 3) motivation; 4) the objective unreasonableness of the losing party's factual and legal arguments; and 5) the need, in particular circumstances, to advance considerations of compensation and deterrence." The district court had found Seltzer's claim "objectively unreasonable." The appeals court continued, "But, the mere fact that Seltzer lost cannot establish his objective unreasonability." They saw it as a close and difficult case: "We concluded that Seltzer's work was transformed by Green Day's use. But that transformation was far from obvious given Green Day's only slight alterations to the original. Furthermore, of the remaining three factors, one was in Seltzer's favor, one was in Green Day's favor, and one was neutral. There is simply no reason to believe that Seltzer 'should have known from the outset that [his] chances of success in this case were slim to none.'" The appeals court vacated the award of attorney's fees.

This case should give one pause. Wide dissemination counted against the original artist. Changing the message seems to be enough.

Art, But No Fair Use

Morris v. Guetta (No. LA CV12-00684 JAK (RZX) (C.D. Cal. Feb. 4, 2013)

Another 2013 case, the same year as the Green Day case, Morris v. Guetta, tackled the question of fair use, with a very different outcome (No. LA CV12-00684 JAK (RZX) (C.D. Cal. Feb. 4, 2013)). In this case, again a photograph was used without permission. In this case, it was a 1977 photograph of the Sex Pistols bassist Sid Vicious taken by Dennis Morris. Thierry Guetta, known as "Mr. Brainwash," (from the film *Exit Through the Gift Shop),* a self-proclaimed appropriation artist, created pop art pieces using the photographs, where he added colors and contrast. Guetta created seven art pieces using the Photograph, adding "element such as splashes of brightly colored paint. One work features Sid Vicious wearing sunglasses and is printed on a backdrop with the character Snoopy and palm trees. One is a mural. One is made out of broken vinyl records. Two works add a mole on the image of the face of Sid Vicious and an overlay of blonde hair in a different style. Some, but not all, of Guetta's seven works were sold." The court looks to see if there is a valid copyright, and if there had been copying, which they find to be the case. Then, the court turned to fair use.

First Factor: nature and character of (third party) use

The court begins with Justice Story: "whether the new work merely "supersede[s] the objects" of the original creation ... or instead adds something new, with a further purpose or different character, altering the first with new expression, meaning, or message; it asks, in other words, whether and to what extent the new work is "transformative." citing Campbell, 510 U.S. at 579. To have a transformative use, the defendant must place the work in a "different context such that the plaintiff's work is transformed into a new creation." citing Wall Data Inc v. Los Angeles Country Sherriff's Dept, 447 F.3d 769, 778 (9th Cir.). The court explains that the more transformative, the more likely fair use will be found. The court looks to many of the case we have already discussed. Then gets to the heart of the matter.

The court did not find Guetta's work sufficiently transformative. "Thus, it is not apparent that Defendants' work adds something new, have a further purpose or are of a different character do to a new expression, meaning or message." The court compares the two works; both have the same facial expression, and the elements added by Guetta are not transformative. "Defendants' work remains at the core pictures of Sid Vicious." The court finds no meaning behind the work; it doesn't meet the standards of Blanch v. Koons, 960 F.2d at 253: "8 Blanch, 467 F.3d 244, provides a clear standard that bridges these two requirements: An artist is not required to compromise his or her artistic vision merely because the artist could have made a similar statement in a non-infringing way. However, the artist must provide a sufficient justification for using another's copyrighted material in effecting the artist's vision. Such a justification could be based on making a commentary on the material used in the other work, i.e., parody. It could also be based on a clear articulation of how using the material served the artist's objective beyond merely saving the artist time or effort, i.e., satire." (8) Guetta had a vague reasoning for using the photograph of "making a commentary on Sid Vicious personal and on the nature of celebrity generally." (9) Sounds like Jeff Koons in his first case that he lost. And here too, the court does not find it sufficient. The first factor weighs against Guetta.

Second Factor: nature of the copyrighted work

The Photograph was creative, and therefore gets thick protection. The second factor weighs against Guetta.

Third Factor: Amount and Substantiality of Portion Used

You look to what was taken, not what was added. Guetta took nearly everything, even though he striped some detailed elements out of the photograph. The third factor weighs against Guetta.

Fourth Factor: Market Effect

The record does not show harm to the market. But "any dispute over the market effect is immaterial because a lack of harm would not change the determination of an unjustified use under the first factor." (13)

The court did not find fair use.

Original photograph by Dennis Morris (left) next to "Mr. Brainwash's" colorized version (right)

So, here, the artist, "Mr. Brainwash," who has a whole backstory (is this a trickster?) admitted to having no meaning or value, and therefore fair use did not apply.

Furie v. Infowars, LLC, Case No. CV 18-1830-MWF (JPRx) (C.D. Cal. May 16, 2019)

This case involves Pepe the Frog, a character that has been part of a comic series and books by Matt Furie since at least 2003. Pepe the Frog became a meme during the 2016 presidential election campaign of Donald Trump, implying support of Trump by Pepe the Frog. Jon Allen made a poster using his own rendering of Pepe, which was used and sold widely, including on Infowars. No permission or license was obtained from Furie.

The court found the use of Pepe as commercial, but not transformative. In reviewing the Second Factor, the fact that Pepe had become a meme did not diminish the copyright —you don't lose copyright if your work becomes popular. (Compare that to the Green Day case, of course).

The plaintiff believed that the adoption of Pepe for the alt-right had harmed the market for his comics. The court rejected a First Amendment argument from Infowars that it stood as political speech, which is also interesting.

Result? You can't co-opt someone else's creative work wholesale for your own posters, even if they are political, or maybe especially if they are political. Infowars made nearly $14,000 from the poster, before it stopped selling the poster in June 2018. Under the settlement, the Infowars agreed to pay Furie $15,000. Infowars saw this as a huge win. Pepe the Frog's image was also pulled from The Daily Stormer in 2018 under a Digital Millennium Copyright Act action by its creator.[42]

Pepe the Frog by Furie (left) and Jon Allen's image including his rendering of Pepe (right)

[42] "Pepe the Frog removed from Daily Stormer after creator makes legal challenge" https://www.theguardian.com/books/2018/jul/12/pepe-the-frog-daily-stormer-matt-furie

Back to Fairey

Stanford's Fair Use Project stepped in to represent Sheppard Fairey, and it was the Fair Use project that filed a declaratory judgment for fair use against AP. Fairey is a professional artist, who trained at Rhode Island School of Design. The original photograph was taken by a Mannie Garcia, who worked for AP.

On April 27, 2006, Garcia took the photograph while assigned to cover a National Press Club conference which Senator Barack Obama was attending, where George Clooney was talking about his recent trip to Darfur, Africa. William Fisher describes the scene in "Reflections on the Hope Poster Case," 25 Harvard Journal of Law and Technology 244 (2012).[43] Many photographers were there. In the space of 45 minutes, Garcia took 250 photographs, with 39 of them of Obama. He submitted 16 of the photos to the AP, which included one of Obama alone and another with Obama and Clooney. While the Garcia Obama photograph was published, it was not high profile and disappeared quickly.

Fairey created the poster by searching Google Images to hunt for a "publicly available" image of Obama. He chose 6-8 photos out of the 200 he viewed, and chose the Garcia Clooney photograph with Obama, but then later switched to the Garcia Obama photograph. Using Adobe Photoshop and Illustrator, he went to work. Fisher describes the process in detail, and then the file was sent to the printers. Fairey's goal was to help the Obama campaign to win the democratic nomination. He gave away most of the 350,000 posters, but did make royalties on merchandise and clothing. He made four "fine art" versions. He also was commissioned to create a mural for the Democratic National Convention. "All told, Fairey earned from the project roughly $1 million, of which more than $830,000 was due to Fairey's sales of the fine art editions and his royalties from the mural and images commissioned by the Presidential Inauguration Committee and Moveon.org." (Fisher). It was acknowledged that hi "Hope" poster made a difference.

There was confusion as to whether Fairey had used the Garcia Obama photo or the Garcia Clooney photo. There was also confusion that it might be a Reuters photographer. Once sorted out, AP contacted him. Fairey had offered the "customary license fee," but AP wanting a percentage of all Fairey's revenue. (Fisher). Fairey contacted Stanford Fair Use Project to help him. Stanford filed a declaratory judgment, "one day before the AP had indicated that it would file suit." (Fisher)

[43] http://jolt.law.harvard.edu/articles/pdf/v25/25HarvJLTech243.pdf

The Clooney Obama Photograph

The Obama photograph

Fairey's Poster

So, Fairey had misremembered which photo he had used, and his attorneys had assumed it was the Clooney photo. But it wasn't. A blogger figured out it was the Obama alone photograph. When he realized the error, he didn't inform his attorneys--for eight months. And worse, he covered it up. The attorneys at Stanford withdrew as his lawyers. He found new ones, including William Fisher III from Harvard Law School's Berkman Center for Internet and Society.

The Case would be settled before it got to trial.

Working Through the Case

As our final fair use case, let's go through the full process. Here are the steps.

1. Was there a valid copyright in the Photograph?
2. Was the photograph actually copied?
3. Was the amount copied improper or unlawful appropriation?
4. If Yes to 3, then, does the fair use doctrine apply?

Fairey did not contest that there was a valid copyright, and that the photograph was actually used the photograph as reference, establishing "actual copying". But Fairey did not believe he took protected expression, no improper appropriation. AP believed the photograph was highly creative. Like the Warhol case, years earlier, Fairey was arguing that he had removed the copyrightable elements, and that the pose fell under *scene a faire*. Regarding the fair use analysis, Fairey argued that his use was "transformative", where his purpose of use was distinct from the original, and that the First Amendment protects political speech. He also had added substantially new materials, just like *Blanch v. Koons,* and that the photograph was merely "raw material." For the second factor, he suggested the photograph was "factual" because it was reporting on an event. The third factor -- the amount -- Fairey claimed he took *no* copyrightable expression. The fourth factor, the market, Fairey argued that his work did not keep others from purchasing copies of Garcia's photograph. The AP, in contrast, pointed to the money Fairey had made, and that his work was not transformative because there was no parody or comment. This last argument has now been settled--we have many cases that expand transformative in the art context to beyond parody or comment. AP worried that if Fairey could do this, others would too, and that would harm the AP. Unfortunately, we never had a court opinion.

The settlement included the following:

- "Neither side surrenders its view of the law.
- Fairey agrees not to use another AP photo without obtaining a license from the AP.
- In the future, the parties will share the rights to make and distribute posters and merchandise bearing the Hope image.
- Fairey and the AP will collaborate in creating a new set of images based upon AP photos.
- In addition, the parties agreed to financial terms that remain confidential."[44]

In the law review from Harvard, Sheppard Fairey reflected on his experience:

- On using a photograph instead of drawing it himself: he wanted the image to look like Obama
- Is illustrating from a photograph "cheating"? No. It was part of his training at Rhode Island School of Design, and is an appropriate technique.

---

[44] Id at 269.

- Is reference art plagiarism? No, it is a common practice in the art world.
- Appropriation is part of art, in using pre-existing materials as a reference point, and changing the perspective.
- Why not obtain a license? He used a news photo for reference; his point was to "convince and inspire. It is a political statement." He was relying on fair use. While he made money, this was not, with even a free download available.
- Why litigation? To protect artists engaged in similar activities.

The article includes other elements, but it ends with Professor William Fisher, "How to Handle Appropriation Art." He advocated an interpretation of *Campbell v. Acuff Rose* and "transformative use," "that a defendant's work is transformative if its purpose is different from that of the Plaintiff's work." At that point, a number of cases, including *Blanch v. Koons*, 467 F.3d 244 (2d Cir.2006) had made such a statement.

Conclusion for Artists

- If you are using a photograph or someone else's work, either get a license for the use, or alternatively, transform its look, but <u>also its message and meaning</u>.
- The artistic transformation doesn't appear to be as important as the message transformation. And if you don't have any meaning behind your changes, like "Mr. Brainwash" and the early Jeff Koons cases, don't use other's creative work.

17: Fair Uses of Trademark & Right of Publicity

When Can You Make Use of a Copyrighted Work

Trademark law focuses on source identifiers: names, logos and other elements that identify a good or service. Yet, trademarks are also used to describe a good, refer to it, and also used within a particular cultural context. Think, "the Rolls Royce of thread." It conveys the thread is expensive and precious. There are a number of instances where trademarked goods and services – the trademark itself can be used within permissible uses. So too with Right of Publicity. We will see there are certain situations where you are allowed to use someone else's likeness in your creative work without permission. As part of our creative process, we may use trademarked goods and/or someone's right of publicity.

This chapter looks at instances (like fair use in copyright) where you can use *someone else's trademark* or *right of publicity*, and kind of connects with our conversation about artists and transformative use of the previous chapter.

Trademark

We will be looking at a number of concepts in trademark: nominative use, descriptive fair use, and the First Amendment and trademark. We will also look at right of publicity and the First Amendment.

Nominative Use

I am doing an interview on the podcast. I ask someone "What is your favorite batting?" They can answer that question, "The Warm Company," even though the name is trademarked. If we can't name the things in our life, we would be paralyzed. I have to be able to say, "I'm a law prof at Tulane University." I'm using Tulane's trademark in that instance, but it is to identify my place of work. You can do that. Comparative advertising uses that. "Wonderfil is so much better than Angelfil." (I made up that last company). The claims must be truthful and verifiable if numbers are used. "Four out of five dentists..." (But now we're getting into advertising law...). But you can name a trademarked goods or service - nominative use.

The concept of nominative use comes from two cases: one about New Kids on the Block, and another about Terri Welles, a former Playmate of the Year. In both cases, the courts agreed that you had to be able name. For the New Kids on the Block (New Kids on the Block v. News Am. Pub., Inc., 971 F.2d 302 (9th Cir. 1992)), the case concerned a quiz by two media outlets on which "New Kid" you preferred; you were charged $0.50 cents when you responded to the poll. You had to name the New Kids to have the quiz. The courts did not agree with the New Kids attempt to block use of their trademarked name, "[w]hile the New Kids have a limited property right in their name, that right does not entitle them to control their fans' use of their own money. Where, as here, the use does not imply sponsorship or endorsement, the fact that it is carried on for profit and in competition with the trademark holder's business is beside the point.". In the second case, Playboy Enterprises Inc. v. Welles (279 F. 3d 796 (2002)), Terri had created an early website naming herself as 1981 Playmate of the Year and used PMOY, Playboy and Playmate in metatags, but she also used the phrase "Playmate of the Year" as wallpaper on her site. The court said, after her countersuit, that you could name it, but you couldn't decorate with it. Nominative use. (See faintly the PMOY in the white background over and over? You can't do that.)

Incidental Use of Trademarks

You are in an interview that is being recorded. You happen to be drinking a LeCroix water. You are not endorsing the product. You just happen to be drinking it. This is called an incidental use. You are not using it as an ad. You are just depicting your life.

What about when people demonstrate something on a sewing machine that shows the trademark (e.g., Bernina, Juki, Janome, etc.), but the person is not connected to the company? They are using their own equipment. Is this an incidental use? That sewing machine company could fuss at the use. Would they? Likely not, because it is free publicity.

Descriptive (or Classic) Fair Use

Descriptive fair use is a little more complicated. Sometimes companies choose trademarks that describe their product, but over time, people identify the product with that company. I can use that descriptive word, even if it is someone else's trademark. For example, a cosmetic company, Chesebrough-Pond's USA Co., ran a campaign for Cutex using "Seal it with a Kiss!!," and asked customers to kiss a postcard and send it to someone they love. The owner of the registered mark SEALED WITH A KISS, Cosmetically Sealed Industries, Inc., a competing line of cosmetics, sued. The court said that "sealed with a kiss" was common and being used in a descriptive sense, not as a source identifier of a product, and so qualified as descriptive fair use. "So long as the defendants [Chesebrough] in good faith are using the phrase in its descriptive sense and prominently identifying the product with the defendants' marks, the defendants incur no liability simply because the materials containing the descriptive phrase are so widely disseminated as to form some degree of association in the public's mind between the phrase and the product. That too is a risk the plaintiff [CBI] took in selecting as its mark a phrase that was not only descriptive but readily recognized by consumers." See Cosmetically Sealed Industries, Inc. v. Chesebrough-Pond's USA Co.125 F.3d 28 (2d Cir. 1997).

Trademark, Right of Publicity and the First Amendment

We're now going to turn to a famous case involving the Danish dance-pop musical group Aqua and their song, "Barbie Girl." A classic. We'll learn about trademark and the First Amendment, and Right of Publicity and the First Amendment.

Mattel, Inc. v. MCA Records, 296 F.3d 894 (9th Cir. 2002).

The case, written by Judge Kozinski, starts out with this sentence: "If this were a sci-fi melodrama, it might be called Speech-Zilla meets Trademark Kong." Kozinski is known for his *creative* writing in opinions. We're going to work our way through this case, because it touches upon a lot of the key element for artists using other people's/company's trademarks.

Kozinski begins with Barbie, the doll, describing her origins in the 1950s as an adult collector's item, and then turning into the mega toy that she is. "Barbie has been labeled both the ideal American woman and a bimbo...She remains a symbol of American girlhood, a public figure who graces the aisles of toy stores throughout the country and beyond. With Barbie, Mattel created not just a toy, but a cultural icon."

Image from the video, "Barbie Girl" by Aqua

Aqua is a Danish band that "as yet, only dreamed of attaining Barbie-like status." (And who says court cases are dry and boring!). Aqua created a song called "Barbie Girl" on their album *Aquarium*. The song is about Barbie's life, with the band members acting out the parts of Ken and (high-pitched singing) Barbie. The song made it to the Top 40 list (and anyone who was a teenager at that time can probably still sing the lyrics!). Mattel sued in 2002.[45]

And here are the beginning lyrics to the song:

> Hiya Barbie
> Hi Ken!
> You wanna go for a ride?
> Sure, Ken!
> Jump in!
> Ha ha ha ha
> I'm a Barbie girl in the Barbie world
> Life in plastic, it's fantastic

[45] You can listen to and see the video on YouTube here: https://www.youtube.com/watch?v=ZyhrYis509A {last accessed 1/11/2020}.

> You can brush my hair, undress me everywhere
> Imagination, life is your creation
> Come on, Barbie, let's go party
> I'm a Barbie girl in the Barbie world
> Life in plastic, it's fantastic
> You can brush my hair, undress me everywhere
> Imagination, life is your creation
> I'm a blonde single girl in the fantasy world

Kozinski gets down to analyzing the case. "A trademark is a word, phrase, or symbol that is used to identify a manufacturer or sponsor of a good or the provider of a service," explains the Judge. The question is how the First Amendment interacts with the property right awarded by the United States Patent and Trademark Office (USPTO) to the trademark holder. Some marks become part of our language, like "the Rolls Royce of its class," or "What else is a quick fix, but a Band Aid?" We use the mark to express concepts; they have become part of our vocabulary. They are not, in this case, being used as a source identifier, but we recognize the qualities of the mark to describe something else. "Simply put, the trademark owner does not have the right to control public discourse whenever the public imbues his mark with meaning beyond its source-identifying function." Kozinski then turns back to the Mattel case.

Here, Aqua used Mattel's mark, both as the title of the song, and as the subject of the song. "The song pokes fun at Barbie and the values that Aqua contends she represents.... The song does not rely on the Barbie mark to poke fun at another subject but targets Barbie herself." This sounds a lot like the copyright case, *Campbell v. Acuff-Rose,* right? He cites this and other cases.

Kozinski relied upon the *Rogers* case. He explains "The Second Circuit has held that "in general [the Trademark Act] should be construed to apply to artistic works only when the public interest in avoiding consumer confusion outweighs the public interest in free expression." Rogers v. Grimaldi, 875 F.2d 994, 999. This phrase became known as the *Rogers* test. Kozinski would apply it with "Barbie Girl. Let's take a look at *Rogers*.

Ginger Rogers sued over Federico Fellini's film *Ginger and Fred* for using her name in the title, and believed the film gave a false impression that she had endorsed the film; therefore, violated her right of publicity, and defamed her by presenting her in a negative light. The film was about "two Italian cabaret performers who made a living by imitating Ginger Rogers and Fred Astaire." Rogers was not happy. She believed that people would see the title and subject matter of the film as an endorsement from her. "This appeal presents a conflict between Rogers' right to protect her celebrated name and the right of others to express themselves freely in their own artistic work. Specifically, we must decide whether Rogers can prevent the use of the title Ginger and Fred for a fictional movie that only obliquely relates to Rogers and Astaire."

Kozinski explains the result. "At first glance, Rogers certainly had a point. Ginger was her name, and Fred was her dancing partner. If a pair of dancing shoes had been labeled Ginger and Fred, a dancer might have suspected that Rogers was associated with the shoes (or at least one of them), just as Michael Jordan has endorsed Nike sneakers that claim to make you fly through the air. But Ginger and Fred was not a brand of shoe; it was the title of a movie...and [should] be treated differently."

Titles communicate a message, but rarely identify the publisher or producer. Moreover, when an artist uses a title, very rarely would the public think that the artist is connected to the brand. He gives the example that when you see a *painting* of Campbell soup can, "we're unlikely to believe that Campbell's has branched into the art business. Nor, upon hearing Janis Joplin croon 'Oh Lord, won't you buy me a Mercedes-Benz?,'' would we suspect that she and the carmaker had entered into a joint venture."

Ginger Rogers and Fred Astaire from "The Gay Divorcee" (1934)

Giulietta Masina and Marcello Mastroianni from the film Ginger and Fred (

The *Rogers* case found that "literary titles do not violate the [Trademark Act] 'unless the title had no artistic relevance to the underlying work whatsoever, or if it has some artistic relevance, unless the title explicitly misleads as to the source or the content of the work." (*Rogers* at 999, cited by *Mattel)*. *Rogers* became known for a two-part test for analyzing whether someone's artistic use of a trademark work was infringing.

1. Is the use relevant to the underlying work?
2. Does the use explicitly mislead as to the source of the work?

The *Rogers* case was quickly adopted and expanded.

Kozinski applied the *Rogers* case. Aqua's use of the title "Barbie" was not trademark infringement. The use of the word "Barbie" in the title was relevant to the underlying work, and the song does not explicitly mislead as to the source of the work. After the Mattel case, another Barbie case took up the issue: Mattel v. Walking Mountain Productions (353 F.3d 792 (9th Cir. 2003)). Artist Tom Forsythe used nude Barbies in different cooking positions: "Barbies in a Blender", "Enchilada Barbie", "Fondue a la Barbie", etc. The court applied the *Rogers* test, finding the use of the mark was a parody, and that the mark was not explicitly misleading. (Forsythe would win $1.8 million award against Mattel). Other cases followed that were not Barbie related.

So, that's the test. Using a trademark in an artistic way: is the use relevant to the underlying artistic work being created, and does the use explicitly mislead as to the source of the work? Can you think of examples? One more big case: University of Alabama v. Moore

Daniel Moore is a painter that since 1979 has focused his work on famous University of Alabama football scenes. For the first 11 years, Moore had no relationship with the University. Then, in 1991, he signed a dozen licensing agreements with the University for market-specific items. His work appears in calendars, mugs, and other items. He also continued to create and sell paintings and prints that were not subject to the licensing agreement, and some that he had created before the agreement. In 2002, the University of Alabama told Moore he needed to get permission to depict uniforms of the UA because the uniforms were trademarks in the unlicensed paintings and prints. Moore disagreed because he said he was using them to depict historical events—the football games. UA sued Moore in 2005. The 11th Circuit divided the discussion between the paintings, prints and calendars, and the "mundane products."

The court concluded that the First Amendment interests in artistic expression outweighed any consumer confusion, and so no trademark infringement occurred. The court turned to the *Rogers* test. They noted that other circuits had applied the *Rogers* test, including to a parody of *Cliff Notes* called *Spy Notes* (Cliff Notes, Inc. v. Bantam Doubleday Dell Publishing Group, 886 F.2d 490 (2d Cir. 1989)); a use the trademark for an entertainment club in a video game (EESS Entertainment 2000, Inc. v. Rock Star Videos, Inc. 547 F.3d 1085 (9th Cir 2008)); and an artist who had painted a collage of Tiger Woods images. (ETW Corp. v. Jireh Publ'g, Inc. 332 F.3d 915, 918-19 (6th Cir. 2003)). All found that the use had artistic relevance to the underlying work, and did not mislead as to the source of the work. All of the examples were found to be protected by the First Amendment against a claim of false endorsement and/or trademark infringement. Then they turned to Moore.

Paintings, Prints and Calendars: "In this case, we readily conclude that Moore's paintings, prints, and calendars are protected under the *Rogers* test. The depiction of the University's uniforms in the content of these items is artistically relevant to the expressive underlying works because the uniforms' colors and designs are needed for a realistic portrayal of famous scenes from Alabama football history. Also, there is no evidence that Moore ever marketed an unlicensed item as 'endorsed' or 'sponsored' by the University, or otherwise explicitly stated that such items were affiliated with the University. Moore's paintings, prints, and calendars very clearly are embodiments of artistic expression, and are entitled to full First Amendment protection. The extent of his use of the University's trademarks is their mere inclusion (their necessary inclusion) in the body of the image, which Moore creates to memorialize and enhance a particular play or event in the University's football history. Even if 'some members of the public would draw the incorrect inference that [the University] had some involvement with [Moore's paintings, prints, and calendars,], that risk of misunderstanding, not engendered by any overt [or in this case even implicit] claim is so outweighed by the interest in artistic expression as to preclude' any violation of the Lanham Act." Rogers, 875 F.2d at 1001. First Amendment prevailed, using the *Rogers* test.

Mundane products: The court then turned to the "mundane products." Moore argued that because he has a copyright in the original paintings that do not infringe the University's trademarks, he could produce derivative works like gift shop mugs. The Court did not agree. "It should be remembered that a copyright is not a 'right' to use: it is a right to exclude others from using the copyrighted work." citing 1 J. Thomas McCarthy, McCarthy on Trademarks and Unfair Competition § 6:14 (4th ed.2011) (emphasis added); see also Fed. Trade Comm'n v. Real Prods. Corp., 90 F.2d 617, 619 (2d Cir.1937) ("A copyright is not a license to engage in unfair competition."). The court further explained, "Selling the copyrighted drawing itself may not amount to a trademark infringement, but its placement on certain products very well might." Creating an artwork under *Rogers* is one thing; commercializing on mugs and other gift shop items is quite another.

Conclusion

Fair use under trademark and right of publicity can be profoundly helpful to artists. The *Rogers* test helps us understand the parameters. And we also mustn't forget about descriptive (fair use), incidental fair use, and nominative fair use.

18: No Such Thing as the 10% Rule

Common Misinformation

You may have heard that if you just change 10% of a copyrighted work, then you are good to go. Or you can copy 10%. This is not how fair use works, at least in the United States. How did this misnomer occur? When fair use was passed the mid-1970s, a committee was put together to think through the new relationship between fair use and copy machines (a new thing at the time) in connection to copies for teaching. That's where our story begins. Two groups were created to study and come up with guidelines.

> **Commission on New Technological Uses of Copyrighted Works** (CONTU) Guidelines on Photocopying under Interlibrary Loan Arrangements: These guidelines were developed for librarians related to interlibrary loans. It related to Section 108 of the U.S. Copyright Act. This has nothing to do with fair use, Section 107, and only applies to librarians.
>
> **The Conference on Fair Use** (CONFU): In the mid-1990s, ninety-three organizations attempted to negotiate proposed guidelines for applying fair use, but **failed.** They included representatives from publishing, software, scholars, authors, artists, photographers, musicians, universities, and government agencies. They worked for 2-½ years. Some found the proposal overly strict, and others thought they gave away too much.

What did occur was Congressionally-endorsed guidelines for classroom copying: The Agreement on Guidelines for Classroom Copying for Not-for-profit Education Institutions with Respect to Books and Periodicals (the Classroom Guidelines). The Classroom guidelines were an agreement between authors, educators and publishers in 1976. This is *not* part of the law, and many saw them as too restrictive. These are considered the *minimum* standards for educational fair use under Section 107. This was supposed to help teachers understand permissible copying. But they are not controlling in court. See Marcus v. Rowley, 695 F.2d 1171, 1178 (9th Cir. 1983). Here is what they say about how much a teacher can copy for classroom use in non-profit education settings with regard to book and periodicals. (Note: these are not designed for use by shops or for-profit shows).

> **Single copy:** Teachers may for scholarly research copy a chapter from a book, an article from a periodical, a short story, essay or poem, a chart, cartoon or drawing.
>
> **Multiple copies:** For classroom discussion: a poem less than 250 words, or not more than two pages; a complete article, story or essay of less than 2500 words, or an excerpt of no more than **1000 words or 10%, whichever is less;** or one chart, graph, diagram, drawing, cartoon or picture per book or per periodical. The copying must be at "the instance and inspiration of the individual teacher"; and "the inspiration and decision to use the work and the moment of it use for maximum teaching effectiveness are so close in time that it would be unreasonable to expect a timely reply to a request for permission. Cumulative effect: it can only be for one course, and not more than one poem, article, story, essay or two excerpts may be copied from the same author, or

> three from the same collection in one class term; and not more than 9 instances of copying for one course in one term. Copying cannot be a substitute for an anthology or textbook. And no copying from "consumables" including workbooks and testing materials. You can't charge the students for the copies either.

These are fairly limiting, both in what they apply to, and how much can be used.

Since then, a bunch of the issues that arose have been litigated, including course packets (copies of portions of books, articles and other copyrighted materials that were bound for college students). This issue got litigated in Cambridge University Press v. Mark P. Becker.[46] Cambridge University Press, SAGE Publication and Oxford University Press (plaintiff) sued Georgia State (defendant) for 6700 works that appeared in their e-reserve system, because Georgia State has "invited students to download, review, and print such materials without permission of the copyright holder."

Georgia State University (GSU) had a policy that allowed GSU professors to make digital copies of excerpts from Plaintiff's books for students without paying Plaintiffs by using an e-reserve system. The books involved were research-based monographs, not textbooks, and also edited collections. Professors often put these books on reserve, where students can go to read assignments, or alternatively they created course packets that students purchase. Course packets usually require permission from publishers through the Copyright Clearance Center (CCC) (who helped fund the publisher's case at issue). But, instead of sending all students to use one or a few physical copies on reserve, profession could now have a librarian scan the excerpt from the published book, and give access to GSU students on course-specific websites. This was the e-reserve. The question that the 11th circuit took up was whether e-reserves counted under fair use, or if licensing fees were required. In 2009, GSU put in place a fair use checklist for faculty to evaluate whether the excerpt required permission or qualified under fair use. The court looks to the four factors of fair use. The 11th circuit turned to the four factor fair use test.

First Factor: nature and character of (third party) use

Was the Defendants' use transformative? Here the 11th Circuit did not find the use of work to be transformative. "The excerpts of Plaintiffs' work posted on GSU's electronic reserve system are verbatim copies of portions of the original books which have merely been converted into a digital format, with the same purpose: reading materials for students in university courses. The Defendant's use supersedes the original. The 11th circuit also considered that GSU was a non-profit educational institution, part of the first factor. In previous course packet cases, the copying was done by a commercial entity; here it is done by GSU staff. The court found the use is the kind considered under fair use's first factor, even though it was not a transformative use. Educational uses are important. "Congress devoted considerable attention to working out the proper scope of the fair use defense as applied to copying for educational and classroom purposes, going so far as to include in a final report the Classroom Guidelines developed by

---

[46] *Cambridge University Press v. Patton*, No. 08-01425 (D.Ga. May 11, 2012); Cambridge Univ. Press v. Patton, 769 F.3d 1232 (11th Cir. 2014); and *Cambridge University Press v. Mark P. Becker No. 1:08-cv-01425-ODE (N.D. Ga. Mar. 31, 2016)*

representatives of educator, author, and publisher groups at the urging of Congress." Congress went to great lengths to include educational copying under fair use. So, the 11th circuit agreed with the District Court that the first factor favors a finding of fair use.

Second Factor: nature of the copyrighted work

The 11th Circuit found that the works were not merely factual, but contains "evaluative, analytical, or subjectively descriptive material," and so the 11th circuit found the second factor to either be neutral, or even weighing against fair use. But they also said that the second factor did not have much importance in this case, because the works are neither fictional nor unpublished.

Third Factor: Amount and Substantiality of Portion Used

Here the District Court had found the Defendant had not used more than 10% of a work, or one chapter of a book with ten or more chapters. The 11th Circuit responded: "The District Court's blanket 10 percent-or-one-chapter benchmark was improper." No bright-line rules exist. The court also said that previously commercial copying cases were not binding; instead the court had to look to Defendant's pedagogical purpose, measured against the works. The District court was right **not to use the Classroom Guidelines or the course packet cases.** But the District court erred in using the 10%-or-one-chapter safe harbor. "The District Court should have analyzed each instance of alleged copying individually, considering the quantity and quality of the material taken--including whether the material taken constitutes the heart of the work—and whether the taking was excessive in light of the educational purpose of the use and the threat of market substitution."

Fourth Factor: effect on the market

"The central question under the fourth factor is not whether Defendants' use of Plaintiffs' works caused Plaintiffs to lose some potential revenue. Rather, it is whether Defendants' use—taking into account the damage that might occur if "everybody did it"—would cause substantial economic harm such that allowing it would frustrate the purposes of copyright by materially impairing Defendants' incentive to publish the work." The 11th Circuit agreed with the District Court that "the small excerpts the Defendants used do not substitute for the full books from which they are drawn," and no lost book sales were presented. Then they turned to CCC's licensing program for academic permissions, which Plaintiffs feel were substantially harmed. The Court wrote, "the fact that Plaintiffs have made paying easier does not automatically dictate a right of payment.... The goal of copyright is to stimulate the creation of new works, not to furnish copyright holders with control over all markets. Accordingly, the ability to license does not demand a finding against fair use."

So, why do we need to know this? The district court and the appeals court both did a fair use analysis and **rejected the 10% concept**. It's more complicated than 10%. And 10% was about copying for classroom use, and nothing more. Help stop the spread of the 10% myth.

When I went to Wizard World Comic Con 2020, I heard a number of times from the artists that they had to merely change the original work 10% to be "ok." No! But, what they are doing is transforming the work. They know they have to change it. They just misunderstand the law. Think back to the Green Day change -- Was that 10%? I'm not sure. But they changed/added to the work. And we know it has to be a meaningful change, and not merely color like in the Guetta case. Transformativeness is not a fixed amount.

Fair Use Quick Summary

Let's Make Sure You Need to Use Fair Use.

Is the work one of the following?

- ☐ public domain work
- ☐ unprotectable element
- ☐ owned/created by you (and you still have ownership)

If Yes to any of these, fair use is not needed

Types of Fair Use:

- ☐ Nominative fair use (trademark)
- ☐ Descriptive fair use (trademark)
- ☐ Incidental/de minimis use (copyright)
- ☐ Parody (copyright)
- ☐ Comment or criticism (copyright)
- ☐ News reporting (copyright)
- ☐ Spontaneous copying for classroom use (and not a market replacement) (copyright)
- ☐ Transformative use (copyright)

Four Factor Analysis Under Copyright (make sure to analyze)

1. Purpose and Character of (Infringing) Use
2. Nature of Original work (fact or fiction)
3. Amount used (quantity and quality; don't take "heart of the work" unless parody)
4. Market Replacement? (doesn't apply to comment, criticism and parody)

Rogers test for use of trademark works in art

1. Is the use relevant to the underlying work?
2. Does the use explicitly mislead as to the source of the work?

Transformative Use in Art (Copyright/Fair Use)

- Is the potentially infringing use different character from the original, giving new expression, and employing new aesthetics with creative and communicative results?
- Is there a message/meaning related to the new use (not always needed)?
- Is the use political in that it identifies the original work with a political party or movement (goes against fair use)?

Part 5:
Specific Scenarios

19: When Things Go Wrong

How to Address Copyright Problems

So, you get an email from a friend. Someone has swiped your original design. What do you do? That depends on whether you have included copyright notice, whether you have registered the work, where the alleged infringement occurred, and what is alleged.

Assuming the work is protected by copyright, and that there is infringement, there a number of things you do when you believe someone has infringed your work. But it can go both ways. What if someone thinks *you* have infringed their work? We'll discuss that too.

Mechanisms for Addressing Infringement

Currently, there are three methods for addressing infringement, and we may shortly have a fourth, a small claims court.

Being an Enforcer. If you want to be an enforcer, register your work. Send a cease-and-desist letter. Notify the social media platform with a notice-and-takedown submission. And, in some cases, sue for infringement. To do the last choice, you have to have a registration certificate from the U.S. Copyright Office.

Winning over your Infringer. You could contact the person who is infringing. Explain things to them, and see if they want a license to use your work. You could, of course, combine this with enforcer mode.

Other Options. Ignore it. Appreciate that people are stealing from you (that you have something to steal!). Make more things. Keep it to yourself next time so people don't steal. Use it as a social media opportunity.

Remember that piracy comes with fame. As Los Angeles Attorney, Chris Reed noted, Hollywood studios have whole teams that work on piracy and they still have problems. It's part of the world that we live in, especially in a digital environment. Patterns, for example, are a lot easier to replicate and steal, than, say fabric or a complicated tool. Someone might try to make their own version of a Pfaff sewing machine, but it will take a lot more to make a knock off than copying a Christa Watson pattern.

Going Down the Infringement Path

So, you've decided. You have registered your work. You have hired a lawyer. You are taking the infringer to court. What happens in that process?

1. Do you have a copyright registration?
2. Do you have a valid copyright? Is the work under copyright?
3. Are you the copyright holder or an authorized agent of the copyright holder?

If you get through that, we are now looking at proving that there is copying, and in fact, inappropriate copying.

Step one: Was there copying?

We look to what was taken in the original and used in the allegedly infringing copy. We look to see if the elements copied are in the public domain, independently created (e.g. no access to the original work, both basing work on something in the public domain, permission or a license was granted, etc.), and other elements. If there was copying of copyrightable elements, the courts then move onto the next step.

- It doesn't have to be exact; it can be substantially similar.
- If the original had been distributed widely to the public that often goes toward finding access, and even subconscious copying.

Step two: Was there inappropriate copying?

So, we would have to see if the original and the allegedly infringing work is "substantially similar" and whether in that similarity that has been inappropriate copying.

Notice and Takedown

The Notice and Takedown system was enacted as the Online Copyright Infringement Liability Limitation Act, a part of the Digital Millennium Copyright Act of 1998. It protects platform hosts from liability as long as they have a system in place for alleged infringement, among other things.

If your work has been infringed: If the infringement is occurring online on a platform, you can notify the platform to take it down. Each social media platform has a way to address potential infringement. This is governed by Section 512(c) of the Copyright Act. Your goal is to get it takedown. How do you find them? Do a quick search with the platform's name and "notice and takedown."

Let's look at Facebook's provisions. We begin at https://www.facebook.com/help/contact/634636770043106, where we choose whether we want to report a copyright or trademark violation.

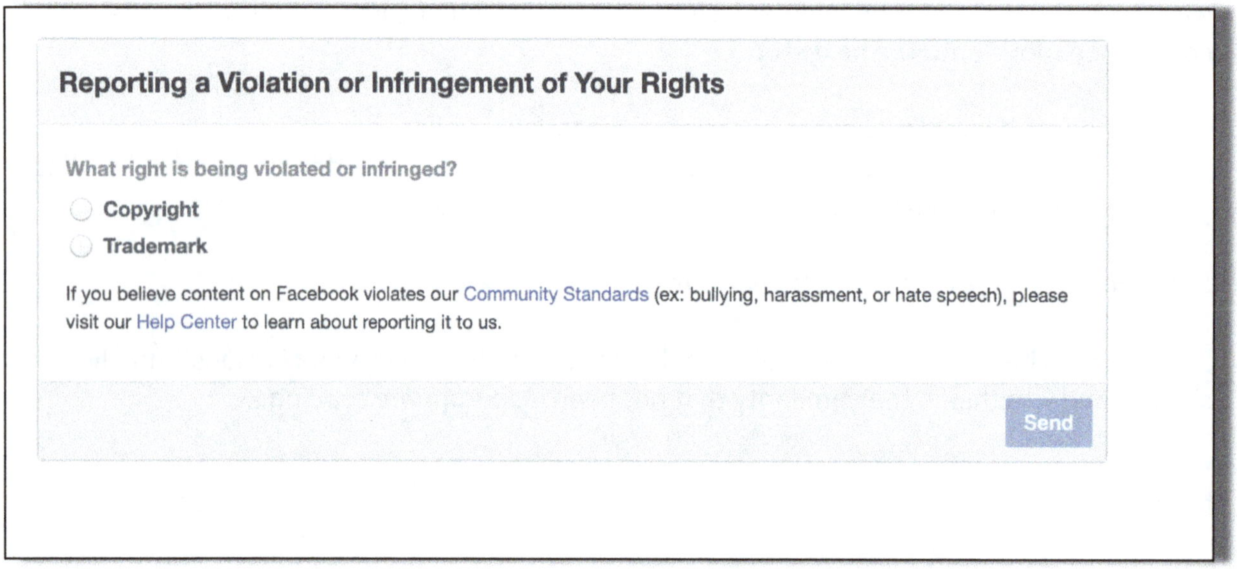

Reporting a Violation or Infringement of Your Rights

What right is being violated or infringed?

- Copyright
- Trademark

If you believe content on Facebook violates our Community Standards (ex: bullying, harassment, or hate speech), please visit our Help Center to learn about reporting it to us.

Send

Copyright Report Form

Use this form to report content that you believe infringes your copyright

To be sure you're in the right place, what best describes your issue?

- ◯ My account has been hacked
- ◯ I lost access to a group or Page I used to manage
- ◯ I found a fake profile that is pretending to be me
- ◯ I am being bullied or harassed
- ◯ I found inappropriate or abusive content
- ◯ I (or someone I am legally responsible for) appear in content that I do not want displayed
- ◯ My name (or the name of my organization) is being used without my permission
- ◯ I found content which I believe infringes my trademark
- ◉ I found content which I believe infringes my copyright

In most countries, copyright is a legal right that protects original works of authorship, such as books, music, film and art. Generally, things like names, titles, slogans or short phrases aren't considered to be original enough for copyright protection. Copyright also doesn't generally protect facts or ideas, but it may protect the original words or images that express a fact or idea. For more information on copyright, visit the copyright section of our Help Center.

◯ Continue with my copyright report

Submit

Notice that copyright infringement is at the bottom. Before you continue, another message pops up that is important but fairly unclear.

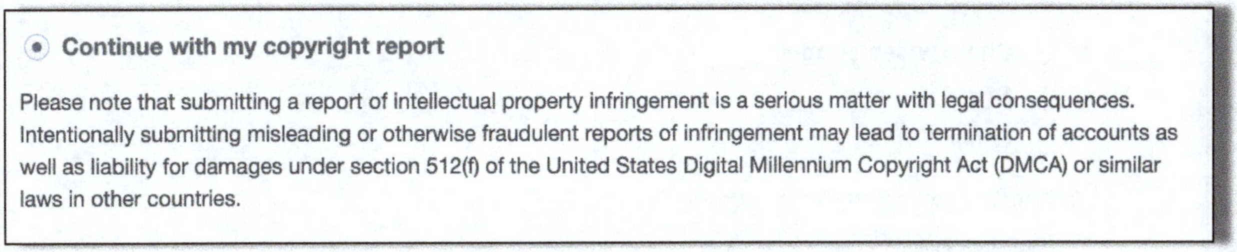

◉ **Continue with my copyright report**

Please note that submitting a report of intellectual property infringement is a serious matter with legal consequences. Intentionally submitting misleading or otherwise fraudulent reports of infringement may lead to termination of accounts as well as liability for damages under section 512(f) of the United States Digital Millennium Copyright Act (DMCA) or similar laws in other countries.

What this means is that if you are filing a notice, you have to consider whether there are fair uses that might apply. Really. And if you don't, and you lose in court (if it gets there), you could be responsible for damages. Hmmm... This could be a little clearer, don't you think? This is about a case call Lenz v. Prince. It's about a baby dancing remember? And what we learn from this is that you have to do a quick fair use analysis (and you are agreeing by saying "yes" to Section 512(f) before submitting a notice and takedown report. This includes:

- ☐Not de minimis use
- ☐Not independent creation
- ☐Source material not in the public domain
- ☐No license (e.g. Creative Commons attached)
- ☐*Rogers* test does apply (for trademark and right of publicity)

☐Nominative use does not apply (trademark)
☐Descriptive fair use does not apply (trademark)
☐Incidental Use does not apply (copyright/trademark)
☐Not commenting or criticizing original work
☐Not news reporting
☐Not parody

That's what you are agreeing to with Section 512(f). What is Section 512(f)? "Any person who knowingly materially misrepresents under [17 U.S.C. § 512] that material or activity is infringing ... shall be liable for any damages, including costs and attorneys' fees, incurred by the alleged infringer...who is injured by such misrepresentation, as the result of the service provider relying upon such misrepresentation in removing or disabling access to the material or activity claimed to be infringing...." The Ninth Circuit in Lenz concluded that copyright owners had to consider fair use and other lawful uses before sending a takedown notice. This was an important moment for fair use: "The appeals court made clear that fair use is not an "infringement to be excused" but instead is not copyright infringement at all." See EFF's explanation for Lenz, https://www.eff.org/cases/lenz-v-universal

So, then, you put in your information, where the infringing work can be found, whether the rights holder in the United States or abroad and a few more questions.

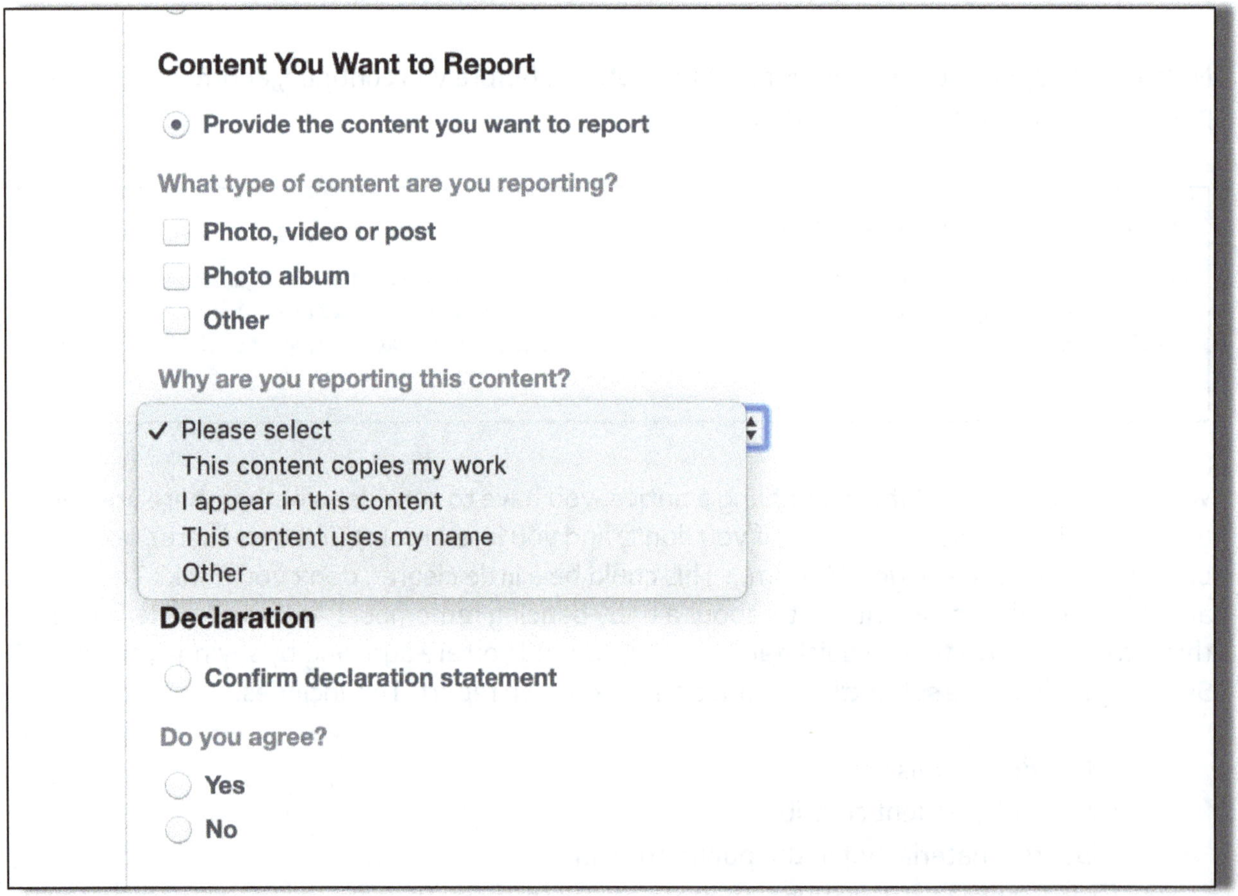

You then provided information about your copyrighted work.

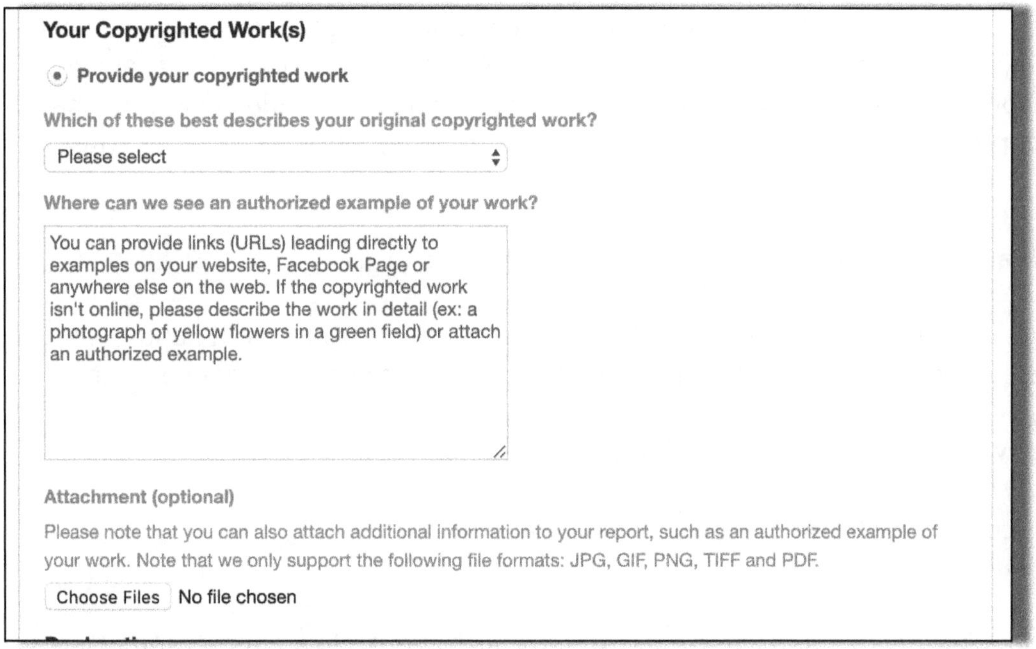

Your Copyrighted Work(s)

(•) **Provide your copyrighted work**

Which of these best describes your original copyrighted work?

Please select

Where can we see an authorized example of your work?

You can provide links (URLs) leading directly to examples on your website, Facebook Page or anywhere else on the web. If the copyrighted work isn't online, please describe the work in detail (ex: a photograph of yellow flowers in a green field) or attach an authorized example.

Attachment (optional)

Please note that you can also attach additional information to your report, such as an authorized example of your work. Note that we only support the following file formats: JPG, GIF, PNG, TIFF and PDF.

Choose Files No file chosen

And then you submit your declaration:

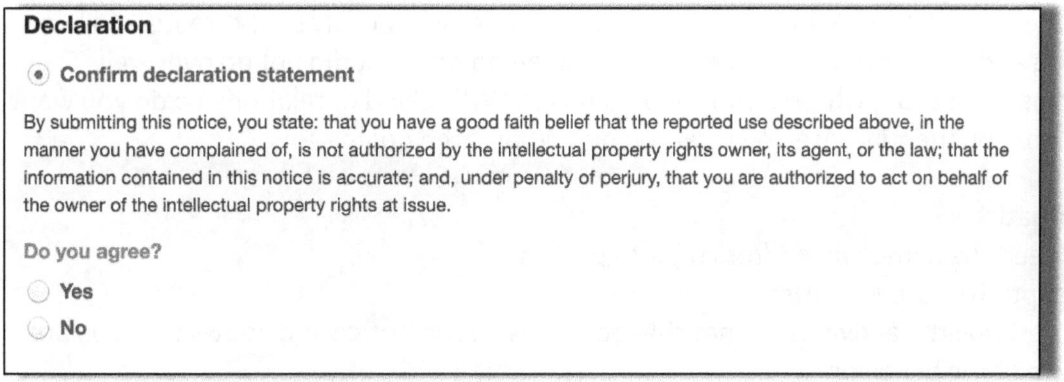

Declaration

(•) **Confirm declaration statement**

By submitting this notice, you state: that you have a good faith belief that the reported use described above, in the manner you have complained of, is not authorized by the intellectual property rights owner, its agent, or the law; that the information contained in this notice is accurate; and, under penalty of perjury, that you are authorized to act on behalf of the owner of the intellectual property rights at issue.

Do you agree?

( ) **Yes**

( ) **No**

Then what happens? The alleged infringer is notified. They are given the opportunity for counter-notification, to explain why they used the materials. That is forwarded to the person making the complaint. The original person then has 14 days to file a complaint in federal court to keep the work from being posted again. If that does not occur, Facebook notifies the counter-notifier that they can repost the content. That's the whole system.

If you receive a notice and takedown. First, don't panic. Evaluate your use. Why do you think they are upset? Is it legitimate? Were you both relying on something in the public domain? Independent creation? Fair Use? If you feel like the Work shouldn't have been taken down, file a counter-notice. If the original complainer doesn't file a legal action against you in court within 14 days, you can put it back up if you want. Alternatively, you can keep it down, even if you are in the right. It's ok. And how likely is someone to file a complaint and take you to court? Not, but it is still a risk. You might want to talk to an attorney.

Cease and Desist Letters

You want to tell someone to stop doing something, or pay a license fee, or destroy their copies. A cease and desist letter is one tool to achieve that goal. A cease and desist letter is sent when you think someone has infringed your copyright, trademark, patent or trade dress, there has been a contract problem, or harassment. In order to be infringing, there are different criteria for each.

What is a cease and desist letter?

This is a letter you send directly to the alleged infringer to tell them you are not happy. Now, cease and desist letters should be crafted to attempt to attain the outcome that you want.

- Do you want to have them stop using your work?
- Destroy the work?
- Get a licensing fee from them?
- Get credit?

Those are the four basic things a cease and desist letter is all about. Now, there is something important to realize. If you threaten them with suing them, you may actually have to do that, and they could file suit against YOU first. So, before you go sending a letter or having a lawyer send a letter, there are a few things to do, including some homework. Also, you should think about the tone of the letter. Who is this? The Record industry famously sent threatening letters to 8-year-olds and grandmothers for illegally downloading music. It did not go over well. They are still seen as villains. So, who are you sending this to? What kind of relationship do you want with them? Are you friendly? Are you threatening? What is the goal?

- Information
- You need the name and address of both parties
- Description of the Activities
- You describe the activities so that the receiver is put on notice and knows that you are aware of the behavior.
- (Optional) Complaint Ready to File with the Court If you are threatening legal action, you need to also have ready the complaint to begin a lawsuit. You may also potentially send a copy of the complaint with the cease and desist letter.

What if you receive a cease and desist? Evaluate and investigate. Stop, if you are in the wrong. Negotiate a license if that is something you want to do. Ignore? Maybe. Talk to a lawyer? Yes.

Social Pressure

Over the last two years, I've seen another approach. When someone is infringing, or the community thinks they are infringing, social pressure in the form of social networks is powerful. It's something to think about.

For example, Cheryl Sleboda had an image cropped and distributed by two major companies. Her fans notice, and sent her the photographs. When she reached out to the companies, and she noted how many times the image had been shared *without attribution*, the rectified the situation, by adding back attribution. This is small example of social pressure.

But in reality, we don't sue most of the time, and we don't even complain. Where would you even begin, and as Rob Appell said in an interview, do you want that negativity in your life? Take Nicole Daksiewicz of Modernhandcraft. She was alerted by someone that sent her an image from Home Depot's Instagram account of a new "Modern" campaign that looked awfully similar to her quilt. You be the judge:

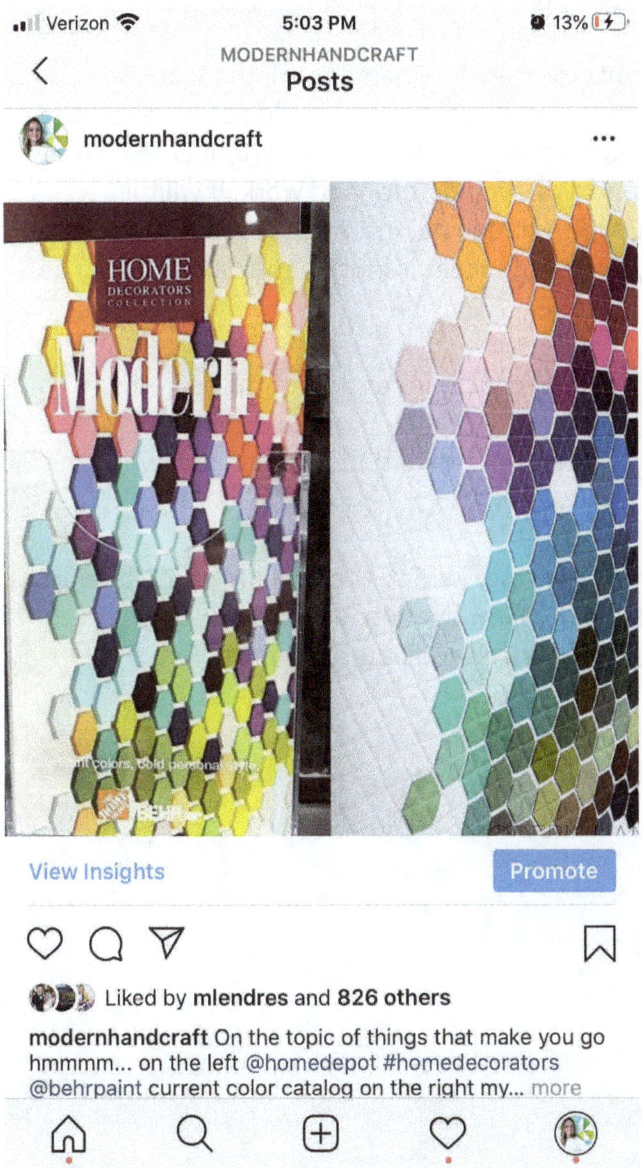

She didn't pursue the infringement. She said that it seemed impossible to think about tackling such a big company, even when someone from Home Depot reached out to her. In many ways, I've buried the lead. Addressing potential infringement can be scary, confusing and just not worth it. One wonders what Home Depot would have done had she pursued even a conversation. It doesn't always have to be adversarial. And many times, attribution gets lost, and impossible to track down. Reaching out is always an option. But sometimes it seems overwhelming, and it's ok *not to pursue* an injustice too.

Copyright Litigation

So, you've decided to sue. Let's think about what this entails. First, you should make sure to do research and think through how strong the case is from both sides.

1. Is your work registered? This is the first important question. If you do not have a registration certificate (and not just applied to register your work), you cannot (if you are a domestic author) file a lawsuit for copyright infringement.
2. Cost: Litigation can be expensive. Are you prepared for this? Sometimes attorney's fees are awarded but that is no guarantee.

Remedies Available Through the Court System

If you sue someone, what is the end game? There are three possibilities: injunction, damages, and/or destruction.

Injunction: stop doing that! This can either be temporary or permanent.

Damages: this can be actual damages and profits, or statutory damages (if the work is registered with the U.S. Copyright Office). With statutory damages, you do not have to show your actual damages and profits, which can be a hard thing to do with copyright cases. The award of statutory damages is between $750 and $30,000 per infringed work. If willful damages are found, the damages can rise to up to $150,000 per infringed work. If it is found that the infringer was not aware of infringing, e.g. an innocent infringer, the damages can be reduced to $200.

Destruction: this can happen after the copyright case concludes as part of the remedy.

Seizure or impoundment: give me the infringing items are taken; this can happen when the copyright case is ending.

Costs and Attorney's Fees: This is not automatically rewarded to the winning party, but it is up to the court to decide. Factors include frivolousness, motivation, objective unreasonableness, and the need to advance consequences and deterrence.

A Quick Note on Contributory Infringement

There are two kinds of infringement: direct and secondary liability. Direct is when you do the infringing. You copy the work, distribute it, etc. Secondary liability is when you encourage someone to do the infringing by either inducing, profiting from or authorizing the infringement. First, you must find a direct infringement. Then, you look to see if others might have also been involved. Contributory infringement is when some contribute to infringing conduct by materially contributing or inducing infringement.

Vicarious liability is when someone has a direct financial interest in the infringing activity and has the ability to supervise the infringing activity. Selling counterfeit goods is an example. You didn't make the goods, but you are benefiting from the illegal activity by selling them.
A third kind is inducement--direct encouragement for someone else to infringe. If you have a business model where you actively encourage people to post copyrighted works to build up your following, that is inducement. "Post a pattern here that you bought at a quilt shop." Inducement.

Don't Forget About VARA

For visual artists, VARA can be a powerful tool. No registration necessary, but a lot of restrictions on what can qualify. Check with an attorney on how case law has progressed, and whether VARA is right for your case.

20: Work Made for Hire Agreement

Does Your Job Require You to Make Art?

A work made for hire agreement can happen in two situations: you are an employee and the work that you do is owned by your employer. They pay your taxes, health insurance, assign you a bunch of tasks. Your creative work is part of your daily job.

A proper work for hire situation can also come up with commissioned works. This has to be one of nine categories defined in the Copyright Act: a contribution to a collective work, as a part of a motion picture or other audiovisual work, as a translator, as a supplementary work, as a compilation, as an instructional text, as a test, as an answer material for a test, or as an atlas. Supplementary work includes works for publication like introductions, conclusions, illustrations, explanations, revisions, commentary, forwards, afterward, maps, charts, tables, editorial notes, afterward, editorial notes, musical arrangements, answer material for tests, bibliographies, appendices, and indexes. If your work fits into one of these categories, there has to be an express, signed agreement in place as well.

Note: if you contribute to a collective work, you have given the owner of the collective work the privilege of reproducing the work for the contribution only, and any revision of the collective work. But you keep the copyright in the work you have contributed. That can be altered by contract, of course.

Ok. So, you are creating a work for someone else, and you don't fit into the two categories above. You can create a contract that assigns the copyright or provides a license to the person/company you are creating the work for.

Agreement between the parties: Describe who the parties are, including who is the Company/Individual and who is the Contractor. The agreement will also include the title of the Work.

Independent Contractor: The document will acknowledge that Contractor is an Independent Contractor (not work for hire and not commissioned work under the 1976 Copyright Act). The Company/Individual has no responsibility for benefits, insurance, o taxes on behalf of the Contractor.

Payment: This should explain how much and in what manner the payment to the Contractor will be made. Do certain milestones have to be met? Are there fees for supplies?

Intellectual Property: Be clear who owns the intellectual property including the copyright. The Contactor owns the copyright, unless the Contactor assigns the copyright to the Company/Individual. Alternatively, the Contactor can assign an exclusive license to use the work or a non-exclusive license.

Contractor's Warranties and Representations: Contract agrees to warrant the work including copyright, trademarks, any right of publicity and privacy.

Indemnification: Contractor indemnifies and holds harmless Company/Individual whether or not in connection with litigation.

Dispute Resolution: This will dictate what will happen if the parties disagree.

Governing Law and Venue: What law applies (state and/or country), and where would the case be litigated?

Entire Agreement: This asserts that the document is the whole agreement.

And of course, sign the agreement – both parties.

21: Permission

When to Ask

When you ask someone for permission to use their copyrighted work, or alternatively, their right of publicity, you can keep the agreement simple. But get everything in writing.

1. For Copyrighted works:
2. Person's name
3. The Work
4. Whether the use will be commercial or non-commercial
5. Whether there is a payment
6. Whether you will be making a derivative work from the person's original work.
7. Whether the permission is for an exclusive or non-exclusive right to use
8. That the person has the right to give permission
9. Whether attribution is required.

For permission to use someone's image:

1. Person's name
2. Right to use the image and likeness of the person
3. Whether the use will be commercial or non-commercial
4. Whether there is payment
5. Whether you will be making a derivative work from the person's original work.
6. Whether the permission is for an exclusive or non-exclusive right to use
7. That the person has the right to give permission
8. Whether attribution is required
9. Whether 18 and older, legal age (and if not, consent of parent or guardian)

Something to consider

You do not need to ask if you are relying on fair use. Sometimes, in fact, if you ask, you are giving people the idea that *they can decide*, which isn't true. So, asking may create more problems. Think about whether you need to ask and if it is appropriate to ask.

22: Copyright Transfer Agreements

Get it in Writing

You can only transfer copyright by a written agreement, which must be signed. You have to decide what you want to transfer: all of the 106 rights, or something specific. The rights you can assign reproduction, distribution, derivative, public display, and public performance. You can assign the movie rights to your story, but keep the derivative work sequel rights.

Here are some things to consider:

1. Name of the Copyright Holder and name of the New Owner.
2. Name of the Work
3. What rights are being transferred
4. Confirmation that the Copyright holder has the right to transfer ownership
5. Any attribution of moral rights that remain with the Copyright Holder?

And sign the agreement. You should also let the U.S. Copyright Office that you have assigned the copyright to someone else. You can do this through the website www.copyright.gov.

23: Making Copies

When is it Legal to Make Copies?

Making copies is a complicated fact-specific topic. But we see that this question arises quite often. When thinking about making copies, the first question to ask is by making the copy, are you creating a market replacement for purchasing a copy of the Work? Here are some scenarios:

Making copies of family photographs.

You are not creating a market replacement. You are preserving the works, or using for a creative purpose. For example, Karen Swiech takes 5000 family photographs and scans them into her computer. By doing this, she is making a copy. She is preserving the photographs. But she also intends to make a mosaic quilt, where each photograph acts as part of a larger photograph. She alters in Photoshop and then uploads the images to a program, which helps her place them. When she is satisfied with that, she purchases a copy – of the selection, arrangement and coordination of those photographs that she uploaded. She then uploads the compilation to Spoonflower to print the mosaic on fabric. There was lots of copying – the images scanned into her computer, the images uploaded to mosaic, the compilation of the images to Spoonflower. But all of this has been done under personal use, under transformative use under fair use, and she is not planning to sell the work. She is not the author of the photos, or at least not all of them. So, she has technically violated the copyright of the other photographers, but in this case, that is really not an issue, because fair use likely applies.

Result: Ok to copy. Fair use/Transformative Use and Personal use applies?

What if Karen used professional photographs, say of a famous person? I think likely the same result would apply. Interesting yes? Again, no commercial use; fair use/transformative use.

Karen also created an index of sorts on the back of the quilt, with instead of 1 x 1 inch squarer photographs, 2 x 2. How does that go in our scenario? Can you sort it out?

The Pattern Requires Copying. Katja Marek is the author of the New Hexagon, and also the New Hexagon 2. These are books that each have 52 patterns for English Paper Piecing, and as part of the book, you have to make a copy of the pattern. She is giving you permission to copy. Now, how far can that copying go? You purchased the book. It's for your personal use. What if your friend wants to do the patterns? They can borrow the book, and make their own copies. That's First Sale Doctrine at work. You can't make 10 copies of each pattern for you sewing group. That would be a market replacement and uncool – you are committing copyright infringement, and not supporting the quilting community. Katja worked hard on that book.

You Copy an Idea from a Book.

We know that ideas are not protectable. But the expression is. Review the terms, and be careful.

You Copy Blocks from EQ8 or BlockBase.

Look at the license. I think it allows for commercial use. The program EQ8 does not claim copyright on the individual common blocks. [check] But check the license. And so, we get lots of books based on those blocks, including the Farmer's Wife Series by Laurie Aaron Hird. She also creates CDs of her books that allow you to copy the blocks onto your computer and copy them. These are the public domain. So, what about that? Can you make lots of copies of the common blocks? Yep. They are in the public domain, and she hasn't done anything to alter them except name them something different. But you can't copy her book – that would-be infringement.

Copying a Pattern for Your Guild

This gets tricky. Is the pattern a common block? You are good. Is the pattern something older than 1924? Good again. Is the pattern something first published in the U.S. before 1989 that does not have copyright notice (e.g. a magazine where there is no ©? Ok. So, you can see what we're getting at: Is the pattern in the public domain?

If the pattern is something you found out in the world – on the Internet, in your local quilt shop that has been published after 1989: that's under copyright – the selection, arrangement and coordination of the pattern – the image, the expression of the instructions. Ask permission.

What if that pattern details a common block? That's ok. You still can't copy that expression of the block. Now, the patternmaker may give permission to use for groups, or you can contact them. But it is it the mass-producing copies as a market placement that is the infringement. Why you are using the pattern, e.g. charity quilting, doesn't absolve the crime. It's better than if you were selling it, but still don't make copies.

Making Binders of Patterns to Share

One of the most egregious examples of copyright infringement I've heard about is someone who suggested that as part of a retreat, everyone copy all the patterns they have, and they could make binders for each person of all of the patterns. No. No. No. No. You do not have the right to do that.

A Reminder about Digital Copies

Unlike paper copies and books, digital copies do not fall under the First Sale Doctrine. So, you can't borrow someone's digital copy. You can't sell your digital copy. You really can't do much, unless the copyright holder has given you permission. And yet, they are the easiest to email to a friend, print, and share. It's the great irony of our times.

You Copy an Idea from a Book

Part 6:
A Copyright Quilt

24: The Copyright Quilt

Thinking About Copyright Like a Quilter

In writing this book, I tried to think about how to convey what we are learning within a hands-on art context. I created the Copyright Quilt. To conclude this book, I thought we could go through the quilt—a pattern in some ways—as a means of summarizing what we have learned. I encourage you to make your own copyright quilts. I found that physicalizing the ideas helped me to really understand what they meant.

The Quilt

The quilt has four sections and three borders, each that tell the copyright story of a creative work.

Three borders

- White inner border: Noncommercial use
- Black outside border: Commercial use
- Grey: The grey area

We'll talk about the commercial/non-commercial use distinction one more time, and explore more of what is included in the grey area.

Four sections

- Idea
- Inspiration
- Creation
- Dissemination

This is another way of thinking about the content of this book. We'll look at how to think about creating a work, and the relationships with the rest of the world, pre-existing materials, and future uses of your creation.

This is the story of creating a work. We have other stories, of course. And we're simplifying it as a summary. Please dive deep when you need to, and always keep in mind why you are asking the questions. That matters too.

Three Borders

The sections are surrounded by three borders. I usually like to discuss this after the sections, but I am often bombarded with questions about them from the beginning. And in some ways, this makes sense. Since copyright law is really an economic system, we have to first see if what we are doing falls inside or outside the economics of copyright. (Now, copyright is also a moral rights/natural rights/personhood system, too.)

Commercial Use: This is represented in red and black. Danger. Danger. If you are creating a work for commercial use, you need to be careful about what resources you use, including inspiration and already existing works. Commercial use is complicated, including determining when is something considered a commercial use. But in other ways, it's simple. Are you planning to sell or license the work? Commercial use within the fair use and trademark/First Amendment context require more than merely selling, and that can get confusing. And sometimes with fan art, content owners distinguish between low-commercial use that is not worth their time in pursuing and more significant commercial use.

The Grey Area: You make fan art, and you sell it at Comic-Con. It's a commercial use, but the content owners turn a blind eye or consider it a "tolerable use" (not a legal term, but one used by some in the content-creation industry). The grey area could be seen as doing something that is technically illegal, but you don't get caught. Alternatively, it could be that what you do is technically legal, but the community you work within does not condone such behavior. We see a great deal of discussion on one of the Facebook groups of pattern makers concerns of people copying and stealing their ideas, and they feel like even though it would not be copyright infringement, it is still morally wrong for the community.

Four Internal Sections

Section 1: Idea

Ideas are not protectable. They come from all kinds of places. "I want to make a baby quilt." "I love Ebony Love's new fabric line and want to make a quilt with it." "I want to make a Dresden plate quilt." "Doesn't that floor tile look like it will make a great quilt?" So many places ideas can come from, and this is where an artist's work begins.

Orange was used to represent ideas because orange has come to represent entrepreneurialism and inventiveness. Ideas are where you dream and imagine. The three different fabrics represent three different ideas.

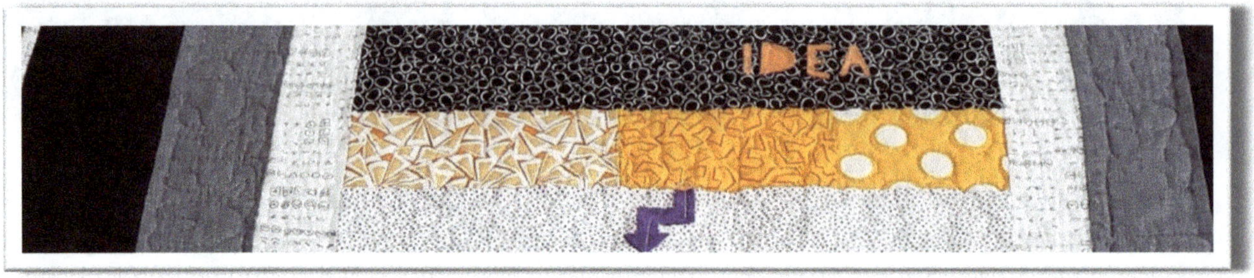

Section 2: Inspiration

Like ideas, inspiration comes from everywhere—from quilt shows, the Internet, books, friends, nature, our own sketches, others' artwork, and photographs, to name a few spaces. At the inspiration stage, we look in all directions. We don't care whether the works that inspire are under copyright, unprotectable (e.g. common shapes), or in the public domain. We're simply pulling in all forms into our mind. But we should recognize as we move into the creation that some *are* under copyright, and others are not.

Blue represents public domain works and pink represents copyrighted works. If I had been clever, I would have used all public domain blue fabrics and all pink copyrighted fabrics. But I hadn't thought that far in advance.

Section 3: Creation

Creation is where the heart of this book resides. There are a lot of pieces to creation. Let's take a look at the quilt section. Some words I've included are shorthand for larger concepts. All of these should be familiar to you now.

- **Fix:** Fixation. We know that to protect a work by copyright, the work must be fixed in a tangible medium of expression.
- **SAC:** Selection, arrangement, and coordination. That's what we do. We may take common shapes, colors, and other elements; mix them together, and we make our own creation.
- **Human**: Independent creative creation by a human is required. Sweat of the brow doesn't count.
- **Copy** and **Derivative**: That's the exclusive rights we get, along with public performance, public display and distribution.
- **Author:** Who the author is matters. We presume it is the one creating the work, but it can be an employer (work for hire), or even a commissioned work (under the enumerated categories; not all works are legal commissions). As the author, you decide what happens to your work, the exclusive rights. The author also determines the term of a license and exclusivity/nonexclusivity of the use. Since 1978, the term (length of the copyright) of copyright is based on the original author category; this is true for most copyright laws around the world.
- **Time.** Copyright doesn't last forever, although it lasts for quite a long time, currently as of January 1, 1978, the life of the author plus seventy years for individual works (but not work for hire, which is the shorter of 120 years from creation/95 years from publication). Before 1978 gets a bit complicated.

These are all above the creation, which is represented by the paper pieced trees and a big frog from Tula Pink fabric. Underneath the creation is more law. These are all the extra elements.

- **Data, Math, and Method:** These words stand-in for all the non-protectable elements we've already discussed, including shapes, color, fonts, stock characters, and other non-protectable elements. These are also represented again in the blue underneath the creation, with the word "giants" in orange.
- **Giants:** *Standing on the shoulder of giants* is what we all do when we create—the idea that things that came before us that we build upon. Some are in the public domain and some are under copyright.
- **First Sale:** Once the object is sold, others can use it. First sale is included here because when you purchase the fabric, you are engaged in First Sale. You are creating the work; you are not copying the fabric (until you take a photograph of the creation, of course).
- **Permission**. Sometimes you ask permission to use components of your creation. If you make a movie based on a short story, you are likely asking permission from the author, especially if the short story is still protected by copyright. We covered permission above, but you can also refer to the Copyright Office's Circular 16A for more information *How to Obtain Permission* (https://www.copyright.gov/circs/circ16a.pdf).
- **Fair Use:** When we create, we often rely on fair use. We've discussed copyright and fair use, including transformative fair use, and also descriptive fair use, nominative use, and the First Amendment in trademark law. We also discussed the First Amendment in relation to the right of publicity. Fair use is an important tool for artists, scholars, teachers, news reporters, technology (like Google searching), and so much more.

Once you create a work and you are confident about where you sit within the law, you will likely release your creation out into the world. Exciting. Scary. Fun. You may give away your work. You may sell it as a pattern. You may display it at a show or gallery. You, the copyright holder, gets to decide how and when it is introduced to the public. And then....

Section 4: Dissemination

Under the old law (1909 Copyright Act), there was a legal change that occurred the moment a work was published. Under publication, the work went from state law (right to first publish) to federal law (all the copyright things that we have been learning). The moment of injecting the work into the general public changed the relationship of the work to the law. While the current law still keeps the distinction between unpublished and published, all works once fixed and meeting the copyrightable subject matter requirement are protected, regardless of their publication status from the beginning.

In some way, the 1909 Act's division is a good way to think about your relationship to your work. When it is yours in your studio, it is yours. Once you post it on social media, offer it for sale, or even give it away, you realistically lose a bit of control, and in some cases, the law is just fine with that. Let's take a look at the fourth and final section of the quilt.

The dissemination section begins with: "And share, and share." Share doesn't mean give away for free. Copyright is a utilitarian system that encourages creativity for the happiness/benefit of society. Copyright holders are given exclusive use of their creations to incentivize them to create and disseminate—share their work—whether through sales or charity. The point of the system is dissemination and economic advantage with that dissemination. That's why, under the 1909 Act, when work was unpublished and not shared with the world, it didn't fall under federal copyright law.

Each of the elements of the last section has meaning. They represent what happens to your work once it has been released to the public, and even if you do not release it to the public, because of the way the law is now, everything eventually comes into the public domain.

Idea: (the orange stripe) The ideas that are embedded in your work are now available for everyone to use. Jessica Quilter's Inventory Quilt, Kim Lapacek's Dresden town, and the idea of animals hidden in the fabric of Tula Pink may have existed before these artists, but we came to know them through their work. When we saw that idea, we could use it. The question is how close was the next version to theirs—idea/expression dichotomy, and also what are the customs of the community with regard to respecting one another's ideas. While copyright law might not find it troublesome, the community standards might.

Public domain elements: Some of the elements in your work are in the public domain—you borrowed them. Some are elements you created, like a technique on how to do something. And eventually, your entire work will come into the public domain. Not for a while, mind you (your life plus 70 years), but all things come into the public domain eventually.

We've talked about thin copyright. Creative works generally have thick protection; but if you have merely taken traditional blocks and arranged them in a basic way, you may either have no protection or very thin. If you do not put a copyright notice on your work, or take the time to register it, you have far less protection. You can also communicate to the world that you allow the use of your work and even the making of derivative works through Creative Commons licenses.

Notice that the same fabric that was in copyright (the green frog) turns blue, indicating that it is now in the future (Tula Pink's life plus 70 years) and is now in the public domain.

The copyrighted work: This is represented as the tree, sitting upon the pink stripe. The work is under copyright, carrying with it all of the exclusive rights from the beginning.

Now, people may borrow bits of your work—fair use. They may comment or criticize your work—fair use. They may even ask permission to use your work in their work. That's part of copyright.

Copyright is an important element in the process of creating. This book has explored that. We want to end by stepping back to the bigger picture and ecosystem. This chapter is for you to think about. It's for the community to decide. We have created some basic principles for shop owners, quilters, artists, and pattern-makers. See what you think.

Best Practices in General for Everyone

- Support pattern makers. Purchase their patterns. Don't copy them for friends. Buy the patterns for classes you attend.
- Be confident in using unprotectable elements. This is our public domain. Use it.
- If you care about your work, put a copyright notice on it, and register it with the U.S. Copyright Office.
- Don't share if you don't want others to use your ideas.
- First Sale doctrine. Remember it. It applies to physical goods only, not digital goods.
- Be creative. **There is no 10% rule.** Think instead—will someone look at my work and not think of the other's work? Is it distinguishable? If you compare element by element, is mine different enough? Be different. Don't copy. Use that creative brain to add to our beautiful body of creative works.

For Shop Owners

We created the Play Fair sign for quilt shops to help when copyright issues arise. In many ways, shop owners are an intermediary between fabric and pattern designers and customers. Go to our website, www.justwannaquilt.com to download your free copy.

Remember the goals. You want people to purchase items, to love your store, and to feel at home. So, it's a balance. You decide your access controls. You can let people take pictures of fabric, but not the bolt information (so they can't look up the numbers online). You can make the rules, just like a museum does. You can encourage show and tell with their projects. You can even take a picture of their purchase, and with their permission, post to social media. Furthermore, you can encourage them to bring the project back in at various stages. Ideally, you should post your rules.

Examples of rules you might use:

One: Taking Photographs

This is your choice regarding a policy. Like a museum, you can post the access rules of your store. If you want people to post photographs of the store, let them know. If you do not, make sure to post a notice sign.

Suggested language:

☐ Feel free to snap photographs of our shop, fabrics, and samples! Make sure to include the following hashtags: ____________________

OR

☐ Please refrain from taking photographs while you are in the shop, as there are copyrighted materials that we are not authorized to give you permission to share.

Two: Respect the Pattern Designs

Please do not take photographs of patterns in the store. Instead, please purchase the patterns to support our patternmakers and our quilting ecosystem. If you take a class from us, we will require each participant to purchase the pattern; no exceptions.

Three: First Sale Doctrine

When you buy physical items, you can do a lot of things with them. You can cut them up and make quilts out of them, for instance. Digital patterns do not fall under First Sale. So, buy fabric! Buy patterns! If you don't like the fabric, give it to a friend. If you don't need the quilt book, donate it to your quilt guild. That's the First Sale Doctrine at work.

Suggested language:

First Sale Doctrine. Make what you want. That's why you buy it. But don't make copies for your friends. Give away what you buy. Sell it. Note: the First Sale Doctrine does not apply to digital patterns.

Four: Sharing - Show Us Your Work!

Here you are encouraging others to bring in their work, and you can post it. Make sure to give attribution both to the quilt creator, as well as the patternmaker, and any other elements that might seem to stand out, like fabric lines, threads, or a quilting approach. This is just a good custom and respectful of the community and its members.

Five: Reservation

We reserve the right to ask customers not to commit copyright piracy in our shop.

You can honestly explain that you are potentially contributorily liable if you do not. (You could also be sued for their actions.)

What other rules might you post?

For Pattern Designers

Pattern designers are on the frontline of both customers making unauthorized copies and other patternmakers stealing their work. They have a difficult time. There needs to be a Best Practice created amongst the pattern maker community. And if the CASE Act (small claims court) passes into legislation, this will be an interesting group to watch.

Here's what pattern makers seem to care about:

- People not purchasing their patterns. They've worked hard to create them.
- Other designers stealing their patterns. This is a harder one. But it is something that really upsets them. The questions I would be asking
    - Was there Independent creation?
    - Was there access to the original work by the alleged infringer?
    - How substantially similar are the works?
    - Are the similarities based on public domain or non-copyrightable elements?
- The community standards: how does the community handle offenders? Is it a teachable moment? Is it social pressure? How does the community police itself?

For Quilters

This book is written for us—the quilters. We may be professionals. We may be very enthusiastic and talented but not sell anything. We may enter quilt shows. Or we just quilt for ourselves and our local community. But we likely are people who *just wanna quilt*. We are generous, sharing, kind people obsessed with making beautiful art that we often give away for free to people we love, to strangers, our kids' teachers, and so many more situations. Sometimes we even keep one for ourselves!

We see restrictions all around us on our behavior. I don't want to leave you with that. Share your tools. Share your magazines. Share your patterns (just don't copy them). Be respectful, of course. But also, be empowered by your choices. Make your own beautiful creations. Puzzle when you want. Follow patterns. Make your own. Quilting is so very wonderful, isn't it?

I.8.8: The IP Clause Revisited

When I teach intellectual property, we begin most days with the IP clause from the constitution. "To promote the progress of science and useful arts, by securing for limited times to authors and inventors the exclusive right to their respective writings and discoveries." It's our guidepost.

Here's what that phrase looks like by the end of the class, and the end of this book:
Copyright law was formed by Congress

- **to promote the *progress of science*** (that's copyright) **and useful arts** (that's patent),
- **by securing** (fixation triggers securing the right in copyright granted by the federal government under the 1976 Copyright Act)
- **for limited Times** (duration and the public domain)
- **to authors** (human copyright that have independent creation with a modicum of creativity) **and inventors** (patents)
- **the exclusive rights** (copying, distribution, derivative works, public display, and public performance, but with the limitations of fair use, first sale, library exceptions, classroom performance, and display, useful articles doctrine, merger, de minimis, and a host of others),
- **to their respective writings** (section 102(a) categories including literary, visual, sound recordings, audiovisual, software, and architecture, but not 102(b) methods, math, fonts generally, common shapes, and other unprotectable elements) **and discoveries (patents)."**

You've seen this image before...but now you understand what it means. Ricardo, our Editor-in-Chief of the *Just Wanna* series, my former law student, my colleague, and my friend, helped to make this wall quilt as a law student with me: The I.8.8 IP clause quilt.

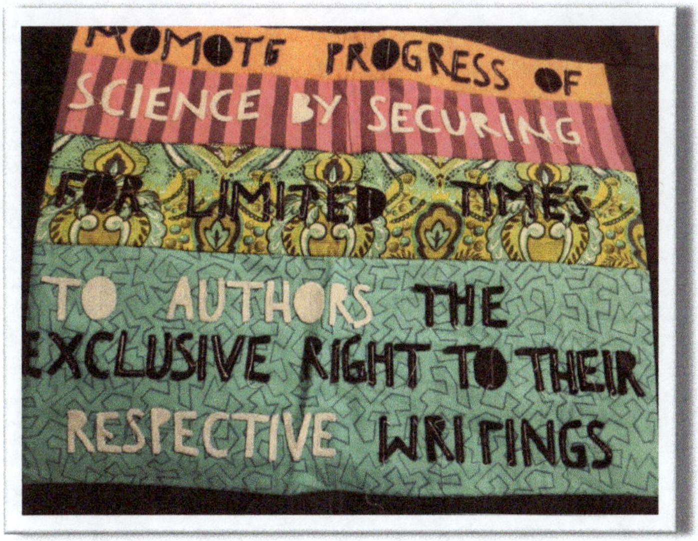

Concluding Thoughts

Copyright is about laws that reflect our use and creation of cultural materials. Quilting is one of those spaces. I'm so proud to be part of this project. I've learned and continue to learn so much from this project. As this work goes out into the world, I imagine we will have subsequent additions and editions, as we get responses back, add examples, and add content.

Copyright law is a system of balances to encourage creativity and economic vibrancy. Copyright is a tool. Copyright is not scary. Copyright is fun.

Copyright Map Instructions

Make your own. Copy mine.
Learn copyright while you sew!

Three layers of strips surround the outside:

- Black: commercial use
- Grey: the grey area
- White: non-commercial use

Four sections

- Idea: Orange
- Inspiration: Pink (copyrighted works) and Blue (unprotectable and public domain works)
- Creation (green) with pink and blue below it - standing on the shoulders of giants.
- Sharing: all four colors, as your work goes out into the world
    - Your ideas
    - Protectable and unprotectable elements
    - Your potential economics, the heart of the Copyright system (selling the work, the pattern, etc.)
    - Someone else using your work (first sale, fair use, permissions, etc.)

That's it. Your map can look any way you want.

COMMERCIAL USE
PERSONAL USE
IDEA
INSPIRATION
COPYRIGHT
NOW CREATE
SAC
COPY
DERIVATIVE
HUMAN
TIME
AUTHOR
DATA FIRST SALE MATH
METHOD PERMISSION
GIANTS
FAIR USE
AND SHARE
AND SHARE

Kari Vojkechovsky's Copyright Map from QuiltCon

"I was fortunate enough to take Dr. Elizabeth Townsend Gard's Copyright Quilt Class at QuiltCon 2019, and this improv quilt is my end result. The color-coded meaning is of course directed by the workshop. I had fun adding a little extra symbolism. I quilted little row houses into the white to signify you can do what you want for home use. The gray area is stippled over organically gridded fabric because sometimes a case is unresolved, even though there are connections to established law. That little corner in the dark gray reminds me that we have to be careful with our orange ideas (orangey dots) to see where they fit in the public domain. The dark grey/black has triangles pointing out, symbolizing the contribution to the public domain, and is quilted with a nice, stable grid that means you must make sure you fit into the established practices and norms. The scissors fabric is to indicate our industry of quilt makers and respect (don't misuse my fabric scissors—or my intellectual property!). Anyone who hasn't taken the workshop and is casually viewing it would not have any idea of the symbolism, which I enjoy. The composition works on its own just as art but it's even more interesting to know all the meaning stitched into it."

-Kari Vojtechovsky

25: Just Wanna Quilt Notebook

Record Your Progress as You Quilt

The Just Wanna Quilt Notebook was my dream: a place to document your process and copyright information on projects that you care about – that you are potentially going to put out in the public, either in a quilt show, or in a commercial context. Document. Document. Document. We see that it is important in a number of instances.

1. Independent Creation

If someone accuses you of copyright infringement, you will have a record of how you came up with the idea, when you started the work, what resources you used, etc. If you have infringed, you can fix it, with an apology or share of the royalties. But if you did not use the work, you will have proof.

2. Copyright Registration

You will have all of the information you need to fill out the copyright registration, which of course, you are doing...

3. Documentation for Quilt Shows

You are ready to go! You have all of the information you need to fill out that form.

4. Infringement!!!!

Someone has infringed your work. You have proof of how you created it. You can send them a cease and desist letter, file a notice and takedown, and threaten (or actually) sue them. You have documentation. This is sooooooooooooo important. (See how many "o"s? It's that important. We created an independent Notebook that can be purchased. We are also included in this book, one set of the forms, which you may photocopy for your own use.

Name of Quilt Project:

Start Date: Completion Date:

Finishing Date Goal: How did you celebrate?

This will be: ☐ Gift ☐ Charity Quilt ☐ Show Quilt ☐ Commercial ☐ Keep ☐ Not sure

☐Professional Pattern ☐Commissioned ☐ Other ____________________________

Recipient/Show Information:

Is this a contest/challenge or show with specific rules?

☐ Challenge ☐ Contest ☐ Sew-along/BOM ☐ Quilt Show with Specific Requirements

☐ Charity quilt with specific requirements ☐ Other _________________

Time Keeping (optional)

Idea:

Shopping:

Creating the Pattern:

Piecing/Applique/Construction:

Quilting:

Binding:

Total:

The Idea Stage

What is your original idea? Inspiration? Thoughts?

The Shopping Stage

☐ Local Shop____________________________ ☐ Online ___________________________

☐ Other ________________________________ ☐ My Stash

The Pattern/Design Stage

☐ Kit ☐ Pattern

(Author/Title) ____

☐ Original Design (You are the author.)

☐ Inspired by ____

☐ Derivative work from ____

Describe the process of creating the pattern (if applicable).

Thread Log

Include the name, color, weight, and thread company for your records.

Piecing/Appliqué:

Quilting:

The Fabric Stage

(List, document, paste, whatever you like)

The Construction Stage

Tools/Techniques (Include special rulers, YouTube videos, books, a friend's suggestion, etc.)

The Quilting Stage

Type of Quilting: ☐ FMQ ☐ Hand ☐ Computer ☐ Tie ☐ Walking Foot ☐ QAYG

Batting Used:

Name of Quilter:

Patterns Used/Inspired by (if any):

The Binding Stage

Binding Complete? ☐ Yes ☐ No

The Label Stage

Label? ☐ Yes ☐ No

Name of Quilt:

Pattern/Kit Name:

Designer:

Piecer:

Quilter:

Technique Used:

Name of Recipient:

Story Behind the Quilt:

Description of Completed Quilt

(include right of attribution for key people including yourself as designer, original pattern maker, sewist, and/or quilter)

Completed Quilt

Type of Quilt: ☐ Traditional ☐ Art ☐ Improv ☐Modern ☐ Other_________________

Completed Size: _________ x ______

Appraisal

Did you get it appraised? ☐ No ☐ Yes

Appraiser: ________________________________ Date:______________

Appraisal Value:

Insurance:____________ Fair Market ____________ Donation _________

I shared this quilt or a photograph of the quilt

☐ Online ☐ Facebook ☐ My Webpage ☐ Instagram ☐ Other ________________

☐ At My Local Quilt Shop ____

☐ At My Guild____

☐ In a Show ____

☐ In a Quilting Facebook Group ____________________________________

☐ Just Wanna Quilt Facebook Group

Just Wanna Quilt would love to see your quilts! Join our Facebook Group, become part of our Quilting Army, and share you amazing creations! .

Hashtags on Social Media:

(Include your own hashtags, along with your sewing machine, batting used, thread, pattern, and if you would like #justwannaquilt #quiltingarmy #jwqnotebook.)

Copyright Assessment Checklist

Versions of:

☐ **Kit:** Quilt is based on a **kit** and I followed the directions. No new copyright.

☐ **Class:** Quilt is based on a **class.** I chose my own fabrics. Thin copyright on the selection arrangement and coordination of the fabrics, but likely not enforceable.

☐ **Pattern:** Quilt was made from purchased pattern. No new copyright on the pattern; thin copyright on the selection arrangement and coordination of the fabrics, but likely not enforceable.

OR

New Design/Original Patterns:

☐ **Tradition:** Quilt is based on traditional or well-known blocks, sashing, and layouts. No new copyright on the individual parts. Thin copyright on the selection arrangement and coordination of the fabrics, but likely not enforceable.

☐ **Original:** Quilt is an original work of art. Copyright protection likely. Register with the U.S. Copyright Office it for stronger protection.

Is there an underlying work in the original work? ☐ Yes ☐ No

If yes, what are you relying on? ☐ Fair use ☐ Permission from author

The following are items I used in my quilt:

☐ Basic fonts (not protectable)

☐ Basic shapes (not protectable)

☐ Common blocks (not protectable)

☐ Techniques (not protectable)

☐ Quotes/music/phrases (small bits) (fair use)

☐ Other

Copyright Protection/Notice for Original Patterns

☐ I want others to be able to use my original pattern free of charge

© Year, Name. Feel free to use this pattern and share it for non-commercial purposes. If you want to commercialize it, please contact ______________________.

☐ I want to protect it. (Register it, of course)

© Year, Name. All rights reserved.

☐ Other

© Year, name. ____________ [explain]

Have you registered the work with the U.S. Copyright Office?

☐ Yes. Registration Number: ____________________

☐ No.

Additional Notes:

www.ingramcontent.com/pod-product-compliance
Lightning Source LLC
LaVergne TN
LVHW060024210926
848481LV00013B/3785